2017 release

Adobe® Animate® CC
The Professional Portfolio

AGAINST THE CLOCK
mastering graphic technology

Managing Editor: Ellenn Behoriam
Cover & Interior Design: Erika Kendra
Editor: Angelina Kendra
Copy Editor: Liz Bleau

The fonts utilized in these training materials are the property of Against The Clock, Inc., and are supplied to the legitimate buyers of the Against The Clock training materials solely for use with the exercises and projects provided in the body of the materials. They may not be used for any other purpose, and under no circumstances may they be transferred to another individual, nor copied or distributed by any means whatsoever.

Against The Clock and the Against The Clock logo are trademarks of Against The Clock, Inc., registered in the United States and elsewhere. References to and instructional materials provided for any particular application program, operating system, hardware platform, or other commercially available product or products do not represent an endorsement of such product or products by Against The Clock, Inc.

Photoshop, Acrobat, Illustrator, InDesign, Flash, Dreamweaver, and PostScript are trademarks of Adobe Systems Incorporated. Macintosh is a trademark of Apple Computer, Inc. Other product and company names mentioned herein may be the trademarks of their respective owners.

The image on the cover shows a stairwell in the Polish royal castle in Warsaw, Poland.
(© Linfernum | Dreamstime.com)

10 9 8 7 6 5

Print ISBN: 978-1-936201-99-0
Ebook ISBN: 978-1-946396-00-6

AGAINST THE CLOCK
mastering graphic technology

4710 28th Street North, Saint Petersburg, FL 33714
800-256-4ATC • www.againsttheclock.com

Acknowledgements

ABOUT AGAINST THE CLOCK

Against The Clock, long recognized as one of the nation's leaders in courseware development, has been publishing high-quality educational materials for the graphic and computer arts industries since 1990. The company has developed a solid and widely-respected approach to teaching people how to effectively utilize graphics applications while maintaining a disciplined approach to real-world problems.

Having developed the *Against The Clock* and the *Essentials for Design* series with Prentice Hall/Pearson Education, ATC drew from years of professional experience and instructor feedback to develop *The Professional Portfolio Series*, focusing on the Adobe Creative Suite. These books feature step-by-step explanations, detailed foundational information, and advice and tips from industry professionals that offer practical solutions to technical issues.

Against The Clock works closely with all major software developers to create learning solutions that fulfill both the requirements of instructors and the needs of students. Thousands of graphic arts professionals — designers, illustrators, imaging specialists, prepress experts, and production managers — began their educations with Against The Clock training books. These professionals studied at Baker College, Nossi College of Art, Virginia Tech, Appalachian State University, Keiser College, University of South Carolina, Gress Graphic Arts Institute, Kean University, Southern Polytechnic State University, Brenau University, and many other educational institutions.

ABOUT THE AUTHOR

Erika Kendra holds a BA in History and a BA in English Literature from the University of Pittsburgh. She began her career in the graphic communications industry as an editor at Graphic Arts Technical Foundation before moving to Los Angeles in 2000. Erika is the author or co-author of more than thirty books about Adobe graphic design software. She has also written several books about graphic design concepts such as color reproduction and preflighting, and dozens of articles for online and print journals in the graphics industry. Working with Against The Clock for more than 15 years, Erika was a key partner in developing *The Professional Portfolio Series* of software training books.

CONTRIBUTING AUTHORS, ARTISTS, AND EDITORS

A big thank you to the people whose artwork, comments, and expertise contributed to the success of these books:

- **Steve Bird,** Adobe Certified Expert
- **Colleen Bredahl,** United Tribes Technical College
- **Richard Schrand,** International Academy of Design & Technology, Nashville, TN
- **Pam Harris,** University of North Texas at Dallas
- **Debbie Davidson,** Against The Clock, Inc.

Finally, thanks to **Angelina Kendra,** editor, and **Liz Bleau,** copy editor, for making sure that we all said what we meant to say.

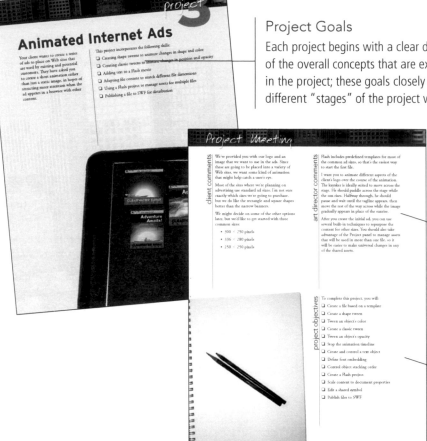

Project Goals

Each project begins with a clear description of the overall concepts that are explained in the project; these goals closely match the different "stages" of the project workflow.

The Project Meeting

Each project includes the client's initial comments, which provide valuable information about the job. The Project Art Director, a vital part of any design workflow, also provides fundamental advice and production requirements.

Project Objectives

Each Project Meeting includes a summary of the specific skills required to complete the project.

Real-World Workflow

Projects are broken into logical lessons or "stages" of the workflow. Brief introductions at the beginning of each stage provide vital foundational material required to complete the task.

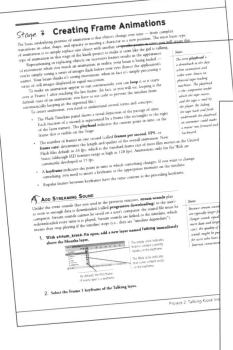

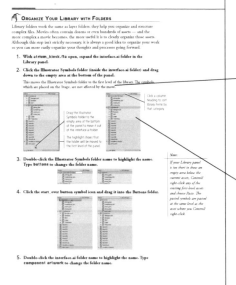

Step-By-Step Exercises

Every stage of the workflow is broken into multiple hands-on, step-by-step exercises.

Visual Explanations

Wherever possible, screen shots are annotated so you can quickly identify important information.

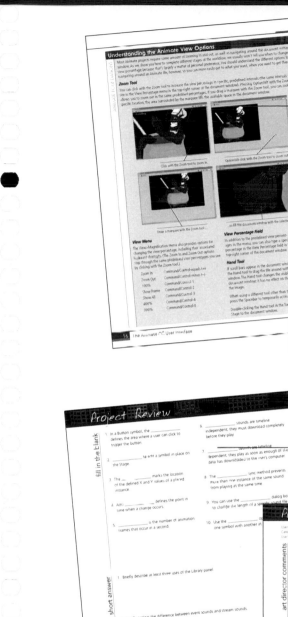

Animate Foundations

Additional functionality, related tools, and underlying graphic design concepts are included throughout the book.

Advice and Warnings

Where appropriate, sidebars provide shortcuts, warnings, or tips about the topic at hand.

Project Review

After completing each project, you can complete these fill-in-the-blank and short-answer questions to test your understanding of the concepts in the project.

Portfolio Builder Projects

Each step-by-step project is accompanied by a freeform project, allowing you to practice skills and creativity, resulting in an extensive and diverse portfolio of work.

Visual Summary

Using an annotated version of the finished project, you can quickly identify the skills used to complete different aspects of the job.

The Against The Clock *Portfolio Series* teaches graphic design software tools and techniques entirely within the framework of real-world projects; we introduce and explain skills where they would naturally fall into a real project workflow. This project-based approach allows you to get in depth with the software beginning in Project 1.

Clear, easy-to-read, step-by-step instructions walk you through every phase of each job, from creating a new file to saving the finished piece. Wherever logical, we also offer practical advice and tips about underlying concepts and graphic design practices.

The projects in this book reflect a range of basic Animate jobs, from drawing artwork that will be used in an animation to animating creatures in the ocean. When you finish the projects in this book (and the accompanying Portfolio Builder exercises), you will be better prepared for a more in-depth exploration of digital animation.

It is important to keep in mind that Animate is an extremely versatile and powerful application. The sheer volume of available tools, panels, and features can seem intimidating when you first look at the interface. Most of these tools, however, are fairly simple to use with a bit of background information and a little practice.

Wherever necessary, we explain the underlying concepts and terms that are required for understanding the software. We're confident these projects provide the practice you need to be able to create sophisticated artwork by the end of the very first project.

project 1 — Corvette Artwork

- ❏ Setting up the Workspace
- ❏ Drawing in Animate
- ❏ Painting and Coloring Objects

project 2 — Talking Kiosk Interface

- ❏ Working with Symbols
- ❏ Working with Sound
- ❏ Creating Frame Animations

project 3 — Animated Internet Ads

- ❏ Animating Symbols
- ❏ Working with Text
- ❏ Repurposing Animate Content

project 4 — Ocean Animation

- ❏ Importing Bitmaps and Symbols
- ❏ Animating Symbols
- ❏ Programming Basic Timeline Control

the portfolio series

Contents

Contents

Getting Started

PREREQUISITES

To use *The Professional Portfolio Series,* you should know how to use your mouse to point and click, as well as how to drag items around the screen. You should be able to resize and arrange windows on your desktop to maximize your available space. You should know how to access drop-down menus, and understand how check boxes and radio buttons work. It also doesn't hurt to have a good understanding of how your operating system organizes files and folders, and how to navigate your way around them. If you're familiar with these fundamental skills, then you know all that's necessary to use the Portfolio Series.

RESOURCE FILES

All the files you need to complete the projects in this book — except, of course, the Animate application files — are on the Student Files Web page at againsttheclock.com. See the inside back cover of this book for access information.

Each archive (ZIP) file is named according to the related project (e.g., **Vette_ANCC17_RF.zip**). At the beginning of each project, you must download the archive for that project and expand it to access the resource files that you need to complete the exercises. Detailed instructions for this process are included in the Interface chapter.

Files required for the related Portfolio Builder exercises at the end of each project are also available on the Student Files page; these archives are also named by project (e.g., **Robot_ANCC17_PB.zip**).

SOFTWARE VERSIONS

This book was written and tested using the 2017 release of Adobe Animate CC software (Build 16.0). You can find the specific version number in the Splash Screen that appears while your application is launching, or by choosing About Animate in the Animate CC menu (Macintosh) or Help menu (Windows).

Because Adobe has announced periodic upgrades rather than releasing new full versions, some features and functionality might have changed since publication. Please check the Errata section of the Against The Clock Web site for any significant issues that might have arisen from these periodic upgrades.

SYSTEM REQUIREMENTS

The Professional Portfolio Series was designed to work on both Macintosh or Windows computers; where differences exist from one platform to another, we include specific instructions relative to each platform. One issue that remains different from Macintosh to Windows is the use of different modifier keys (Control, Shift, etc.) to accomplish the same task. When we present key commands, we always follow the same Macintosh/Windows format — Macintosh keys are listed first, then a slash, followed by the Windows key commands.

Adobe Animate (formerly Flash Professional) is the industry-standard application for building animations and other interactive content. Mastering the tools and techniques of the application can significantly improve your potential career options.

Typical Animate work ranges from simply moving things around within a space to building fully interactive games and Web sites, complete with sound and video files. Animate is somewhat unique in the communications industry because these different types of work often require different sets of skills — specifically, a combination of both visual creativity and logical programming. Depending on the type of application you're building, you should have a basic understanding of both graphic design and code.

Our goal in this book is to teach you how to use the available tools to create various types of work that you might encounter in your professional career. As you complete the projects, you explore the basic drawing techniques, and then move on to more advanced techniques such as adding animation and interactivity.

The simple exercises in this introduction are designed to let you explore the Animate user interface. Whether you are new to the application or upgrading from a previous version, we highly recommend that you follow these steps to click around and become familiar with the basic workspace.

EXPLORE THE ANIMATE INTERFACE

The user interface (UI) is what you see when you launch Animate. The specific elements you see — including which panels are open and where they are located — depend on what was done the last time the application was open. The first time you launch the application, you'll see the default workspace settings defined by Adobe. When you relaunch after you or another user has quit, the workspace defaults to the last-used settings — including specific open panels and the position of those panels on your screen.

We designed the following exercise so you can explore various ways of controlling Animate's panels. Because workspace preferences are largely a matter of personal taste, the projects in this book direct you to use specific panels, but you can choose where to place those elements within the interface.

1. **Create a new empty folder named WIP (Work In Progress) on any writable disk (where you plan to save your work).**

2. **Download the InterfaceAN_ANCC17_RF.zip archive from the Student Files Web page.**

3. **Macintosh users: Place the ZIP archive in your WIP folder, then double-click the file icon to expand it.**

   Windows users: Double-click the ZIP archive file to open it. Click the folder inside the archive and drag it into your primary WIP folder.

   The resulting **InterfaceAN** folder contains all the files you need to complete this introduction.

Macintosh

Double-click the archive
file icon to expand it.

Windows

Drag the InterfaceAN folder from
the archive to your WIP folder.

4. In Animate, open the Window menu and choose Workspaces>Essentials.

Saved workspaces, accessed in the Window>Workspaces menu or in the Workspace switcher on the Application bar, provide one-click access to a defined group of tools that might otherwise take multiple clicks each time you need the same toolset.

Keyboard shortcuts (if available) are listed on the right side of the menu.

Many menu commands are toggles, which means they are either on or off. The checkmark indicates that an option is toggled on (visible or active).

Note:

If a menu command is grayed out, it is unavailable for the current selection.

5. Choose Window>Workspace>Reset 'Essentials'. If asked if you're sure about resetting the workspace, click Yes.

Saved workspaces remember the last-used state; calling a workspace again restores the panels exactly as they were the last time you used that workspace. For example, if you close a panel that is part of a saved workspace, that panel will not be reopened the next time you call the same workspace. To restore the *saved* state of the workspace, you have to use the Reset option.

Steps 4 and 5 might not do anything, depending on what was done in Animate before you started this exercise; if you or someone else changes anything and quits the application, those changes are remembered even when Animate is relaunched. Because we can't be sure what your default settings show, completing these steps resets the interface to one of the built-in default workspaces so your screen will match our screen shots.

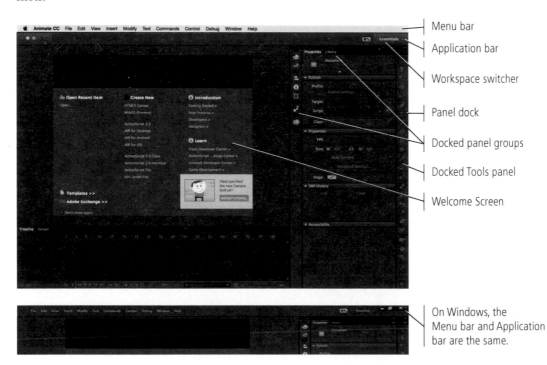

Menu bar

Application bar

Workspace switcher

Panel dock

Docked panel groups

Docked Tools panel

Welcome Screen

On Windows, the Menu bar and Application bar are the same.

The Welcome Screen appears by default when no file is open, unless someone checked the Don't Show Again option. If you don't see the Welcome Screen when no files are open, you can turn this feature back on by choosing Welcome Screen in the On Launch menu of the General pane of the Preferences dialog box. After you quit and relaunch the application, the Welcome Screen reappears.

6. Macintosh users: Choose Animate CC>Preferences.
Windows users: Choose Edit>Preferences.

Remember that on Macintosh systems, the Preferences dialog box is accessed in the Animate CC menu; Windows users access the Preferences dialog box in the Edit menu.

Preferences customize the way many of the program's tools and options function. Once open, you can access any of the Preference categories by clicking a different option in the left pane; the right side of the dialog box displays options related to the active category.

Macintosh

Animate CC	File	Edit	V
About Animate			
Sync Settings	▶		
Preferences...	⌘U		
Font Mapping...			
Keyboard Shortcuts...			
Services	▶		
Hide Animate	⌘H		
Hide Others	⌥⌘H		
Show All			
Quit Animate	⌘Q		

Windows

Edit View Insert Modify Text Comma...	
Undo	Ctrl+Z
Redo	Ctrl+Y
Cut	Ctrl+X
Copy	Ctrl+C
Paste in Center	Ctrl+V
Paste in Place	Ctrl+Shift+V
Paste Special	
Clear	Backspace
Duplicate	Ctrl+D
Select All	Ctrl+A
Deselect All	Ctrl+Shift+A
Invert Selection	
Find and Replace	Ctrl+F
Find Next	F3
Timeline	▶
Edit Symbols	Ctrl+E
Edit Selected	
Edit in Place	
Preferences...	Ctrl+U
Font Mapping...	
Keyboard Shortcuts...	

7. With General selected in the list on the left side of the Preferences dialog box, choose any option that you prefer in the User Interface menu.

You might have already noticed the rather dark appearance of the panels and interface background. The application uses the dark "theme" as the default. (We used the Light option throughout this book because text in the interface elements is easier to read in printed screen captures.)

8. Check the option to Auto-Collapse Iconic Panels, then click OK to close the Preferences dialog box.

Note:

As you work your way through the projects in this book, you will learn not only what you can do with these collections of Preferences, but also why and when you might want to use them.

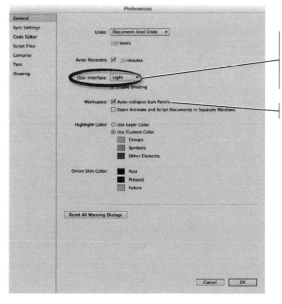

Choose Light or Dark in this menu to change the color of the overall workspace.

Check this option.

9. Continue to the next exercise.

EXPLORE THE ARRANGEMENT OF ANIMATE PANELS

As you gain experience and familiarity with Animate, you will develop personal artistic and working styles. Animate includes a number of options for arranging and managing the numerous panels, so you can customize and personalize the workspace to suit your specific needs.

We designed the following exercise to give you an opportunity to explore different ways of controlling Animate panels. Because workspace preferences are largely a matter of personal taste, the projects in this book instruct you to use certain tools and panels, but where you place those elements within the interface is up to you.

1. **In Animate, move your mouse cursor over the top icon in the leftmost column of the panel dock.**

   The area where the panels are stored is called the **panel dock**. Panels, whether docked or floating, can be collapsed to icons (called iconic or iconized panels) to save space in the document window. You can see what each icon symbolizes through the tooltip that appears when you hover over a specific icon.

   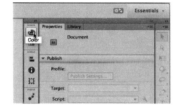

   Each dock column, technically considered a separate dock, can be expanded or iconized independently of other columns.

2. **Click the left edge of the leftmost column of docked panels. Hold down the mouse button and drag left until the names of the panels are visible.**

   When panels are iconized, you can expand the icons to show the panel names. This is useful when you are not yet familiar with the icons. You can also drag the column edge to the right to hide the panel names.

   Click the edge of the column and drag left to show the panel names.

   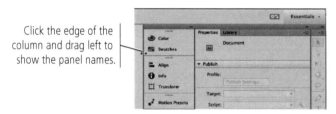

Note:

When we say "click and drag," you should hold down the mouse button while dragging.

3. **Control/right-click the title bar above the docked panel icons. Make sure Auto-Collapse Icon Panels in the contextual menu is checked (toggled on).**

   As we explained in the Getting Started section, when commands are different for the Macintosh and Windows operating systems, we include the different commands in the Macintosh/Windows format. In this case, Macintosh users who do not have right-click mouse capability can press the Control key and click to access the contextual menu. You do not have to press Control *and* right-click to access the menus.

   Control/right-clicking a dock title bar opens the dock contextual menu, where you can change the default panel behavior. If you toggle off the Auto-Collapse Icon Panels option (which is active by default), a panel remains open until you intentionally collapse it, or until you open a different panel in the same column of the dock.

   Control/right-click the dock column title bar to open the contextual menu.

   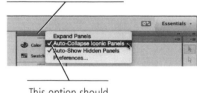

   This option should be checked.

   The Auto-Collapse Icon Panels option is also available in the User Interface pane of the Preferences dialog box, which you can open directly from the dock contextual menu.

Note:

*A **contextual menu** is a menu that offers options related to a specific object. You can access contextual menus for most objects by Control/right-clicking.*

Note:

If you're using a Macintosh and don't have a mouse with right-click capability, we highly recommend that you purchase one.

4. **Click the Align panel button in the column of iconized panels.**

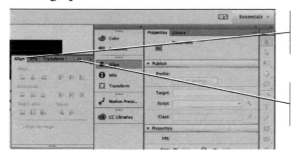

Clicking a docked panel button opens the panel to the left of the panel dock.

Click this icon to intentionally collapse an expanded panel.

Note:

Click a specific tab to make that panel active in a panel group.

5. **Click away from the expanded panel (in the main workspace area, above or below the Welcome Screen).**

By default, expanded panels close as soon as you click away from them.

Note:

Press F4 to hide all open panels. If any panels are hidden, press F4 again to reshow the hidden panels.

6. **Double-click the header above the column of panel icons.**

Double-clicking the dock column header expands iconized panels (or vice versa).

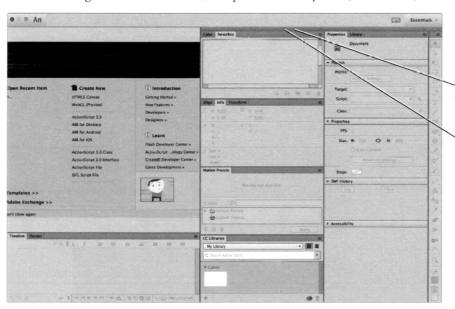

Double-click the header bar over a collapsed dock column to expand that column.

Double-click the header bar over an expanded dock column to collapse that column.

7. **Click the left edge of the expanded dock column and drag right to make the column narrower.**

Columns have a minimum possible width; you should drag right until the column does not get any smaller.

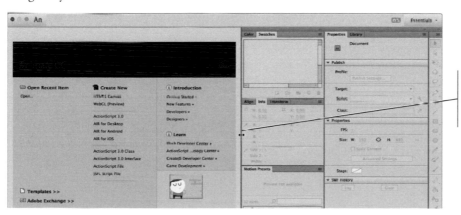

Drag the left edge of the expanded dock column to make the panels wider or narrower.

8. **Click the Motion Presets panel tab and drag left, away from the dock.**

   Most panels are docked by default, but you can move any panel (or panel group) away from the dock so it will appear as a separate panel (called a **floating panel**). A panel does not need to be active before you move it around in the workspace.

   Floating panel groups can be iconized just like columns in the dock. Double-click the floating panel group title bar to toggle between expanded and iconized mode.

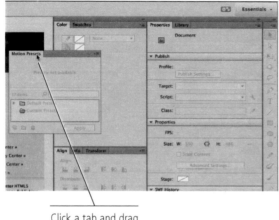

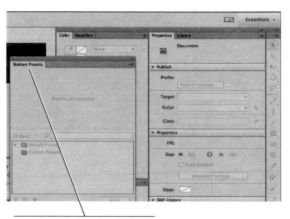

Click a tab and drag to move that panel.

When you release the mouse button, the dragged panel "floats" separate from the dock.

9. **Click the Motion Presets panel tab again and drag back to the dock until a blue line appears below the docked Properties/Library panel group.**

   You can move any panel or group to a specific position in the dock by dragging. The blue highlight indicates where the panel will be placed when you release the mouse button.

Note:

You don't need to move a panel out of the dock before placing it in a different position within the dock. We included Step 8 to show you how to float panels and panel groups.

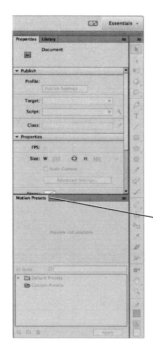

Drag the floating panel until you see a blue line below the docked Properties panel group.

When you release the mouse button, the dragged panel appears below the Properties panel in a separate group.

10. Click the Library panel tab and drag down until the drop zone behind the Motion Presets panel tab turns blue.

When the drop zone of a panel group turns blue, releasing the mouse button will group the moved panel with the existing panel (group).

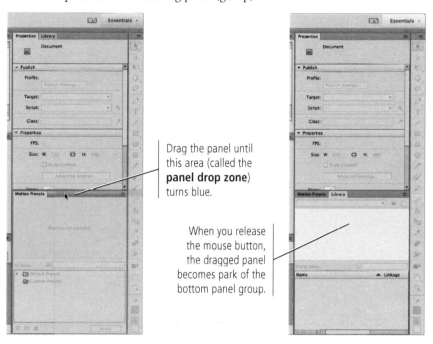

Drag the panel until this area (called the **panel drop zone**) turns blue.

When you release the mouse button, the dragged panel becomes park of the bottom panel group.

Note:

Click and drag a panel group drop zone (the area behind the panel tabs) to move an entire panel group.

Note:

All panels can be accessed in the Window menu.

If you choose a panel that's open but iconized, the panel expands to the left of its icon.

If you choose a panel that's open in an expanded group, that panel comes to the front of the group.

If you choose a panel that isn't currently open, it opens in the same position as when it was last closed.

11. Double-click the Library panel tab to collapse the group.

When a group is collapsed but not iconized, only the panel tabs are visible. Clicking a tab in a collapsed panel group expands the group and makes the selected panel active. You can also expand the group by again double-clicking the drop zone.

Double-click a panel tab to collapse the group to show only the panel tabs.

Note:

Many screen shots in this book show floating panels so we can focus on the most important issue in a particular image. In our production workflow, however, we make heavy use of docked and iconized panels and take full advantage of saved custom workspaces.

12. **Control/right-click the Swatches tab in the left dock column. Choose Close Tab Group from the contextual menu.**

You can use this menu to close an individual docked panel (Close), or to close an entire panel group (Close Tab Group).

Control/right-click a panel tab or the group drop zone to open the contextual menu.

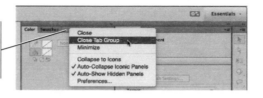

13. **Repeat Step 12 to close the Align/Info/Transform panel group and the CC Libraries panel.**

14. **On the right side of the workspace, click the Tools panel title bar and drag away from the dock into the middle of the workspace.**

When floating, the Tools panel defaults to a standard rectangular panel with the tools in several rows.

15. **Click the Tools panel title bar and drag left until a blue line appears on the left edge of the workspace.**

This step docks the Tools panel on the left edge of the workspace.

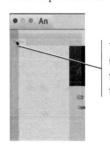

This pop-up "drawer" indicates that you are adding a column to the panel dock (in this case, on the left edge of the workspace).

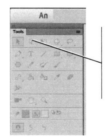

After docking the Tools panel, the panel might still appear in the same configuration as the floating panel (with multiple rows of tools).

16. **Click the right edge of the Tools panel and drag left until all the tools appear in a only one or two columns.**

If you are working with a small monitor such as a laptop, you might not be able to fit all of the Tools panel options in a single column. If this is the case, drag until all options appear in two columns.

Click and drag the right edge of the docked Tools panel to show all tools in a single column.

Identifying and Accessing Tools in Animate

In addition to a wide variety of panels, Animate includes 31 tools — a large number that indicates the power of the application. You can change the docked Tools panel to more than one column by dragging the right edge of the panel. When the Tools panel is floating, it defaults to show the various tools in rows.

You learn how to use these tools as you complete the projects in this book. For now, you should simply take the opportunity to identify the tools and their location on the Tools panel. The image to the right shows the icon, tool name, and keyboard shortcut (if any) that accesses each tool. Nested tools are shown indented.

Keyboard Shortcuts & Nested Tools

When you hover your mouse over a tool, the pop-up tooltip shows the name of the tool and a letter in parentheses. Pressing that letter activates the associated tool (unless you're working with type, in which case pressing a key adds that letter to your text). If you don't see tooltips, check the General pane of the Preferences dialog box; the Show Tooltips check box should be active. (Note: You must have a file open to see the tooltips and access the nested tools.)

When you hover the mouse cursor over the tool, a tooltip shows the name of the tool.

Any tool with an arrow in the bottom-right corner includes related tools nested below it. When you click a tool and hold down the mouse button, the nested tools appear in a pop-up menu. If you choose one of the nested tools, that variation becomes the default choice in the Tools panel.

This arrow means the tool has other nested tools.

Click and hold down the mouse button to show the nested tools.

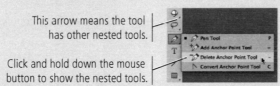

Tool Options

In addition to the basic tool set, the bottom of the Tools panel includes options that control the fill and stroke colors, as well as options that change depending on the selected tool.

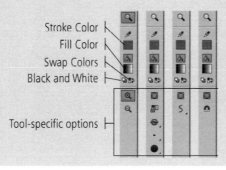

Stroke Color
Fill Color
Swap Colors
Black and White

Tool-specific options

Selection tool (V)
Subselection tool (A)
Free Transform tool (Q)
Gradient Transform tool (F)
3D Rotation tool (W)
3D Translation tool (G)
Lasso tool (L)
Polygon tool (L)
Magic Wand (L)
Pen tool (P)
Add Anchor Point tool (=)
Delete Anchor Point tool (-)
Convert Anchor Point tool (Shift-C)
Text tool (T)
Line tool (N)
Rectangle tool (R)
Rectangle Primitive tool (R)
Oval tool (R)
Oval Primitive tool (O)
Polystar tool
Pencil tool (Shift-Y)
Paint Brush tool (Y)
Brush tool (B)
Bone tool (M)
Bind tool (M)
Paint Bucket tool (K)
Ink Bottle tool (S)
Eyedropper tool (I)
Eraser tool (E)
Width tool (U)
Camera tool (C)
Hand tool (H)
Zoom tool (Z)

17. Click the button on the right side of the Tools panel title bar and choose Lock in the panel Options menu.

If the menu shows "Unlock," the panel is already locked. Simply move the mouse away from the menu and click to dismiss the menu.

When a panel is locked, it can't be removed from the dock (although it can be resized, collapsed, or expanded).

Click here to open the panel Options menu.

18. Continue to the next exercise.

CREATE A SAVED WORKSPACE

By now you should understand that you have extensive control over the appearance of your Animate workspace — you can determine what panels are visible, where and how they appear, and even the size of individual panels and panel groups. Rather than re-establishing every workspace element each time you return to Animate, you can save your custom workspace settings so you can recall them with a single click.

1. Click the Workspace switcher in the Application/Menu bar and choose New Workspace.

Again, keep in mind that we list differing commands in the Macintosh/Windows format. On Macintosh, the Workspace switcher is in the Application bar; on Windows, it's in the Menu bar.

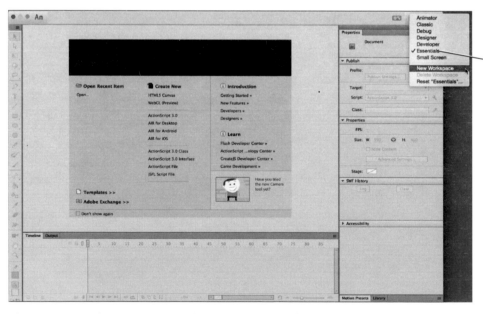

The last-used workspace is checked in the list.

The Manage Workspaces option in the Workspace switcher opens a dialog box where you can choose a specific user-defined workspace to rename or delete. You can't rename or delete the default workspaces that come with the application.

2. In the New Workspace dialog box, type **Portfolio** as the Workspace name and click OK.

After saving the current workspace, the Workspace switcher shows the name of the new saved workspace.

3. Control/right-click the Properties panel tab and choose Close from the contextual menu.

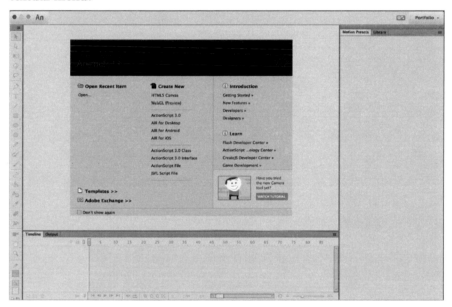

4. Open the Workspace switcher and choose Developer.

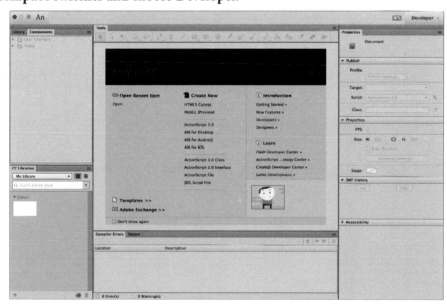

5. **Open the Workspace switcher again and choose Portfolio to restore your custom workspace.**

   Calling a saved workspace restores the last-used state of the workspace. Because you closed the Properties panel after saving the workspace, Dreamweaver reverts to the last-used version of the custom workspace — without the Properties panel.

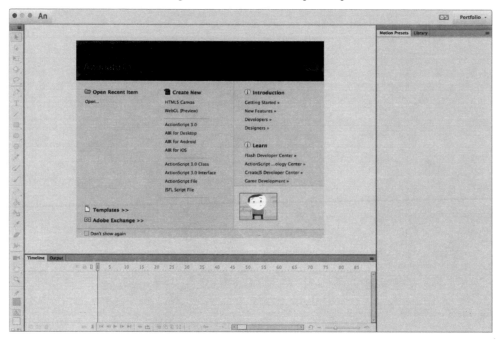

6. **In the Workspace switcher menu, choose Reset 'Portfolio'. When asked if you want to reset the workspace, click Yes.**

   The Reset command reverts the workspace back to the original saved state.

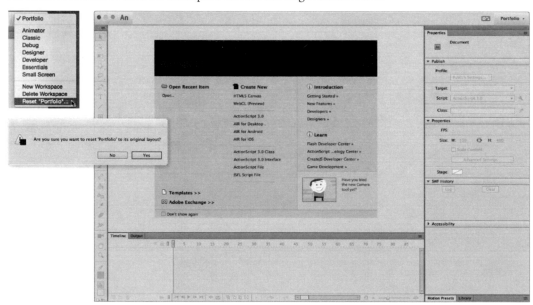

7. **Continue to the next exercise.**

Customizing Animate Keyboard Shortcuts

ANIMATE FOUNDATIONS

Different people use Animate for various reasons, sometimes using a specific, limited set of tools to complete only one type of project. In addition to customizing the workspace and the Tools panel, you can also customize the various keyboard shortcuts used to access different commands (Animate>Keyboard Shortcuts on Macintosh or Edit>Keyboard Shortcuts on Windows). Once you have defined custom menus or shortcuts, you can save your choices as a set so you can access the same custom choices again without having to redo the work.

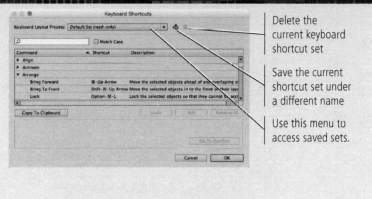

Delete the current keyboard shortcut set

Save the current shortcut set under a different name

Use this menu to access saved sets.

EXPLORE THE ANIMATE DOCUMENT WINDOW

There is far more to using Animate than arranging panels around the workspace. What you do with those panels — and even which panels you need — depends on the type of work you are doing in a particular file. In this exercise, you open an Animate file and explore the interface elements that you will use to create digital animations.

1. **In Animate, choose File>Open.**

2. **Navigate to your WIP>InterfaceAN folder and select capcarl.fla in the list of available files.**

   The Open dialog box is a system-standard navigation dialog. Press Shift to select and open multiple contiguous (consecutive) files in the list. Press Command/Control to select and open multiple non-contiguous files.

Note:

Press Command/Control-O to access the Open dialog box.

Macintosh

Windows

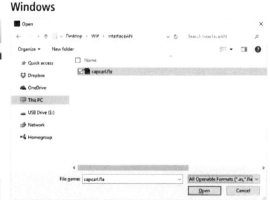

3. Click Open.

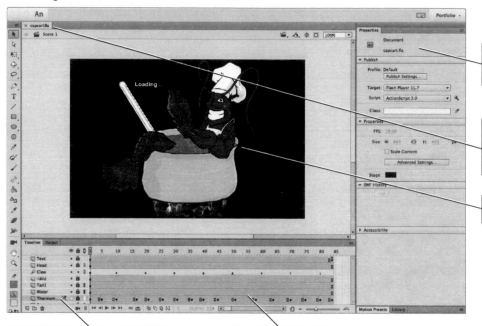

The Properties panel shows information about the file or selected object.

Open files are represented by tabs at the top of the document window.

Objects in the file appear on the Stage.

Placing each object in the file on its own layer simplifies and streamlines management of complex files.

The timeline contains frames, which are used to change what is visible at a given point in time.

4. Above the top-right corner of the Stage, open the View Percentage menu and choose Fit in Window.

5. Click the bar that separates the Stage area from the Timeline panel. Drag up to enlarge the panel and show all the layers in the file.

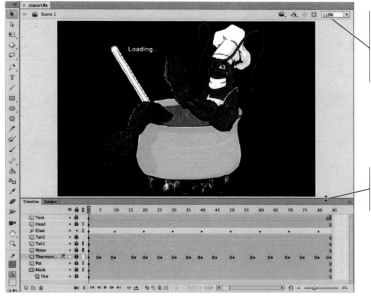

The Fit in Window command enlarges or reduces the view percentage to fill the available space in the document window.

Click here and drag up to show all the layers in the file.

Note:

As you complete the projects in this book, you'll see our screen shots zoom in or out as necessary to show you the most relevant part of a particular file. In most cases we do not tell you what specific view percentage to use for a particular exercise, unless it's specifically required for the work being done.

6. Review the Timeline panel.

The Timeline panel is perhaps the most important panel in Animate. It represents the passage of time within your animation, and it enables you to control what happens to objects in your file, as well as when and where changes occur.

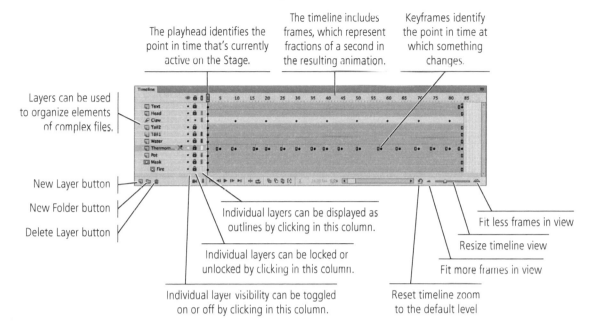

The playhead identifies the point in time that's currently active on the Stage.

The timeline includes frames, which represent fractions of a second in the resulting animation.

Keyframes identify the point in time at which something changes.

Layers can be used to organize elements of complex files.

New Layer button

New Folder button

Delete Layer button

Individual layers can be displayed as outlines by clicking in this column.

Individual layers can be locked or unlocked by clicking in this column.

Individual layer visibility can be toggled on or off by clicking in this column.

Fit less frames in view

Resize timeline view

Fit more frames in view

Reset timeline zoom to the default level

7. Choose the Selection tool from the Tools panel and click the lobster's right claw on the Stage.

Although we will not discuss all 20+ Animate panels here, the Properties panel deserves mention. This important panel is **context sensitive**, which means it provides various options depending on what is selected on the Stage.

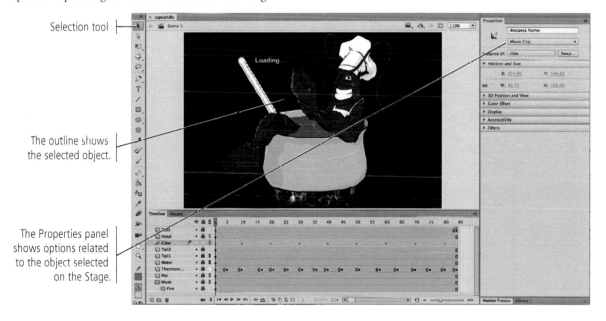

Selection tool

The outline shows the selected object.

The Properties panel shows options related to the object selected on the Stage.

Most Animate projects require some amount of zooming in and out, as well as navigating around the document within its window. As we show you how to complete different stages of the workflow, we usually won't tell you when to change your view percentage because that's largely a matter of personal preference. You should understand the different options for navigating around an Animate file, however, so you can more easily get to what you want, when you want to get there.

Zoom Tool

You can click with the Zoom tool to increase the view percentage in specific, predefined intervals (the same intervals you see in the View Percentage menu in the top-right corner of the document window). Pressing Option/Alt with the Zoom tool allows you to zoom out in the same predefined percentages. If you drag a marquee with the Zoom tool, you can zoom into a specific location; the area surrounded by the marquee fills the available space in the document window.

Click with the Zoom tool to zoom in.

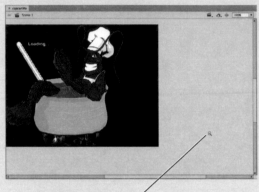

Option/Alt-click with the Zoom tool to zoom out.

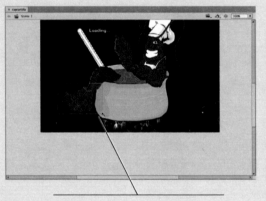

Draw a marquee with the Zoom tool…

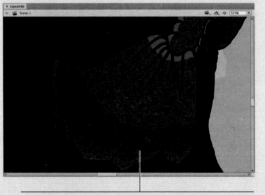

…to fill the document window with the selected area.

View Menu

The View>Magnification menu also provides options for changing the view percentage, including their associated keyboard shortcuts. (The Zoom In and Zoom Out options step through the same predefined view percentages you see by clicking with the Zoom tool.)

Zoom In	Command/Control-equals (=)
Zoom Out	Command/Control-minus (–)
100%	Command/Control-1
Show Frame	Command/Control-2
Show All	Command/Control-3
400%	Command/Control-4
800%	Command/Control-8

View Percentage Field

In addition to the predefined view percentages in the menu, you can also type a specific percentage in the View Percentage field in the top-right corner of the document window.

Hand Tool

If scroll bars appear in the document window, you can use the Hand tool to drag the file around within the document window. The Hand tool changes the visible area in the document window; it has no effect on the actual content of the image.

When using a different tool other than the Text tool, you can press the Spacebar to temporarily access the Hand tool.

Double-clicking the Hand tool in the Tools panel fits the Stage to the document window.

8. **Click the playhead above the timeline frames and drag right.**

    This technique of dragging the playhead above the timeline is called **scrubbing**.

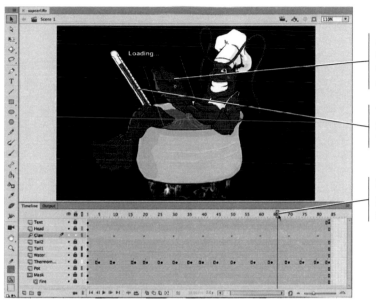

As you drag right, the claw moves back and forth in a waving motion (based on objects on the Claw layer).

The mercury in the thermometer rises (based on objects on the Thermometer layer).

Drag the playhead to preview animation in the document window.

9. **Click the gray area outside of the Stage to deselect everything, then press Return/Enter.**

    One final reminder: throughout this book, we list differing commands in the Macintosh/Windows format. On Macintosh, you need to press the Return key; on Windows, press the Enter key. (We will not repeat this explanation every time different commands are required for the different operating systems.)

    This keyboard shortcut plays the movie on the Stage from the current location of the playhead. If the playhead is already at the end of the frames, it moves back to Frame 1 and plays the entire movie.

Note:

When a movie is playing on the Stage, press the Escape key to stop the playback.

10. **Press Command-Return/Control-Enter.**

    Instead of simply playing the movie on the Stage, you can preview the file to see what it will look like when exported. This keyboard shortcut, which is the same as choosing Test Movie in the Control menu, exports a SWF file from the existing FLA file so you can see what the final file will look like.

    In the separate Player window, you see some animated elements that did not appear when you played the movie on the Stage. This is a perfect example of why you should test actual animation files rather than relying only on what you see on the Stage. (This is especially true if you did not create the file, as in this case.)

The exported SWF file appears in a Player window and begins playing.

Some animation does not play on the Stage, but does play in the Player window.

11. **Close the Player window and return to Animate.**

12. Click the Close button on the capcarl document tab. If asked, click Don't Save/No to close the file without saving.

Clicking the Close button on the Application frame closes all open files and quits the application.

Note:

Press Command/Control-W to close the active file.

Macintosh

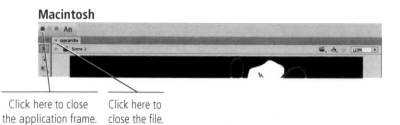

Click here to close the application frame.

Click here to close the file.

Windows

Click here to close the file.

Click here to close the application frame and quit the application.

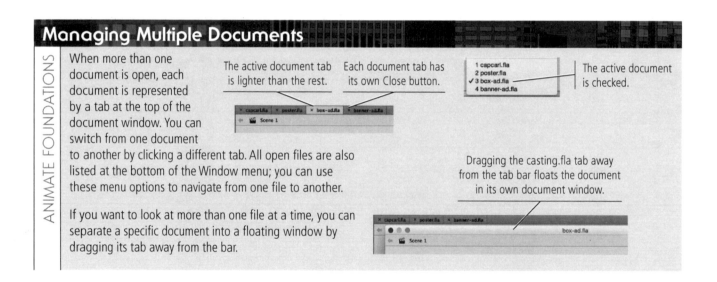

Managing Multiple Documents

ANIMATE FOUNDATIONS

When more than one document is open, each document is represented by a tab at the top of the document window. You can switch from one document to another by clicking a different tab. All open files are also listed at the bottom of the Window menu; you can use these menu options to navigate from one file to another.

If you want to look at more than one file at a time, you can separate a specific document into a floating window by dragging its tab away from the bar.

The active document tab is lighter than the rest.

Each document tab has its own Close button.

1 capcarl.fla
2 poster.fla
✓ 3 box-ad.fla
4 banner-ad.fla

The active document is checked.

Dragging the casting.fla tab away from the tab bar floats the document in its own document window.

Corvette Artwork

Your client is the main sponsor and event promoter of the annual Car Cruise and Music Festival at the Santa Monica Pier. You have been hired to create digital artwork for a number of elements that will be added to the event's Web site, including a game that he is going to develop with Animate programming functionality. The first step is to build a basic illustration that can later be used for the client's various purposes.

This project incorporates the following skills:

❑ Defining a movie file with appropriate settings for the job you're building

❑ Importing a scanned image provided by the creative director

❑ Using various drawing tools to develop a digital version of a rough sketch

❑ Understanding the different drawing modes that are available

❑ Changing fill and stroke colors using a variety of methods

❑ Adding depth using various shading techniques

client comments

I'm planning a number of different projects to promote this year's event. The American sportscar area is always a big draw at the event, so I'd like to feature Corvettes on all of the event collateral.

Most of the print work is going to use photos, but I'm planning some other projects where I want to use artwork instead of a picture — animations, Web banners, and I'm even thinking about an interactive game.

I'm an Animate programmer, but not an artist. If you can create the artwork directly in Animate, that would save me some time when I implement my other plans.

One final thing — I don't want it to look like a cartoon. Obviously, I don't want it to be a photo, but I do want it to be realistic looking.

art director comments

I sketched out a Corvette, and scanned the sketch for you. I want you to use that sketch as the basis for your finished piece. Start by tracing that drawing using a bright color that you can see against the gray lines in the sketch.

Once you've finished the basic artwork, try to make it seem more realistic than just a flat color conveys. Add some dimension and depth so it doesn't look too much like a cartoon.

Also, make sure you build the artwork using logical layers. That way, if we need to make changes later, or if the client decides to animate it, the document will be structured properly.

Since Animate produces vector artwork, we can use the artwork for just about anything once it's done. The important thing for now, however, is to create a static file that we can post on our Web site for the client's approval.

project objectives

To complete this project, you will:

❑ Set up the workspace to match the requirements of the project

❑ Import the scan of the sketched Corvette

❑ Create a set of logical layers to hold the various components that you will create

❑ Understand the difference between object-drawing and merge-drawing modes

❑ Use the basic shape and line tools to develop the components of the drawing

❑ Draw precise Bézier curves with the Pen tool

❑ Use the Pencil tool to draw freehand shapes

❑ Apply color with the Paint Bucket, Ink Bottle, and Brush tools

❑ Use object groups to combine and protect drawing objects

❑ Apply and edit color gradients

❑ Export a static image for online review

Stage 1 Setting up the Workspace

CREATE A NEW DOCUMENT

1. Download **Vette_ANCC17_RF.zip** from the Student Files Web page.

2. Expand the ZIP archive in your WIP folder (Macintosh) or copy the archive contents into your WIP folder (Windows).

   This results in a folder named **Vette**, which contains all of the files you need for this project. You should also use this folder to save the files you create in this project.

   If necessary, refer to Page 1 of the Interface chapter for specific information on expanding or accessing the required resource files.

3. In Animate, choose File>New.

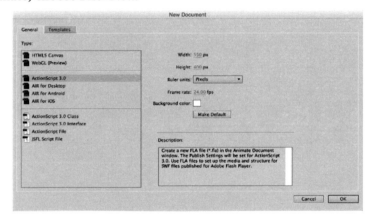

   When you create a new file, you can define a number of options for the file.

   In the General tab, you can use the Type window to determine what kind of file you are creating. ActionScript 3.0, the default option, exports a SWF file that requires a special Player plug-in to view the file. You can also create an HTML5 canvas file, which can play natively in a browser without a plug in, or a WebGL (Web Graphics Library) file that uses JavaScript code and does not require a browser plug-in to display. The AIR for Desktop, AIR for Android, and AIR for iOS options create files that can be distributed as standalone "apps" for (respectively) desktop use, Android tablets/phones, and Apple iPads/iPhones.

   On the right side of the dialog box, the **Width** and **Height** options define the Stage size, or the area that will be included in the final exported movie. In this project, you are using the Animate Stage as a drawing board (literally). You will adjust the Stage size in the next exercise to meet the needs of the drawing you will create.

   The **Ruler Units** menu defaults to Pixels, which is appropriate for files that will be distributed digitally.

   The **Frame Rate** defines the number of frames that exist in a second (frames per second, or fps). You will learn more about frame rate beginning in Project 2: Talking Kiosk Interface, when you start creating animations.

   The **Background Color** option defines the color of the Stage; this color appears behind all elements that you create or place in the file.

Note:

You can click the Templates tab to access pre-defined templates in many different styles.

Note:

Although there are slight differences in appearance between the Macintosh (shown here) and Windows dialog boxes, the options are the same.

Note:

Press Command/ Control-N to open the New Document dialog box.

4. **In the General tab, choose ActionScript 3.0 in the Type list. Leave all other options at the default settings, and then click OK.**

When you create a new file, the Stage is automatically centered in the document window. The Stage is essentially the workspace, or the digital "page" area; anything outside the Stage area will not be visible in the exported movie (although it will increase the file size, which affects its download time).

Note:

We have arranged our workspace to make the best possible use of space in our screen shots; feel free to arrange the panels however you prefer. For this project, you will be using the Tools, Properties, Align, Timeline, and Color panels.

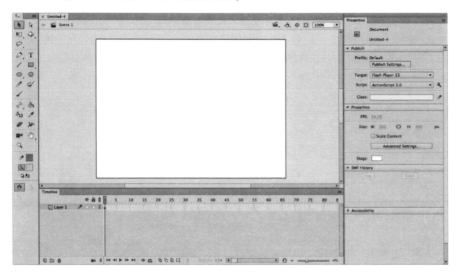

5. **Choose File>Save.**

Because this is a new file that has not yet been saved, choosing File>Save automatically opens the Save dialog box, where you define the file name, save location, and format.

If a file has already been saved at some point, the Save command simply overwrites the previously saved version of the file. If you want to save the new version and maintain the original, you have to use the File>Save As command to define a new name and create a copy of the file.

Note:

Press Command/Control-S to save the active file.

Press Command/Control-Shift-S to use the Save As option.

6. **In the resulting dialog box, navigate to your WIP>Vette folder.**

7. **Change the file name to corvette.fla. Make sure Animate Document is selected in the File Format/Save As Type menu and click Save.**

Native Animate files use the FLA extension. By default, the extension is included in the Save As/File Name field. You don't need to type it again if you don't delete the default extension from the field. (If you don't see the extension, uncheck the Hide Extension option at the bottom of the dialog box.)

8. **Continue to the next exercise.**

IMPORT A RASTER IMAGE

As we discussed during the production meeting for this assignment, you will base your work on a scanned sketch. Animate can import a range of file formats, including JPG, GIF, PNG, TIF, EPS, and native Illustrator and Photoshop files.

1. With corvette.fla open, choose File>Import>Import to Stage.

Four options are available when you choose the Import command:

- **Import to Stage** simply brings an external image onto the current Stage. Imported bitmap images are also added to the file Library panel; if you import a vector graphic that uses no symbols or embedded bitmaps, nothing is added to the Library.

- **Import to Library** automatically places graphics into the Animate Library panel.

- **Open External Library** is commonly used to incorporate graphics from one project into another project.

- **Import Video** allows you to bring digital video into an Animate file.

Note:

Press Command/Control-R to import an object to the Stage.

Save All			
Revert			
Import	▶	Import to Stage...	⌘R
Export	▶	Import to Library...	
		Open External Library...	⇧⌘O
Publish Settings...	⇧⌘F12	Import Video...	
Publish	⌥⇧F12		

Raster Images vs. Vector Art

ANIMATE FOUNDATIONS

There are two kinds of computer images. The first, known as a **raster image** or **bitmap**, is composed of simple pixels. Each pixel has a specific value, and that value determines the color, intensity, and brightness of that pixel. The number of pixels that make up a raster image is fixed at the time of the scan or photograph. If you blow up (enlarge) a raster image, it becomes grainy and loses quality; in fact, you can see the individual pixels in an enlarged raster image.

Animate is a vector-based program. **Vector art** is not based on pixels; instead, it is based on mathematical values. Vector art is essentially a tiny program that tells the printer or monitor to "draw a line from Point A to Point B, bending X degrees coming out of Point A and entering Point B from an angle of Z." Although this might sound confusing, you don't have to write any complicated code to make vectors work properly; you can simply draw with the Animate tools and the vectors are created for you.

Although vector graphics often improve the quality of images in a movie, they can also degrade playback performance because they require greater processing power to perform the necessary mathematical calculations.

An example of the difference between a raster image and vector art is shown below. At 100% size, both the raster image and the type (composed of vector objects) are crisp. If you zoom in closely enough, however, the individual pixels in the photograph start to show, and the image breaks down — but the type remains perfectly crisp and clear.

At actual size, both the type in this image and the photograph appear perfectly crisp and clear.

The detail on the tree breaks down if you look closely enough.

The type object, which is a vector object, remains clear even when enlarged.

2. **Navigate to your ШIP>Uette folder, select corvette.jpg, and click Open/Import.**

   The imported file is placed on the Stage, aligned to the left edge and centered vertically to the Stage area. As you can see, the placed image does not fit in the default Stage area.

3. **Note the placed image's width and height in the Properties panel.**

   Because the imported image is still selected, the Properties panel shows information about the image — most importantly for this exercise, the image's physical dimensions.

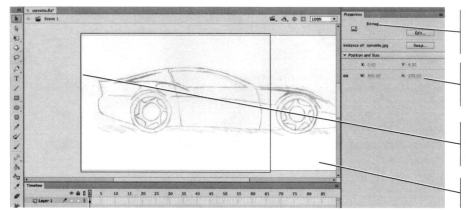

The Properties panel shows that the selected object is a bitmap file.

The object's position and size are clearly listed in the panel.

The placed file is aligned to the left edge and centered vertically on the Stage.

The placed file is wider than the current Stage area.

4. **Save the file and continue to the next exercise.**

 CHANGE DOCUMENT PROPERTIES

The imported artwork is larger than the defined Stage size. Because you're going to trace the imported sketch, you need to make the Stage area large enough to hold the entire sketch (and ultimately, the finished artwork).

1. **With corvette.fla open, choose the Selection tool at the top of the Tools panel.**

2. **Click in the gray area outside the Stage to make sure nothing is selected.**

   When nothing is selected in the file, you can use the Properties panel to access a number of options that affect the entire document — including the file's physical dimensions.

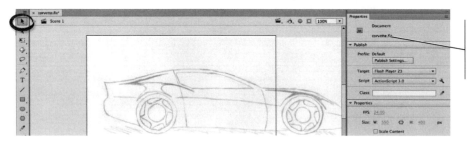

When nothing is selected, the Properties panel shows options related to the overall file.

3. **In the Properties panel, place the cursor over the left number in the Size setting.**

When the cursor is over an existing value, you can click and drag left or right to dynamically change the value (called a "scrubby slider").

Note:

Whenever we say "click and drag", you should hold down the mouse button as you drag. We will not repeat the instruction to hold down the mouse button unless it differs in some way from the normal click-and-drag procedure.

4. **Click the existing value to highlight the existing field value, then type 850.**

Clicking an existing value in a panel accesses the actual field; you can type to change the value in the field.

5. **Press Tab to highlight the Height field, then type 450, to change the Stage height.**

Note:

You can also simply click away from a field to finalize the new value.

6. **Press Return/Enter to finalize the change.**

7. **If the entire Stage does not fit into your document window, choose Fit In Window in the View Percentage menu.**

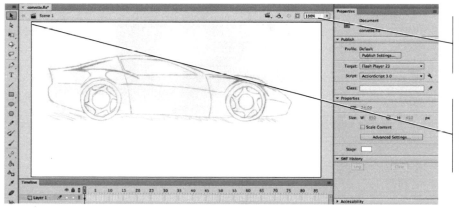

If necessary, use this menu to fit the entire Stage area in the document window.

The placed file's position relative to the Stage is not affected. The top-left corner is in the same spot as before you changed the Stage size.

Using the Document Settings Dialog Box

ANIMATE FOUNDATIONS

If you click the Advanced Settings button in the Properties panel (or choose Modify> Document), you can access the same document properties that are available in the Properties panel when nothing is selected in the file.

The Dimensions, Frame Rate, and Background Color options are the same as those available in the Properties panel.

By default, changing the Stage size does not affect objects that are already placed on the Stage. You can check the **Scale Content** option to resize placed objects when the Stage size changes.

You can also use the **Match Contents** option to automatically change the Stage size to match existing Contents (objects placed on the Stage) or Printer settings.

8. **At the bottom of the Align panel (Window>Align), check the Align To Stage box.**

When this option is active, you can use the Align panel to precisely position one or more objects relative to the defined Stage area in your file. (The Align panel remembers the last-used state of the Align To Stage option, so it might already be checked.)

Note:

Press Command/ Control-K to show or hide the Align panel.

Note:

Remember: all Animate panels can be accessed in the Window menu.

Align options move selected objects based on the defined edge or center.

Button icons indicate which edge will be aligned or distributed.

Distribute options average the spacing between the selected edge or center of objects.

Space options can be used to create uniform space between selected objects.

Check this option

Match Size options can be used to force objects to the same height, width, or both.

9. **Click the sketch with the Selection tool to select it, and then click the Align Horizontal Center and Align Vertical Center buttons in the Align panel.**

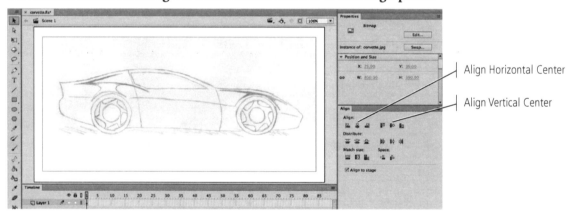

Align Horizontal Center

Align Vertical Center

10. **In the Align panel, turn off the Align to Stage option.**

If you later try to align multiple objects to one another and the Align to Stage option is still checked, the results will not be what you want. Although you can undo the Align process (Edit>Undo Align), it is a good idea to get into the habit of turning off the Align to Stage option as soon as you are finished using it.

11. **Save the file and continue to the next exercise.**

CREATE LAYERS FOR ORGANIZING ARTWORK

The Timeline panel allows you to easily create, arrange, and manage multiple layers in order to better organize your work. Layers can help you organize complex drawings and animations into a logical, easy-to-understand structure, while keeping all the components separate. You will use the timeline layers extensively as you complete the projects in this book.

1. **With corvette.fla open, review the Timeline panel.**

   Layers are listed on the left side of the timeline; the order in which the layers are stacked (from top to bottom) is referred to as the layer **stacking order**. Objects on higher layers in the stack will obscure objects on layers that are lower in the stack. You can easily change the stacking order by dragging a layer to a new position in the stack.

   Every file includes a default layer, named Layer 1. The icons to the right of the layer name provide a number of options, as well as some useful information.

   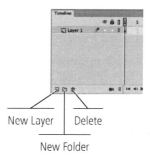

   - The Pencil icon identifies the active layer, where new objects will be placed when you create them.
   - Click the column under the Eye icon to hide or show a layer.
   - Click the column under the Lock icon to lock or unlock a layer.
   - Click the column under the hollow rectangle to toggle a layer between regular and outline mode. Outline mode shows only the wireframes of objects on that layer; fill and stroke attributes are not visible. The color of the rectangle under the Outline identifies the color of outlines, paths, anchor points, and handles for objects on that layer.

   New Layer | Delete
   New Folder

2. **Double-click the name of the layer to highlight the name. Type Sketch to rename the layer, and then press Return/Enter to apply the change.**

   Double-click the layer name to change it.

3. **Below the list of layers, click the New Layer button to add another layer on top of the first layer.**

   The new layer is automatically added immediately above the previously selected layer. New layers (and layer folders) are created in the same nesting level as the currently selected layer. In this case there is only one level of layers (there are no layer folders), so all new layers will be placed at the primary level.

4. **Using the same technique from Step 2, rename the new layer Window and press Return/Enter to apply the change.**

5. **Repeat Steps 3–4 to create four more layers: Body, Wheels, Door, and Accents.**

6. **If you can't see all six layer names, click the bar above the docked Timeline panel and drag up to expand the panel.**

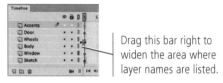

Drag this bar up or down to change the height of the Timeline panel.

Note:

If your Timeline panel is not docked, click the bottom edge of the floating panel and drag down to expand the panel.

7. **If you can't see the full layer names, click the bar to the right of the Outline icons and drag right.**

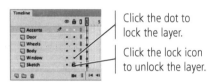

Drag this bar right to widen the area where layer names are listed.

8. **Lock the Sketch layer by clicking the small dot below the Lock icon.**

Locking the layer prevents you from accidentally deleting or otherwise modifying the sketch, which will be the basis for developing the actual drawing.

Click the dot to lock the layer.

Click the lock icon to unlock the layer.

Note:

If a layer is selected but locked, the pencil is covered with a slash, indicating that you can't change objects on the layer or add objects to the layer.

9. **Save the file and continue to the next stage of the project.**

Drawing Preferences

You can control a number of drawing options using the Drawing pane of the Preferences dialog box.

Each time you click with the Pen tool, you add an anchor point; successive anchor points are connected by lines. If the **Show Pen Preview** option is checked, a preview line follows the cursor to show the line that will be created when you add a new anchor point.

When the **Show Solid Points** check box is active, selecting an anchor point with the Subselection tool shows the selected point as solid instead of hollow.

The **Connect Lines** options (Must Be Close, Normal, and Can Be Distant) determine how close lines or points must be before Animate automatically connects them.

The **Smooth Curves** options (Off, Rough, Normal, and Smooth) determine how many points will be used to create a line when you're drawing with the Pencil tool with the Smooth or Straighten options turned on. The Rough option results in more points and a jagged line; the Smooth option results in fewer points and a smoother line.

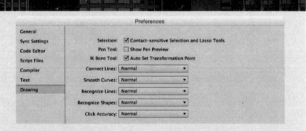

The **Recognize Lines** options (Off, Strict, Normal, and Tolerant) determine how close to straight a line drawn with the Pencil tool must be before Animate recognizes it as straight.

The **Recognize Shapes** options (Off, Strict, Normal, and Tolerant) determine how close to the shape an oval or square drawn with the Pencil tool must be before Animate recognizes it as the actual shape and makes the necessary adjustment.

The **Click Accuracy** options (Strict, Normal, and Tolerant) determine how close to an object you must place the cursor to select the object.

28 | Project 1: Corvette Artwork

Stage 2 Drawing in Animate

At the bottom of the Tools panel, a number of options affect what will happen when you create new drawing objects.

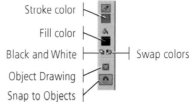
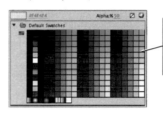

Stroke color
Fill color
Black and White — Swap colors
Object Drawing
Snap to Objects

Click the Fill Color or Stroke Color swatch to open the pop-up Swatches panel.

- Click the Stroke Color or Fill Color swatch to open a pop-up Swatches panel, where you can select a new color for the relevant attribute (stroke of fill).

- Clicking the Black and White button resets the default colors to a black stroke and white fill.

- Clicking the Swap Colors button reverses the active stroke and fill colors.

When you draw with the basic shape tools, or with the Pen, Line, Pencil, Paint Brush, or Brush tool, a toggle near the bottom of the Tools panel determines what type of drawing you will create.

- When the Object Drawing button is not highlighted (▣), shapes are created in **merge-drawing mode**.

- When the Object Drawing button is highlighted (▣), shapes are created in **object-drawing mode**.

All shapes drawn in **merge-drawing mode** exist at the bottom of the stacking order on their layer. In other words, they are always behind other objects — groups, drawing objects, symbol instances, etc. — in the same layer. You cannot rearrange the stacking order of merge-drawing shapes.

When you create an object in merge-drawing mode, the fill and stroke are treated as separate entities. You can individually select each part with the Selection (solid arrow) tool, and you can move or modify each part without affecting the other.

In the examples shown here, the oval shape was created in merge-drawing mode. It has a defined orange fill and blue stroke.

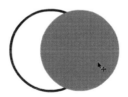

Click with the Selection tool to select the fill or the stroke; the cross-hatch pattern indicates the selected area.

Click and drag to move only the selected area.

Drag a selection marquee to select part of a shape.

Move or delete only the selected pixels.

When you drag one merge-drawing shape onto another on the same layer, the topmost shape removes whatever portion of the lower shape(s) it covers.

In the image to the right, the second column shows that we moved the orange circle on top of the blue circle. In the third column, you see the result of deselecting the orange circle, and then reselecting it and pulling it away from the blue circle. (This type of destructive interaction does not occur until you deselect the topmost object, which gives you a chance to "finalize" the edit. As long as you still see the crosshatch pattern on the object you're dragging, the underlying objects have not yet been changed.)

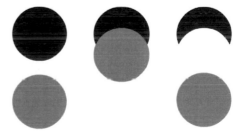

This type of interaction does not occur with objects created in object-drawing mode or when you're working with grouped objects. If you select something with the Selection tool and see a bounding box instead of the crosshatch pattern, underlying objects will not be affected.

You can prevent this type of destructive editing by grouping the components of the shape. Simply drag a selection around the entire object and choose Modify>Group. When a standard object is grouped, you see only the group **bounding box** when you select the object on the Stage. (The bounding box marks the outermost boundaries of the shape.)

Bounding box

After grouping the fill and stroke, you can't select the individual components. The bounding box indicates the boundary of the group.

Even when merge-drawing shapes are grouped, you can access the individual pixel components by double-clicking them on the Stage. This opens a secondary Stage — called **Edit mode** — where you can access and edit the individual components. The Edit bar above the Stage shows that you are no longer on the main Stage (Scene 1), but editing a group.

Edit bar

Double-clicking a group enters Edit mode for that group, where you can access the individual components of the group.

Of course, merge-drawing shapes have drawbacks as well; you could easily move or change an object that you don't want to change — such as dragging a fill away from its stroke and not realizing it until 15 steps later when it's too late to easily undo the error.

To solve this problem, you can draw in **object-drawing mode** by toggling on the switch at the bottom of the Tools panel. When you create a shape or line in object-drawing mode, it automatically displays the bounding box as soon as you create it, and you can't select the fill and stroke independently — at least not on the main Stage.

For a shape created in merge-drawing mode, you can use the Selection tool to independently select the shape's fill and stroke.

For a shape created in object-drawing mode, you can use the Selection tool to reveal the shape's bounding box. You can't independently select the object's fill or stroke.

If you want to access the individual components of an object created in object-drawing mode, simply double-click the object. Double-clicking activates Edit mode; the Edit bar shows that you are "inside" (editing) a drawing object.

In Edit mode, you can access the individual drawing shapes that make up an object created in object-drawing mode.

DRAW WITH THE LINE TOOL

The Line tool creates straight lines, which are simply strokes with no fills. You can combine lines with other shapes to develop custom objects. In this exercise, you draw several lines to complete the shape of the car's window.

1. **With corvette.fla open, click the Window layer (in the Timeline panel) to make it the active one.**

   Any objects you draw will be placed on the active layer. It's important to check which layer you're working on whenever you start to create new artwork. Many professionals prefer to lock all but the layer that is being used at a given time, although it isn't necessary if you remember to select the layer you want before you begin drawing.

2. **Select the Line tool in the Tools panel. At the bottom of the Tools panel, make sure the object-drawing option is turned off.**

3. **Using either the Properties panel or the Tools panel, click the Stroke Color swatch to open the pop-up Swatches panel.**

   When you select a drawing tool, the Properties panel provides a number of options that are relevant to the selected tool. These options remember the last-used settings, so some might already reflect the settings we define in the following steps.

   The Stroke Color swatch in the Properties panel is the same as the Stroke Color swatch in the Tools panel. Changing either swatch reflects the same color in the other one.

   When you use the Line tool, the Fill Color swatch in the Properties panel is always set to None. By definition, a line has no fill; you can't change the fill color of a line. The Fill Color swatch in the Tools panel, on the other hand, retains the last-used fill option. When you switch to a tool that creates filled shapes, the swatch in the Tools panel becomes the default fill color.

4. **Make sure the Alpha value is set to 100%, and choose a bright green color as the stroke color.**

   You can use any color you prefer; we are using green so it is easily visible against the gray lines in the sketch. Later in this project, you will change the stroke and fill colors of the various pieces to create the finished artwork.

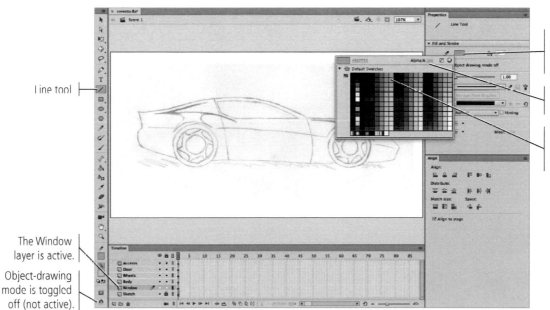

> *Note:*
>
> *You can Control/right-click a layer in the Timeline and choose Lock Others to lock all but the selected layer.*

> *Note:*
>
> *The Line tool does not create filled shapes, so the fill color is not relevant for this exercise.*

Line tool

Click the swatch to open the Swatches panel.

Make sure this value is set to 100%.

We are using this green color for the strokes.

The Window layer is active.

Object-drawing mode is toggled off (not active).

5. **In the Properties panel, set the stroke height (thickness) to 2 and choose Solid in the Style menu.**

You can type a specific stroke height in the Stroke Height field, or you can drag the associated slider for a live preview of the size you drag to (between 0.25 and 200 points).

Animate includes a number of built-in line styles, including dashed, dotted, ragged, stippled, and hatched. You can also edit the selected stroke style by clicking the pencil icon to the right of the Style menu.

Note:

The Scale menu defines how strokes are affected by scaling a symbol in which the line exists. (This option only affects strokes that are part of a symbol, which you will learn about starting in Project 2: Talking Kiosk Interface.)

Note:

The Hinting check box helps when you draw straight lines that are connected to smooth curves. When this option is not checked, the curves might seem to be disconnected from the straight lines.

6. **Open the Cap menu and make sure the Round option is active.**

The Cap options define the appearance of a stroke beyond the endpoint of the line.

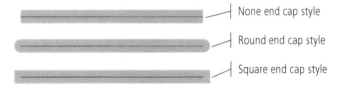

None end cap style

Round end cap style

Square end cap style

7. **Open the Join menu and make sure the Round option is selected.**

The Join options define the appearance of corners where two lines meet. When Miter is selected, you can define a miter limit in the Miter field. (This option is not relevant for Round or Bevel joins.) A miter limit controls when the corner switches from a pointed joint to a beveled joint, as a factor of the stroke height. If you define a miter limit of 2 for a 2-point line, the corner is beveled if the pointed corner extends beyond 4 points (2 × 2).

Miter join results in pointed corners.	Round join applies a circular edge to the corners.	Bevel join cuts off the points of the corners.

8. **Zoom in to the window on the sketch.**

As a general rule, we don't tell you the specific view percentage to use because every user's monitor and personal preferences determine a comfortable working environment. We do, however, tell you where to focus your attention.

9. **Choose View>Snapping>Snap to Objects. If this option is already checked (toggled on), move the mouse cursor away from the menu and click to dismiss the menu.**

As you draw different line segments with the Line tool, you want the ends of individual segments to align with each other. This is much easier when the Snap to Objects option is toggled on.

10. **Click the top-left corner of the window, hold down the mouse button, drag down and right, to the bottom-left corner, and then release the mouse button. When you release the mouse button, do not move the mouse cursor.**

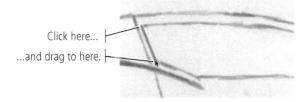

Click here...

...and drag to here.

11. **With the cursor in the same position as when you finished the previous step, click and drag down and right to create the lower-left corner of the window shape (use the following image as a guide).**

Because the Snap to Objects option is toggled on, when you first click you should see a small circle connecting to the end of the line you drew in the previous step. This indicates that the new line is connecting to that open endpoint.

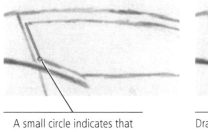 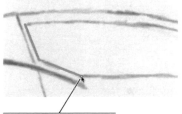

A small circle indicates that you are connecting to the open endpoint of an existing line.

Drag to here to create the second line in the shape.

12. **With the cursor in the exact position as at the end of Step 11, click and drag right to create the bottom edge of the window.**

13. **With the cursor in the exact position as at the end of Step 12, click and drag up and left until you see a small circle over the end of the first line you created, then release the mouse button.**

Again, the circle icon indicates that you are connecting to the open endpoint of an existing line — in this case, you are closing the shape.

The circle indicates that you are connecting to the open endpoint, effectively closing the shape.

14. **Save the file and continue to the next exercise.**

As the name suggests, the Selection tool is used to select objects. It can also be used to push or pull drawing objects into different shapes, almost as if you were pushing a string with your finger. In this exercise you will use this capability to bend the lines you just created into the correct shape for the car's window.

1. **With corvette.fla open, choose the Selection tool in the Tools panel.**

2. **Review the positions of the window corners. If any do not line up with the sketch, move the Selection tool cursor near the corner until a small corner shape appears in the tool icon. Click and drag to reposition the corner point.**

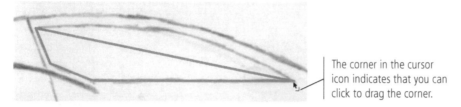

The corner in the cursor icon indicates that you can click to drag the corner.

3. **Move the cursor near the diagonal line that makes up the top of the window shape until you see a curved line in the cursor icon.**

If an object is already selected, you have to first deselect it before you can use the Selection tool to bend the lines into different shapes.

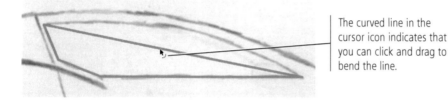

The curved line in the cursor icon indicates that you can click and drag to bend the line.

4. **Click and drag up to push the line into a curved shape that matches the sketch.**

One unique aspect of drawing with Animate is using the Selection tool to pull or push a line into a different shape. When you release the mouse button, the line is reshaped.

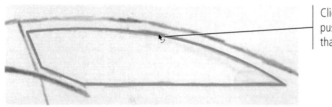

Click and drag up to push the line into a curve that matches the sketch.

5. **Repeat this process to slightly bend the diagonal line in the bottom-left corner of the window shape.**

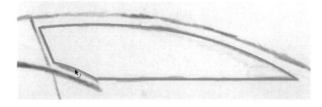

Note:

This type of "bending" works for objects created in merge-drawing or object-drawing mode.

6. **Save the file and continue to the next exercise.**

Anchor Point Basics

Using the Subselection tool. When you click a line with the Subselection tool, you can see the object's anchor points. When you click a specific anchor point with the Subselection tool, you select only that point.

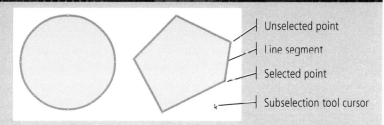

Unselected point

Line segment

Selected point

Subselection tool cursor

Moving points. To move a specific anchor point, select it with the Subselection tool and then drag to move it to the desired location. You can also **nudge** (move just a little bit at a time) a point by selecting it and then pressing the Up/Down/Left/Right Arrow keys on your keyboard.

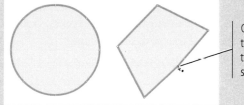

Click and drag with the Subselection tool to move only the selected anchor point.

Reshaping a curve using its handles.
To reshape a curve, first select it with the Subselection tool, and then drag the related handles. (Handles will appear from each smooth anchor point that is connected to the curve.)

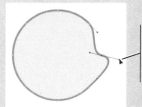

As you drag the handle up and out to the right, the shape of the curve changes accordingly.

Converting corner points to curves. To change a corner point into a smooth curve, first select the point you want to convert with the Subselection tool, then press the Option/Alt key and drag the point; handles appear, and the corner becomes a curve. You can then adjust the shape of the curve by adjusting the handles.

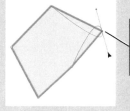

Option/Alt-click and drag with the Subselection tool to convert a corner point to a smooth point.

Converting curves to corner points.
If you need to convert a curve to a corner point, place the Pen tool over the curve point, press the Option/Alt key, and click to change the point to a sharp corner. (Alternatively, use the Convert Anchor Point tool.)

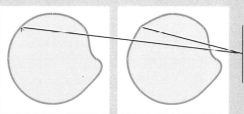

Using the Pen tool, Option/Alt-click a point to convert it from a smooth point to a corner point.

Adding anchor points. To add an anchor point, first select the path with the Subselection tool. Using the Pen tool, place the cursor near the path (but not over an existing anchor point) until you see a plus sign (+) in the tool cursor. Click the path to add a new point to the line. (Alternatively, use the Add Anchor Point tool.)

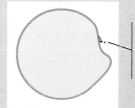

A plus sign (+) in the Pen tool cursor indicates that clicking will add a point to the segment.

Deleting anchor points. To delete an anchor point, first select the path with the Subselection tool. Using the Pen tool, place the cursor near an existing point until you see a minus sign (−) in the tool cursor. (Alternatively, use the Delete Anchor Point tool.)

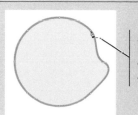

A minus sign (−) in the Pen tool cursor indicates that clicking will remove that anchor point.

DRAW WITH THE PEN TOOL

The Pen tool draws curved lines, known as **Bézier curves**, that are shaped based on the position of anchor points and their connected direction handles. This type of drawing creates very precise shapes, but can be difficult to master. In this exercise, you will draw the shape of the car body. While you work through the steps, you should try to get a feeling for how clicking and dragging affects the shape you create. The best way to master the Pen tool is to practice; as you gain more experience using the Pen tool, you will be better able to understand and predict exactly where you should click to create the shape you want.

1. **With corvette.fla open, select the Body layer to make it the active layer. Zoom out so you can see the entire car shape.**

   If the Body layer is locked, click the lock icon for the layer to unlock it.

2. **Choose the Pen tool in the Tools panel, and toggle on the Object-Drawing mode option.**

3. **Click the Fill Color swatch in the Tools panel and choose the None swatch in the top-right corner of the pop-up Swatches panel.**

   Because you want to be able to see the sketch through the shapes you create in this stage of the project, you are setting the fill to none.

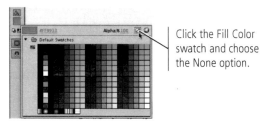

Click the Fill Color swatch and choose the None option.

4. **Using the Properties panel, make sure you are using the same color and size stroke that you used to create the window shape.**

   When you choose a new drawing tool, the object-drawing mode toggle, stroke, and fill properties retain the last-used options. If you took a break from this project after the previous exercise, make sure your drawing options are correct.

Note:

Remember, to zoom out you can press Option/Alt and click with the Zoom tool, or press Command/Control-minus (–).

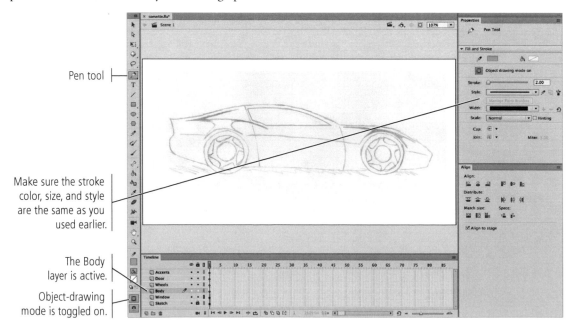

Pen tool

Make sure the stroke color, size, and style are the same as you used earlier.

The Body layer is active.

Object-drawing mode is toggled on.

5. Click once at the top-left corner of the car shape.

Clicking with the Pen tool places an anchor point with no direction handles. (You might have to look very closely to see the anchor point.)

Click here without dragging to place an anchor point with no direction handles.

6. Move to the right until you are above the back edge of the rear wheel. Click and drag to the right to place an anchor point with symmetrical direction handles.

When you click and drag with the Pen tool, you create a smooth anchor point with symmetrical direction handles (the handles on both sides of the point are the same length, exactly opposite one another). The length and angle of the direction handles define the shape of the segment that connects the two anchor points.

Click here to place the anchor point...   ...and drag to create the direction handles.

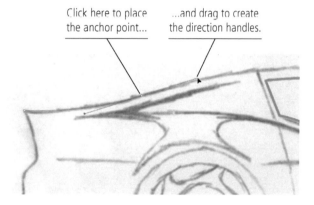

Note:

Pressing Command/ Control while using the Pen tool temporarily switches to the Subselection tool. When you release the key, the Pen tool is again active.

7. Click and drag right again where the back of the door intersects the top of the car.

As you drag, notice how the position of the direction handles affects the shape of the connecting line segment. Experiment with dragging up, down, left, and right to see the effect on the curve shape.

8. Click and drag again where the top of the car meets the hood.

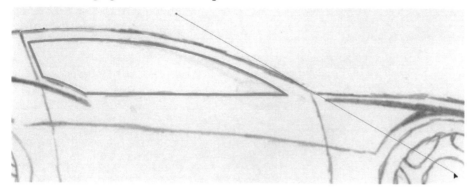

9. Place the cursor over the point you just created and click to remove the handle from the outside of the open point.

While you are drawing, clicking a symmetrical point again removes the direction handle from the outside of the point — converting the point to a corner point. The handle on the inside of the point remains because it is required to define the existing curve shape between the converted point and the previous one.

Note:

You can drag past the edge of the document window if necessary.

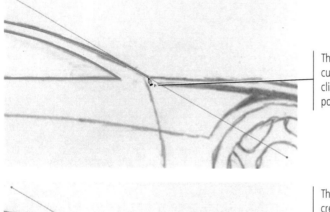

The upside-down v in the cursor icon indicates that clicking will convert this point to a corner point.

The inner handle is required to create the shape of the previous segment, so it is not removed from the new corner point.

Clicking removes the handle from the outside of the point.

10. Click and drag again near the corner of the front bumper.

Do not click the actual corner in the sketch. Because the bumper's edge is actually rounded, it's better to place anchor points on both sides of the curve rather than in the exact center of the curve.

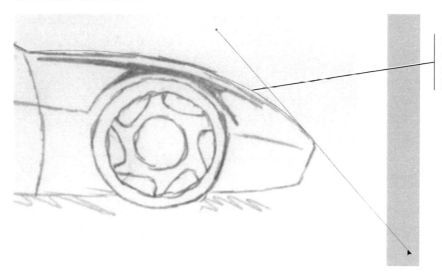

Don't worry about matching the sketched hood exactly; you'll fix this in the next exercise.

11. Click on the front side of the bumper, just below the curve, and drag short handles along the path of the bumper's front edge.

As you can see in our example, symmetrical points often result in incorrect paths. You will learn how to fix this type of problem in the next exercise.

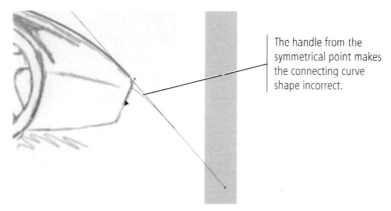

The handle from the symmetrical point makes the connecting curve shape incorrect.

12. Click just before the bottom curve of the bumper shape and drag slightly along the path of the bumper's front edge.

The point here is to create a smooth point with handles on both sides, without significantly affecting the shape of the connecting curve. Dragging a very small distance accomplishes this goal.

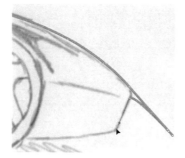

13. **Click and drag slightly along on the bottom edge of the car, just past the bottom-front corner.**

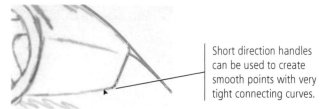

Short direction handles can be used to create smooth points with very tight connecting curves.

14. **Continue drawing the rest of the car shape by clicking and dragging to place anchor points with handles. For the bottom edge, simply extend the bottom-edge line over the wheel shapes.**

15. **When you get to the end of the shape, place the cursor over the original starting point and click to close the shape.**

    When you hover the cursor over the original starting point, the cursor shows a hollow circle in the icon, indicating that you can click to close the shape.

The circle in the cursor icon indicates that clicking will connect to the open endpoint and close the shape.

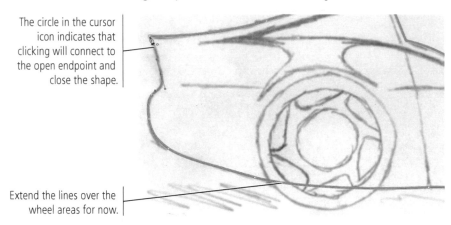

Extend the lines over the wheel areas for now.

16. **Save the file and continue to the next exercise.**

ADJUST BÉZIER CURVE SHAPES

From the previous exercise, you might have guessed that many of the lines that you draw with the Pen tool will not be perfect when you first create them. Fortunately, the Subselection tool makes it easy to edit the position of individual anchor points, as well as the length and angle of the direction handles that define connecting line segments.

1. **With corvette.fla open, zoom into the front end of the car.**

2. **Choose the Subselection tool in the Tools panel.**

    The Selection tool selects entire paths, but the Subselection tool selects individual anchor points. You use the Subselection tool to select and edit anchor points, or adjust the direction handles that define the shapes of curves that connect two anchor points.

3. **Click the green line on the hood to select the shape, then click the anchor point on the front edge of the car hood to select it.**

   Clicking a line with the Subselection tool reveals the shape's anchor points.

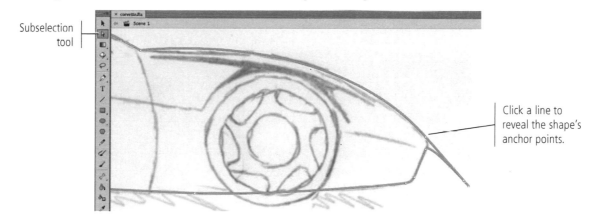

Subselection tool

Click a line to reveal the shape's anchor points.

4. **Click to select the anchor point near the top front edge of the car's hood.**

   Because you are using the Subselection tool, you can select individual anchor points. Selecting an anchor point reveals the handles that are related to that anchor point, which allows you to edit those handles.

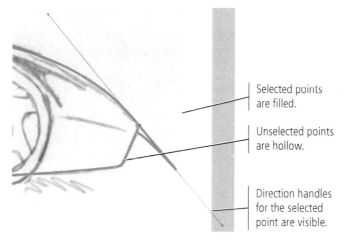

Selected points are filled.

Unselected points are hollow.

Direction handles for the selected point are visible.

5. **Click the outer direction handle (the one on the bottom) and drag up and left to reshape the curve on the top corner of the bumper.**

   When you drag one direction handle, the point remains smooth but it is no longer symmetrical; changing the length, but not the angle, of a direction handle affects only the segment on the same side of the point as the handle that you change.

   Because this is still a smooth point, however, dragging one handle to a different angle would also affect the point's other handle — affecting the shapes of both segments that are connected to the anchor point.

Drag the handle along the existing line position to shorten the handle without changing its angle.

Note:

If you drag toward or away from the anchor point without changing the angle, you are changing the arc of the segment that is related to the changed handle.

6. **Choose the Add Anchor Point tool (nested under the Pen tool), then click the existing line midway along the hood to add a new anchor point.**

   You can also add a point by moving the Pen tool cursor over an existing line segment.

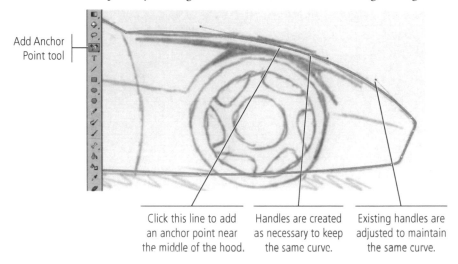

Add Anchor
Point tool

Click this line to add
an anchor point near
the middle of the hood.

Handles are created
as necessary to keep
the same curve.

Existing handles are
adjusted to maintain
the same curve.

7. **Using the Subselection tool, click the new point and drag until the path more closely resembles the line in the sketch.**

   When you move a point, the length and angle of the related handles are not affected. In many cases, you might need to move a point and then adjust the handles to achieve the effect you want.

8. **Review the position of each anchor point and line segment in the car shape. Make any necessary adjustments until you are satisfied with your drawing.**

   Keep the following points in mind as you fine-tune your shape:

   - To move a point, click and drag with the Subselection tool.
   - To add an anchor point, click an existing segment with the Pen tool (or use the Add Anchor Point tool that is nested under the Pen tool).
   - To remove a point, click an existing point with the Pen tool (or use the Delete Anchor Point tool that is nested under the Pen tool).
   - To convert a smooth point to a corner point, Option/Alt click the point with the Pen tool (or use the Convert Anchor Point tool).
   - To convert a corner point to a smooth point, Option/Alt click the point with the Pen tool and drag to create symmetrical direction handles for the point (or use the Convert Anchor Point tool).

9. **In the Timeline panel, click the dot under the Eye icon for the Sketch layer. Click the Stage (away from the existing shapes) to deselect everything, then review your progress.**

Any time you are working from a sketch, it can be helpful to hide the sketch so you can better see exactly what you have created.

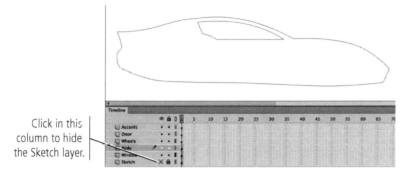

Click in this column to hide the Sketch layer.

10. **Click the X for the Sketch layer to show that layer again.**

Feel free to repeat this process throughout this project — we won't include this step again.

11. **Save the file and continue to the next exercise.**

USE DESTRUCTIVE EDITING TO CREATE SHAPES

When you work on a merge-drawing shape (in other words, one created without object-drawing mode toggled on), you can use the Selection tool to select specific pieces of objects:

- Clicking a stroke selects the line segment between the nearest two anchor points.
- Clicking a fill selects the entire area of the color you click.
- Double-clicking a merge-drawing shape selects the entire stroke and fill.
- Double-clicking the stroke of a merge-drawing shape selects the entire stroke.
- Clicking and dragging a marquee selects only the pixels inside the marquee area.

This behavior enables a type of **destructive editing** that is unique to Animate drawing tools. You can select and move or delete certain pieces of an object without affecting other pieces of the same object.

1. **With corvette.fla open, click the Body layer icon in the Timeline panel to select the layer.**

When you select a layer, all objects on the layer become selected. In this case, the layer only contains one object — the shape of the car's body.

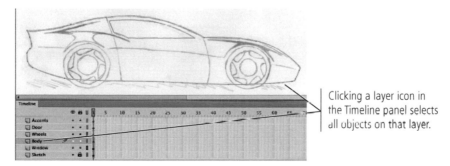

Clicking a layer icon in the Timeline panel selects all objects on that layer.

2. **Using the Selection tool, double-click any line of the car body shape to enter into the drawing object.**

   Double-clicking an object on the Stage switches into Edit mode for the object (often referred to as "entering" the object). While in Edit mode for a particular object, you can see but not access other objects on the Stage.

The Edit bar shows the path to the object you are currently editing.

Other objects are visible, but cannot be selected or edited.

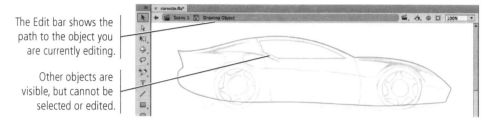

3. **Choose the Line tool in the Tools panel. Make sure Object-Drawing mode is toggled on at the bottom of the Tools panel or in the Properties panel.**

4. **Draw a straight line where the back of the door is indicated in the sketch. Extend the line above and below the car body shape.**

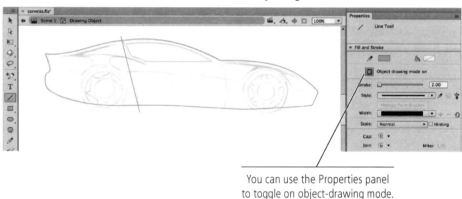

You can use the Properties panel to toggle on object-drawing mode.

Note:

While drawing, press Command/Control to temporarily access the Selection tool; when you release the modifier key, you return to the last-selected tool.

The easiest way to deselect everything is to press Command/Control, and then click away from any object on the Stage.

5. **Choose the Selection tool. Click away from the line to deselect it, and then use the Selection tool to bend the line into shape.**

6. **Click the line to select it again, and then choose Modify>Break Apart.**

   This command converts objects in object-drawing mode to merge-drawing mode so you can use the destructive editing capabilities of the Selection tool.

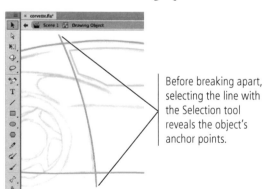

Before breaking apart, selecting the line with the Selection tool reveals the object's anchor points.

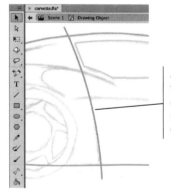

After breaking apart, the line is a merge-drawing shape; you can select the object's pixels with the Selection tool.

7. **Choose the Subselection tool in the Tools panel, and click any of the lines that make up the car body shape.**

    All lines you create in Animate are vectors, which means their position and shape are defined mathematically based on the anchor points that make up the shape. Animate automatically creates whatever anchor points are necessary to reproduce the line you draw — including points wherever two lines overlap, as you can see where the vertical curved line intersects the car body shape.

    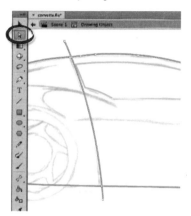

8. **Click away from the lines to deselect everything, then use the Selection tool to click the overhanging line above the car.**

    The selected area displays a small cross-hatch pattern.

9. **Press Shift and click the overhanging line below the car.**

    Pressing Shift allows you to select multiple objects at once; each item you Shift-click is added to the previous selection.

    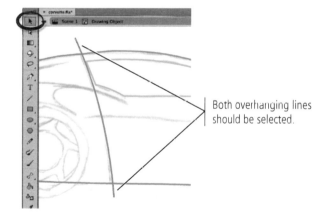

    Both overhanging lines should be selected.

10. **Press Delete/Backspace to remove both elements from the drawing.**

11. **Repeat Steps 3–10 to create the line that marks the front of the door.**

Later in this project, you need to be able to work with the car body shape as a single piece. If you left the door lines on the Body layer, the car shape would be effectively split into three pieces by the door-edge lines. To solve this potential problem, you are now going to move the door lines onto their own layer so they do not cut the car shape into pieces.

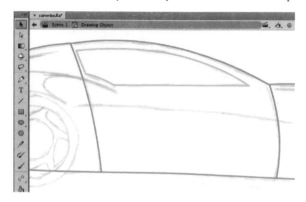

12. **Using the Selection tool, click one of the door edges to select it, then Shift-click to select the other.**

13. **With both lines selected, choose Edit>Cut.**

When you cut an object, it is removed from its original position and temporarily stored on the Clipboard — a reserved area of memory that allows you to temporarily hold objects until you need to use them again somewhere else. This is not the same as deleting (as you did in Step 10); when you delete a selection, it is not stored on the Clipboard.

14. **In the Edit bar, click Scene 1 to return to the main Stage.**

15. **Select the Door layer as the target layer and then choose Edit>Paste in Place.**

The Paste in Place command puts the cut objects in the exact position as they were cut from, but on the now-selected Door layer instead of the original Body layer.

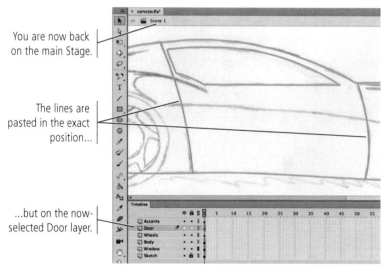

You are now back on the main Stage.

The lines are pasted in the exact position...

...but on the now-selected Door layer.

16. **Save the file and continue to the next exercise.**

DRAW WITH THE OVAL TOOL

Many otherwise complex objects are, in fact, simply a collection of primitive shapes. In the case of this car, you should recognize that the car's wheels are actually made up of three concentric circles. The basic shape tools — including the Oval tool — make it very easy to create this type of object.

1. **With corvette.fla open, select the Wheels layer (in the Timeline panel) as the active layer. Zoom into the rear wheel in the sketch.**

2. **Choose View>Rulers to show the Stage rulers at the top and left edges of the document window.**

3. **Click the horizontal ruler, hold down the mouse button, and drag down to place a horizontal guide in the center of the sketched wheel.**

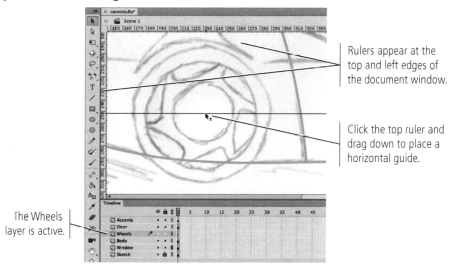

Rulers appear at the top and left edges of the document window.

Click the top ruler and drag down to place a horizontal guide.

The Wheels layer is active.

4. **Click the vertical ruler, hold down the mouse button, and drag right to place a vertical guide in the center of the wheel.**

You will perform a number of steps in this and the next exercise that will depend on an exact center point — where these two guides intersect.

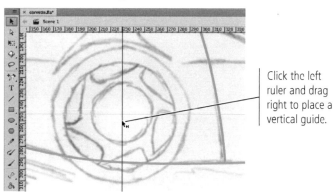

Click the left ruler and drag right to place a vertical guide.

Note:

Because this is a hand-drawn sketch, the wheels aren't exactly circular. It's okay if your circle doesn't exactly match the sketch.

5. **Choose the Oval tool in the Tools panel. Make sure object-drawing mode is toggled on.**

6. **In the Properties panel, make sure the fill and stroke settings match what you used in earlier exercises. In the Oval Options section, set all three sliders to 0.**

   The Oval tool shares many of the same properties as the Pen tool. You can define the fill and stroke color, as well as the stroke style, cap, and join.

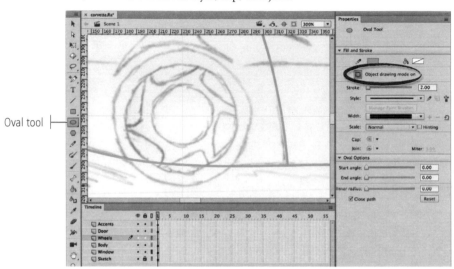

Oval tool

Understanding Basic Shape Options

When you draw a basic shape, the Properties panel also includes options for defining the shape that will be created.

When you use the Oval tool, you can define the **Start Angle** and **End Angle** to create a shape with a defined wedge removed (such as you might see in a pie chart). You can also use the **Inner Radius** option to remove a circle from inside the circle; the defined value refers to the radius of the inner circle (the part that is removed). The **Close Path** option, which is checked by default, can be unchecked to create an open path rather than a closed shape.

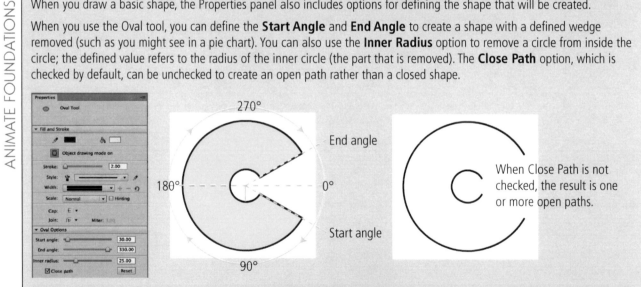

270°

End angle

180°   0°

Start angle

90°

When Close Path is not checked, the result is one or more open paths.

When you use the Rectangle tool, you can easily create a shape with rounded corners. The Options area in the Properties panel defines the **Corner Radius**; by default, all four corners are linked, but you can click the chain icon to define a different radius for each corner. (To understand the concept of corner radius, think of an imaginary circle at the corner of the shape; the radius of that circle is the corner radius, as shown in the image to the right.)

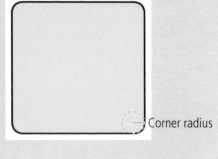

Corner radius

7. **Click at the intersection of the two guides, hold down the mouse button, press Option/Alt-Shift, and drag until the shape approximately matches the outer circle of the sketched wheel.**

You can create a basic shape by simply clicking and dragging; the shape is anchored where you first click. Holding down the Option/Alt key as you drag draws the shape from the center out. Holding down the Shift key while dragging constrains the shape to equal height and width.

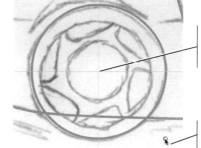

Click at the exact intersection of the guides, press Option/Alt-Shift...

...and drag to create a circle from the center out.

8. **Click the new object with the Selection tool to select it, then choose Edit>Copy.**

Copying stores the selected object in the Clipboard.

9. **Choose Edit>Paste in Place.**

Pasting places a copy of the Clipboard contents onto the selected layer. The Paste in Place command puts the copy in the exact position as the original. You can also choose Paste in Center to place the copy in the exact center of the document window.

10. **Choose the Free Transform tool in the Tools panel.**

When you select an object with the Free Transform tool, the object is bounded by eight transformation handles, which you can to scale, stretch, skew, or rotate the selection. The hollow white circle in the center of the bounding box is the **transformation point**, which identifies the origin point around which the transformation will occur.

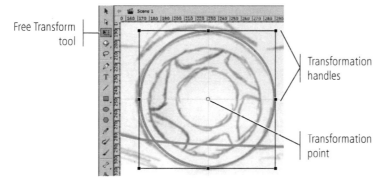

Free Transform tool

Transformation handles

Transformation point

11. **Press Shift, click the bottom-right bounding box handle, and drag up and left to shrink the circle around the center point.**

The transformation is applied around the transformation point, which defaults to the center of the selected shape. Adding Shift constrains the transformation so the object's height-to-width ratio remains the same as the original.

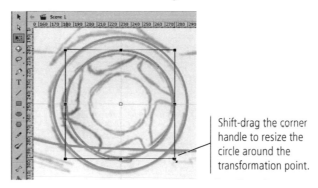

Shift-drag the corner handle to resize the circle around the transformation point.

Note:

To copy an object, select the object and press Command/Control-C.

To cut an object, select the object and press Command/Control-X.

To paste an object from the Clipboard onto the Stage, press Command/Control-V.

To paste an object in place, press Command/Control-Shift-V.

Using the Free Transform Tool

Free Transform mode allows you to change an object (or group) on the Stage by simply dragging. You can enter Free Transform mode by selecting an object with the Free Transform tool, by pressing Q (the keyboard shortcut for the tool), or by choosing Modify>Transform>Free Transform.

In Free Transform mode, the selected object is surrounded by a black bounding box with heavy black handles. A hollow circle in the center indicates the object's transformation point. Depending on where you place the cursor, you can apply different kinds of transformations. The cursor icon changes to reflect the change you will make by dragging.

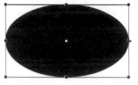
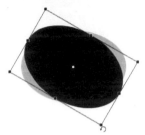
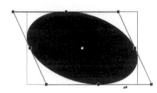

Click a side handle and drag to resize the object's height (left) or width (right).

Click outside a corner handle and drag to rotate the object.

Click and drag between handles on any side to skew the object.

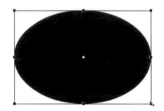
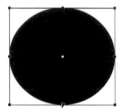

Click a corner handle and drag to resize both height and width at once.

Press **Shift** while dragging a corner handle to maintain the original height-to-width ratio in the resized object (called "constraining").

Press **Option/Alt** while dragging a handle to apply a change around the transformation point. (In this example, Option/Alt-dragging the bottom handle also moves the top handle.)

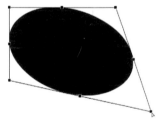
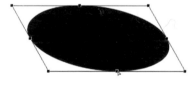

Press **Command/Control** while dragging a corner handle to distort the object shape.

Press **Command/Control** while dragging a side handle to skew and resize an object at the same time.

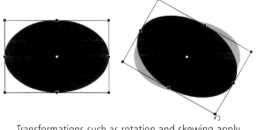
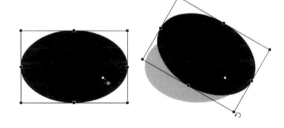

Transformations such as rotation and skewing apply around the transformation point, which defaults to the center of the object.

Moving the transformation point (left) changes the fixed point around which the rotation applies (right).

12. **Repeat Steps 8–11 to create the third circle in the wheel shape.**

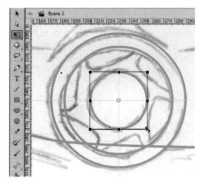

13. **Using the Selection tool, click away from all objects to deselect them.**

14. **Save the file and continue to the next exercise.**

 ## DRAW WITH THE PENCIL TOOL

The Pencil tool provides another way to develop curved artwork. Drawing with the Pencil tool is easy; simply drag a line or shape, and the stroke — in whatever color is currently set in the Tools panel — follows the cursor.

With the proper equipment — notably a pressure-sensitive drawing tablet — the Pencil tool might very well be the most important tool Animate offers. This notion is particularly true for artists skilled at sketching or drawing with natural media such as pen and ink, pencils, and pastel chalks. Other people find the Pencil tool difficult to use, preferring the Pen tool, Bézier curves, primitive shapes, freeform shapes, and combinations thereof.

1. **With corvette.fla open, make sure the Wheels layer is active. Hide the Body layer so the lines do not interfere with the area where you are working.**

2. **Choose the Pencil tool in the Tools panel. Using the Properties panel or Tools panel, make sure object-drawing mode is toggled on.**

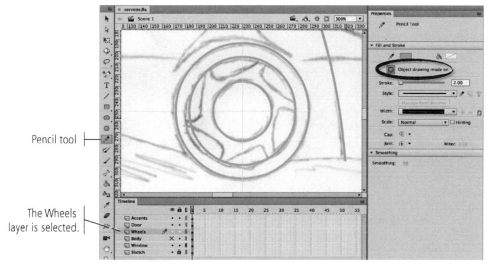

Pencil tool

The Wheels layer is selected.

3. **Click the mode button in the Tools panel and choose the Smooth option.**

The Pencil tool offers three possible modes:

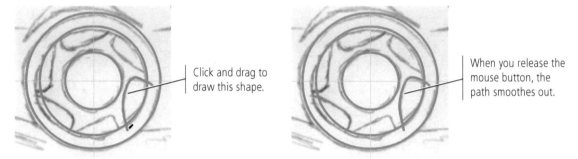

- Straighten mode favors straight lines and corner points.

- Smooth mode favors curves and smooth anchor points in the resulting paths. This option allows greater tolerance for slightly jerky movement as you drag, which can be very useful if you are using a mouse instead of a drawing tablet.

- Ink mode closely follows the path that you draw, placing a large number of anchor points to capture very small movements of the cursor; this mode often results in a very jagged path, especially if you are using a mouse instead of a drawing tablet.

4. **Click and drag to create one of the inset shapes on the wheel. Make sure you overlap the line ends with the second circle, as shown in the following image.**

When you release the mouse button, the Smooth mode should result in a fairly rounded inset shape.

Click and drag to draw this shape.

When you release the mouse button, the path smoothes out.

5. **Choose the Free Transform tool, then click the new shape to reveal its transformation handles.**

6. **Click the transformation point and drag to the intersection of the two ruler guides.**

You are going to copy and rotate this object around the wheel's center point to create the six inset shapes. The ruler guides that you placed mark the center of the wheel, which you used when you Option/Alt dragged from the guide intersection to create the circles. To rotate the inset shape around the same center, you are now moving the first shape's transformation point to the same center point as the overall wheel shape.

The Free Transform tool is selected.

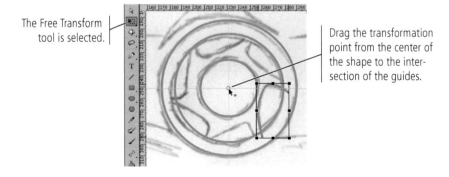

Drag the transformation point from the center of the shape to the intersection of the guides.

7. **With the object selected, choose Edit>Copy.**

8. **Immediately choose Edit>Paste in Place.**

Because you moved the transformation point before copying and pasting the object, the pasted copy also has the same relocated transformation point.

9. **Move the cursor outside one of the object's corner handles until you see the rotation icon in the tool cursor.**

10. **Click and drag left to rotate the copy, approximating the position of the second inset.**

As you drag, you should recognize that the object is rotating around the repositioned transformation point; in other words, it's rotating around the wheel center.

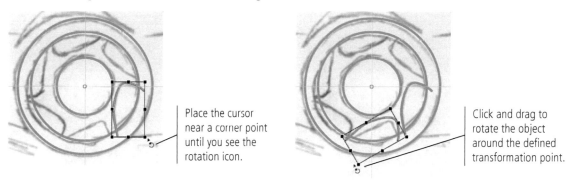

Place the cursor near a corner point until you see the rotation icon.

Click and drag to rotate the object around the defined transformation point.

11. **Repeat Steps 7–10 four more times to create the six wheel insets.**

In this case, don't worry about perfectly matching the sketch. The important point is to have six inset shapes, spaced approximately evenly around the wheel shape.

12. **Choose View>Guides>Clear Guides.**

You no longer need the wheel's center-point reference now that all of the necessary shapes are in place, so you can delete the ruler guides.

Note that this menu also includes options for showing or hiding guides, locking guides, and numerically editing the position of a guide. These options are all useful at some point, depending on the purpose of a particular guide.

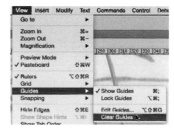

13. **Choose View>Rulers to toggle off the rulers.**

14. **Save the file and continue to the next exercise.**

WORK WITH AN OBJECT GROUP

You want to be able to access the individual shapes that make up the wheel, but you also want to be able to treat the wheel as a single unit on the main Stage. A **group** is a collection of shapes that is combined so it can be treated as a single object.

1. **With corvette.fla open, hide the Sketch layer to make the wheel shapes more prominent.**

2. **Choose the Selection tool, then click the Wheels layer icon to select all objects on that layer.**

   Because you created these objects in object-drawing mode, you can see the anchor points of each each shape. To prevent moving one of these components independently of the others, you can group them into a single unit.

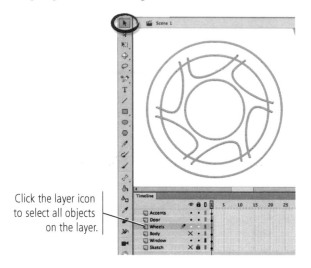

Click the layer icon to select all objects on the layer.

Note:

Press Command/ Control-A to select all objects (on all layers) that are not locked.

3. **Choose Modify>Group.**

   When you group objects, the bounding box displays around the entire group. By manipulating the bounding box, you can resize, move, and otherwise modify a group as you would a single object. Grouped objects are isolated from other elements on the same layer, so you can place grouped objects on top of one another with no worries of damaging the underlying objects.

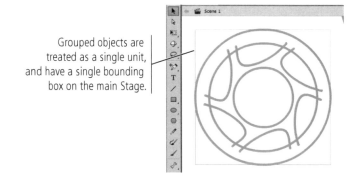

Grouped objects are treated as a single unit, and have a single bounding box on the main Stage.

Note:

You can group objects by pressing Command/ Control-G.

To ungroup objects, select the group and choose Modify>Ungroup or press Command/Control-Shift-G.

4. Double-click the group to enter into it (view the group in Edit mode).

Even though the objects are grouped on the main Stage, you can still access the individual components in Edit mode.

Because you drew these shapes in object-drawing mode, you can't access the pixels of the lines. You can't select and delete parts of the lines with the Selection tool, which you need to do.

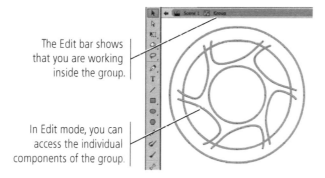

The Edit bar shows that you are working inside the group.

In Edit mode, you can access the individual components of the group.

5. With all objects in the group selected, choose Modify>Break Apart.

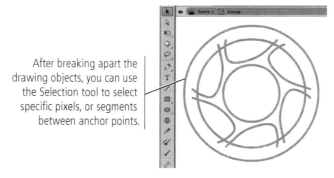

After breaking apart the drawing objects, you can use the Selection tool to select specific pixels, or segments between anchor points.

6. Click away from the lines to deselect everything.

7. Click to select one of the overhanging lines between the outer and middle circles, then press Delete/Backspace.

Remember from the earlier discussion on destructive editing that when you're editing a drawing object, Animate recognizes and separates overlapping elements.

8. Repeat Step 7 to remove all of the extraneous line segments.

9. In the Edit bar, click Scene 1 to return to the main Stage.

Because these objects started as a group, and you made all the edits inside the group, the selection on the main Stage is still treated a single unit; the bounding box surrounds the outer edge of all the objects in the group.

10. **Show the Body and Sketch layers.**

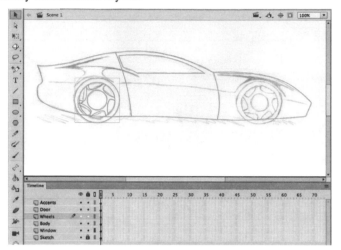

Note:

It's always a good idea to look for ways to avoid duplicating work. You will create the second wheel by duplicating the first wheel after you fill it with color.

11. **Save the file and continue to the next stage of the project.**

Stage 3 Painting and Coloring Objects

You now have all of the primary shapes you need for this project, clearly organized on separate layers. (You will create the front wheel later by duplicating the finished back wheel.) You drew all of these shapes as unfilled objects so you could see the underlying sketch; now you can apply fill colors to the various shapes. You can use a wide variety of methods to paint the car; you will explore these options in this stage of the project.

 ## APPLY FILL AND STROKE COLORS TO SELECTED SHAPES

The most basic way to change an object's color attributes is simply to select the object and then define the appropriate colors — which you will do in this exercise.

1. **With corvette.fla open, click the Body layer icon in the Timeline panel.**

   Remember, clicking a layer icon selects all objects on that layer.

2. **Click the Fill Color swatch in the Tools panel. Make sure the Alpha value is set to 100%, and choose a dark red color from the pop-up Swatches panel.**

   When you change the fill or stroke color when an object is already selected, you affect the relevant attributes of the selected object.

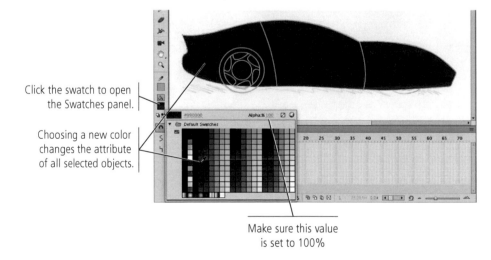

Click the swatch to open the Swatches panel.

Choosing a new color changes the attribute of all selected objects.

Make sure this value is set to 100%

3. **With the car shape still selected, click the Stroke Color swatch in the Tools panel and choose the None swatch.**

   This removes the green lines which were only necessary for the original drawing process.

4. **Review the layers in the Timeline panel.**

   The layer stacking order shows that the window is below the car body. Because the car shape now has a solid fill, you can no longer see the window shape.

   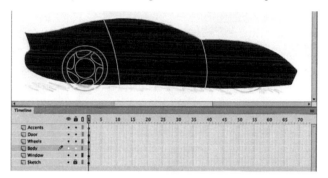

5. **Click the Window layer in the Timeline panel and drag up. When a line appears above the Body layer, release the mouse button.**

   Rearranging the layer stacking order is as simple as clicking and dragging. When the Window layer is above the Body layer, you can again see the window shape.

   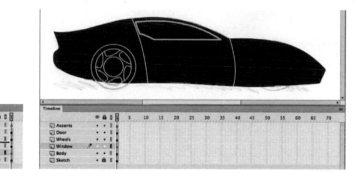

6. **Save the file and continue to the next exercise.**

FILL ARTWORK WITH THE PAINT BUCKET TOOL

The Paint Bucket tool provides an easy way to change objects' fill colors without first selecting the target objects. In this exercise you will use the Paint Bucket tool to change the fill colors of the window and the wheel.

1. **With corvette.fla open, make sure nothing is selected on the Stage.**

   If you change the Fill or Swatch color when an object is selected, the new color will affect the selected object.

2. **Choose the Paint Bucket tool in the Tools panel.**

3. **Use the Fill Color swatch in either the Tools panel or the Properties panel to change the Fill color to Black.**

4. **Click the Gap Size button at the bottom of the Tools panel and choose Close Large Gaps.**

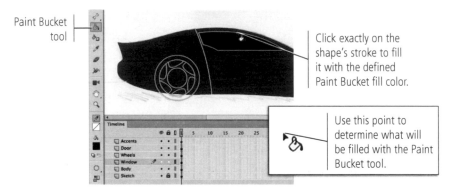

The Gap Size menu allows Animate to overlook slight openings between line segments, which is a common occurrence when you draw with tools such as the Pencil or Line tool. Because you want all of these objects to be solid fills, you are using the largest setting to allow the application to fill the areas that you have defined.

5. **Click the end of the pointer in the tool cursor on the line that identifies the window shape to fill the shape with the defined fill color.**

Because the object doesn't yet have a fill color, you have to click exactly on the existing line to fill the closed shape. If you clicked inside the shape, the tool would recognize the fill color of the body shape and change its fill to black.

Note:

If you change the wrong object (on a different layer), press Command/Control-Z to undo the last step, and click again to edit a specific object.

Some users prefer to lock all but the layer currently being edited, to prevent changes to objects other than the one you targeted.

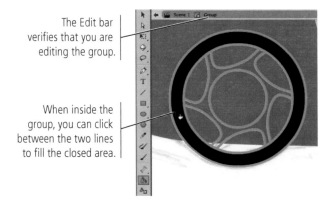

Paint Bucket tool

Click exactly on the shape's stroke to fill it with the defined Paint Bucket fill color.

Use this point to determine what will be filled with the Paint Bucket tool.

6. **Using the Selection tool, double-click the wheel group to enter into the group.**

You have to enter into the group to edit the properties of individual group components.

7. **Choose the Paint Bucket tool again, then click between the outer and middle circles of the wheel shape to change the fill color to black.**

In this case, you are editing only the group. There are no other objects on the group's Stage, so the Paint Bucket tool recognizes the closed area between the two circles and adds the black fill color.

The Edit bar verifies that you are editing the group.

When inside the group, you can click between the two lines to fill the closed area.

8. **Click inside the center circle, and then click inside each of the inset shapes to change all of those fills to black (as shown in the image after Step 10).**

9. **Change the fill color to medium gray, and then click inside the remaining shape (around the wheel insets) to fill that area with gray.**

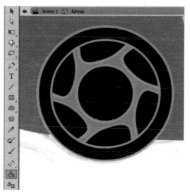

10. **Click Scene 1 in the Edit bar to return to the main Stage.**

11. **Save the file and continue to the next exercise.**

CHANGE STROKE ATTRIBUTES WITH THE INK BOTTLE TOOL

The Ink Bottle tool allows you to change the color of strokes without first selecting a specific object. Any stroke you click will be affected by the defined tool settings. In this exercise you will change the bright green strokes that you used during development to something that more accurately suits the project artwork.

1. **With corvette.fla open, choose Edit>Deselect All to deselect everything.**

   When either selection tool is active, you can also simply click an empty area of the Stage to deselect everything in the file.

2. **Choose the Ink Bottle tool, change the stroke color to black, and change the stroke height to 1 pt.**

   Once you select the Ink Bottle tool, you can use the Properties panel to predetermine the weight, color, stroke style, and other features before you use the tool. The current settings in the Properties panel will be applied to any shape you click with the Ink Bottle tool, and will remain in effect until you change them.

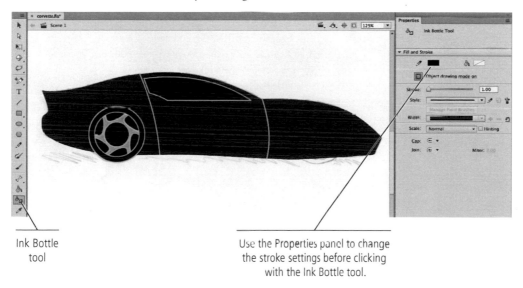

Ink Bottle tool

Use the Properties panel to change the stroke settings before clicking with the Ink Bottle tool.

3. Click inside the Window shape to change the object's stroke color to black.

The stroke instantly changes to the new color; it doesn't matter if you select the layer or not. Since all objects are on unlocked layers, the Ink Bottle tool "knows" which objects it's touching.

Click with the Ink Bottle tool inside a filled shape to change the object's stroke attributes.

4. With the Ink Bottle tool still selected, click the end of the pointer in the tool cursor directly on the lines that mark the front and back of the car door.

When an object has an existing fill, you can click with the Ink Bottle tool anywhere in the object's fill to change the stroke attributes. If an object has no defined fill, you have to click on the existing stroke to change its attributes.

To accomplish this step, it might help to zoom into the lines you want to change.

Note:

You don't need to select the objects before clicking with the Ink Bottle tool to change the stroke color.

Use this point to determine what will be filled with the Ink Bottle tool.

Because these are open lines with no fill, you have to click directly on the lines to change their attributes.

5. Zoom in to the top of the rear door line and review the results.

Because you removed the stroke from the body shape, the "door" lines now hang a bit past the edge of the body shape. You can fix that by adjusting the end-cap style of the door lines.

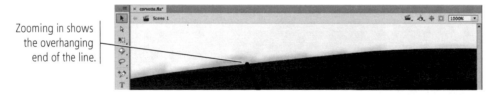

Zooming in shows the overhanging end of the line.

6. Select the door line with the Selection tool. In the Properties panel, choose None in the Cap menu.

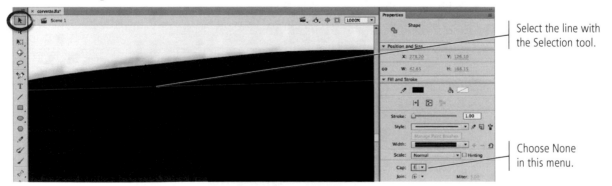

Select the line with the Selection tool.

Choose None in this menu.

7. **Repeat Step 6 for the line that marks the front of the door.**

8. **Using the Selection tool, double-click the wheel group to enter into the group.**

9. **Choose the Ink Bottle tool again and change the stroke color to medium gray.**

10. **Click exactly on the edge of the middle circle.**

    When you used the destructive editing functionality to create the inset shapes, a number of anchor points were added to the circle shape to create the inset pieces. You need to click the circle edge between and within every inset piece to change the entire stroke to gray.

11. **Continue clicking around the circle until the entire middle circle has a 1-pt gray stroke.**

12. **Change the stroke color to black and then click all of the remaining green strokes in the wheel to change them to black.**

    In this case, you have to click the actual strokes. If you clicked the fills, you might inadvertently change the gray stroke of the middle circle back to black.

13. Click Scene 1 in the Edit bar to return to the main Stage.

14. Using the Selection tool, click the wheel group, press Option/Alt, and drag right until the duplicate wheel aligns with the front wheel.

   Pressing Option/Alt while dragging **clones** (makes a copy of) the object you drag.

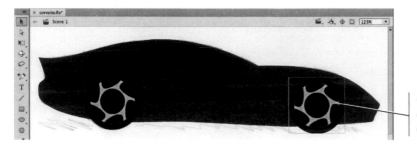

Option/Alt-dragging an object makes an exact copy (called cloning).

15. Save the file and continue to the next exercise.

ADJUST ALPHA TRANSPARENCY

The Alpha property defines the degree of transparency of an object; in other words, it determines how much you can see underlying objects through another object. This can be useful for creating special effects, including the appearance of depth. In this exercise you will adjust alpha values to create the appearance of reflections on the car's surface.

1. With corvette.fla open, click the Outline button for the Body layer so you can see the underlying sketch. Select the Accents layer as the active one.

   Outline mode allows you to see through filled artwork without changing the objects' fill properties. All objects on outlined layers appear as simple lines that match that layer's defined color swatch; defined fill and stroke attributes are not visible.

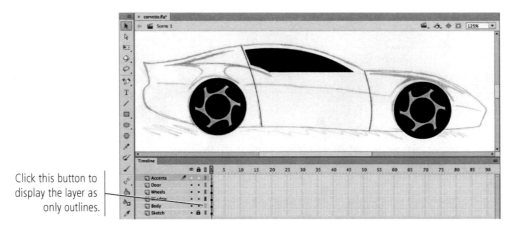

Click this button to display the layer as only outlines.

2. Use any tool you prefer (with object-drawing mode toggled on) to create the two curved shapes that represent reflections on the car's upper body.

3. In the Timeline panel, click the Outline button for the Body layer to restore the layer to the regular view.

4. **Select both of the accent shapes and apply a white fill and no stroke.**

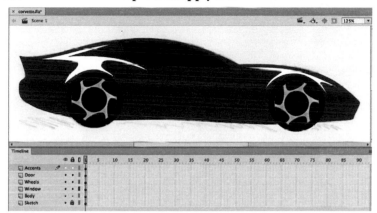

5. **In the Color panel, click the Fill Color swatch to open the color palette.**

   Remember, all panels can be accessed in the Window menu.

6. **Place the cursor over the Alpha value (in the top-right corner of the palette) until you see a two-headed arrow in the hand icon.**

When you see this cursor, you can click and drag left or right to change the associated value (called "scrubbing").

7. **Click and drag left to reduce the Alpha value to 50%.**

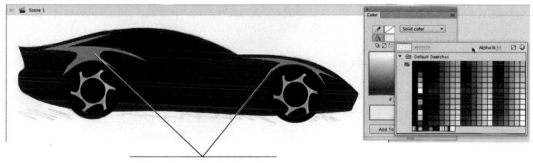

After reducing the Alpha value, you can see some of the red color through the white-filled shapes.

8. **Save the file and continue to the next exercise.**

CONVERT STROKES TO SOFTENED FILLS

The sketch in this project shows three lines that seem to bisect the car, creating an edge that catches the reflection of light. In this exercise, you will create these lines and then adjust them to add depth and texture to the artwork.

1. With `corvette.fla` open, click the Outline icon for the Body layer so you can see the underlying sketch. Make sure the Accents layer is the active one.

2. Choose the Line tool in the Tools panel and activate object-drawing mode. Change the stroke color to white with a 50% Alpha value, and set the stroke height to 1 pt.

3. Draw the three lines on the car that seem to bisect the car horizontally. Use the Selection tool to position and bend the lines as necessary.

4. Click the Outline button for the Body layer to restore it to the normal view.

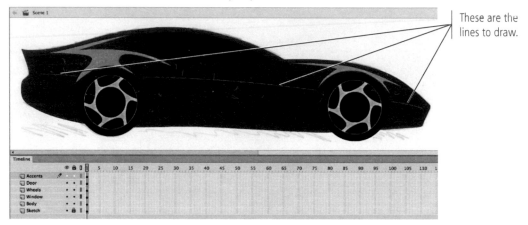

These are the lines to draw.

5. Using the Selection tool, Shift-click to select all three lines.

6. Choose Modify>Shape>Convert Lines to Fills.

   These hard-edged lines appear rather harsh; you are going to modify these lines to more smoothly blend into the underlying shape. To do this, you first need to convert the strokes to filled shapes. The fill of the new shapes adopts the stroke color that was applied to the original line.

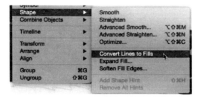

7. With the three lines still selected, choose Modify>Shape>Soften Fill Edges.

8. In the resulting dialog box, set the Distance field to 2 px and set the Number of Steps field to 4. Choose the Expand option.

9. Click OK to apply the change.

Each edge of the shape is now extended by 2 pixels, moving in four steps from the original alpha value (50%) to 0%, or entirely transparent.

| Before converting to a fill | After converting to a fill | After softening edges |

10. Save the file and continue to the next exercise.

PAINT WITH THE BRUSH TOOL

The Brush tool, as you might expect, is used to paint areas of color. This tool offers a number of modes that allow you to paint in only specific areas, as you will do in this exercise to create a shadow underneath the car.

1. With corvette.fla open, select the Body layer as the active one. Click away from the artwork on the Stage to deselect everything.

2. Choose the Brush tool, change the fill color to a medium gray, and set the Alpha value to 100%.

3. At the bottom of the Tools panel, make sure Object Drawing Mode is toggled on.

4. Click the Brush Mode menu and choose Paint Behind.

The Brush tool has five modes:

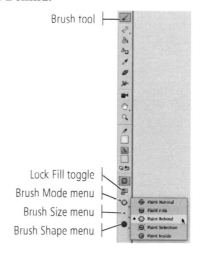

Brush tool
Lock Fill toggle
Brush Mode menu
Brush Size menu
Brush Shape menu

- **Paint Normal** is exactly that: it paints on top of anything already on the Stage.

- Using the **Paint Fills** mode, you paint over the background and any object fills, but you leave object strokes unaffected.

- **Paint Behind** allows you to paint only the background; any area with a fill or stroke remains unaffected by the brush stroke.

- **Paint Selection** applies your brush strokes to currently selected fill areas only.

- **Paint Inside** applies the brush stroke within the boundaries of the fill where you first click.

5. Click the Brush Size button and choose the largest available solid brush.

6. Click the Brush Shape button and choose the full round option.

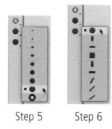

Step 5   Step 6

> *Note:*
>
> *The tool options remember the last-used settings, so some of these might already be set to the options we use in this exercise.*

7. **Using the sketch as a rough guide, click and drag to paint a shadow shape underneath the car.**

   Don't worry about overlapping the car body shape while you're painting the shadow; although it appears to be on top of (and obscuring) the car shape, the shadow assumes its proper place behind the body when you release the mouse button.

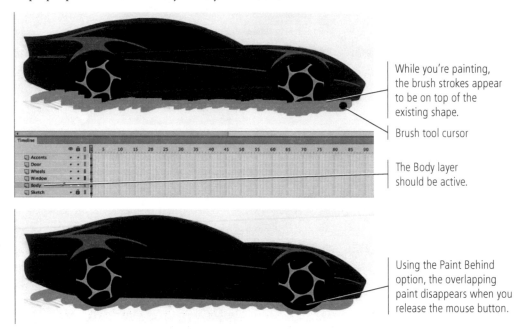

While you're painting, the brush strokes appear to be on top of the existing shape.

Brush tool cursor

The Body layer should be active.

Using the Paint Behind option, the overlapping paint disappears when you release the mouse button.

8. **Using the Selection tool, select the shadow shape and then choose Edit>Cut.**

9. **In the Timeline panel, click the New Layer button. Name the new layer Shadow.**

   As we explained previously, new layers are always added immediately above the previously selected layer.

10. **With the Shadow layer selected, choose Edit>Paste in Place.**

    Even though you couldn't see the entire brush stroke after releasing the mouse button, the shape exactly matches the area that you painted. When moved to a higher layer in the stack, the entire area becomes visible — obscuring some of the car body.

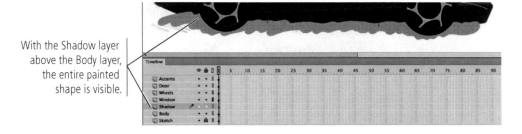

With the Shadow layer above the Body layer, the entire painted shape is visible.

11. **Click the Shadow layer in the Timeline panel and drag it below the Body layer.**

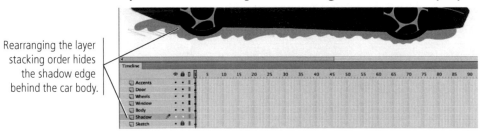

Rearranging the layer stacking order hides the shadow edge behind the car body.

12. **Save the file and continue to the next exercise.**

APPLY LINEAR AND RADIAL GRADIENTS

At this point your artwork is a technically complete piece of artwork; all of the shapes are in place, with the necessary solid fills and strokes to clearly portray a digital Corvette. To add greater depth and dimension, however, you are going to apply gradients to the car's body and window.

1. **With corvette.fla open, click the window shape with the Selection tool.**

2. **Using either the Properties or Tools panel, open the Fill Color palette and choose the white-to-black radial gradient swatch.**

   As soon as you apply the gradient, you see the gradient transformation handles around the selected shape. You can ignore those for now.

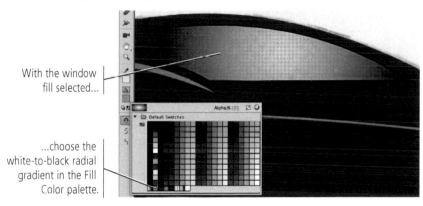

With the window fill selected...

...choose the white-to-black radial gradient in the Fill Color palette.

Note:

The terms "gradient" and "blend" are used interchangeably. Animate documentation uses both gradient and blend; both terms mean a smooth transition from one color to another.

3. **In the Color panel, click below the gradient ramp near the middle to add a new color stop to the gradient.**

   Clicking below the ramp adds a new stop, which defaults to the color of the location where you first click.

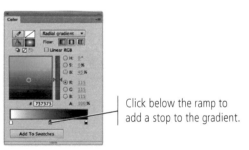

Click below the ramp to add a stop to the gradient.

Note:

You can define up to 15 color stops in a single gradient.

4. **Drag the new stop left, to approximately one-fourth of the way across the ramp.**

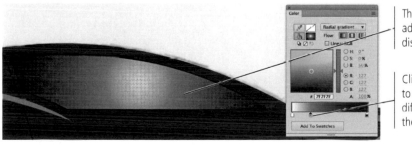

The selected shape adopts the new distribution of color.

Click the stop and drag to move that color to a different position along the gradient.

5. **Click the car body shape with the Selection tool.**

6. **In the Color panel, click the Fill Color icon to activate that attribute.**

7. **In the Color Type menu, choose Linear Gradient.**

   The gradient ramp remembers the last-used gradient, so the adjusted white-to-black gradient from the window is applied to the selected shape (the car body).

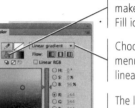

Click here to make sure the Fill icon is active.

Choose from this menu to apply a linear gradient.

The last-used gradient is applied automatically .

8. **At the bottom of the Color panel, click the color stop in the middle of the gradient ramp and drag down away from the ramp.**

   You can remove any stop from a gradient by simply dragging it away from the ramp.

9. **Double-click the color stop at the left end of the gradient ramp. Choose the dark red color swatch from the pop-up palette.**

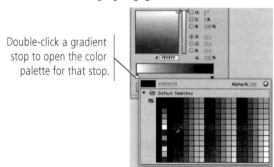

Double-click a gradient stop to open the color palette for that stop.

10. **Double-click the right color stop and choose the same dark red color that you applied to the left stop.**

11. **With the right stop still selected, drag the Brightness slider in the Color panel down until the B option (in the HSB group) shows 10%.**

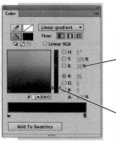

This is the value you are affecting by dragging the slider.

Drag here to change the stop's brightness value.

12. **Save the file and continue to the next exercise.**

TRANSFORM GRADIENTS

As you saw in the previous exercise, it is fairly easy to apply gradients to any drawing object, and to change the colors that are used in those gradients. Of course, the left-to-right gradient on the car's body does not create the realistic effect that you want. You now need to transform the applied gradients to finish the piece.

1. **With corvette.fla open, choose the Gradient Transform tool (nested under the Free Transform tool).**

2. **Click the window shape to select it.**

   The Gradient Transform tool enables you to adjust the size, direction, and center point of a gradient fill. When you click an object filled with a gradient, a special bounding box shows the gradient-editing handles.

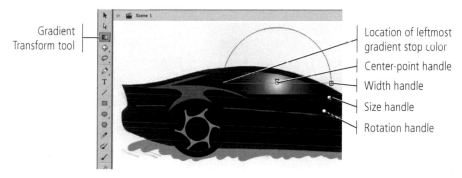

3. **Click the center point of the gradient and drag to the top-left corner of the window shape.**

   Dragging the center-point handle moves the center of the gradient to a new location.

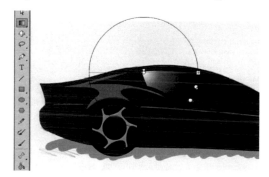

4. **Click the gradient-width handle and drag in about halfway to flatten the gradient.**

   Dragging the width handle of a radial gradient makes the gradient narrower or wider in one direction, essentially creating a skewed effect.

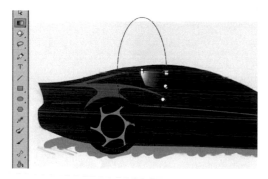

5. Click the gradient-rotation handle and drag left to change the angle of the gradient.

Dragging the rotation handle rotates the gradient around its center point.

6. Click the gradient-size handle and drag out to enlarge the adjusted gradient.

Dragging the size handle makes the overall gradient larger or smaller in both directions (without affecting the gradient's aspect ratio).

7. Still using the Gradient Transform tool, click the car body shape to select it and access the gradient transformation handles.

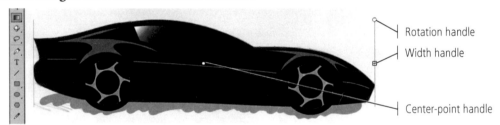

Rotation handle

Width handle

Center-point handle

8. Click the gradient-rotation handle and drag down and left to rotate the gradient approximately 90°, with the dark part of the gradient toward the bottom edge of the car.

Because you did not yet change the gradient width, the rotated gradient transformation handles will be well below the Stage edge. If necessary, zoom out so you can see all the gradient transformation handles.

Note:

You can use the rotation handle to reverse a gradient. Simply drag all the way around (180°) until the gradient colors are reversed.

The gradient transformation handles are below the Stage edge because you have not yet changed the gradient width.

9. **Click the gradient-width handle and drag up until the gradient is just slightly larger than the height of your artwork.**

   For a linear gradient, dragging the width handle makes the gradient narrower or wider.

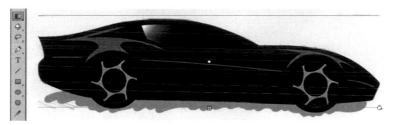

10. **Click the center point of the gradient and drag down, about one-third of the way closer to the bottom of the car body.**

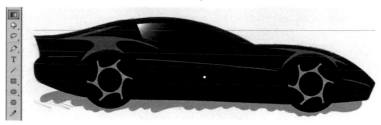

11. **Save the file and continue to the next exercise.**

Locking Bitmap and Gradient Fills

You can use a bitmap (raster) image as the fill of an object by choosing Bitmap Fill in the Fill Type menu of the Color panel. Available bitmap files appear as tiles in the lower half of the panel; if none are available, choosing Bitmap Fill opens a dialog box, so you can import the file you want.

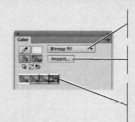

Choose Bitmap Fill in this menu.

Click Import to add bitmaps to the file.

Click any available tile to select that bitmap as the fill.

You can use the Paint Bucket tool to fill an existing object with a bitmap, or use the Brush tool to paint the bitmap onto the Stage. The **Lock Fill** modifier at the bottom of the Tools panel determines how the fill will be added.

- When toggled on, the selected bitmap image is tiled inside the shape.
- When toggled off, the selected bitmap image is basically pasted to the Stage. The filled area essentially "reveals" the area of the selected bitmap image. (If a bitmap-fill image is too small to fill the Stage, the image is tiled as necessary)

Lock Fill modifier

Turned on, the bitmap image is tiled inside the filled shape.

Turned off, the shape reveals the relevant area of the bitmap.

If you select a bitmap-filled object with the Gradient Transform tool, you can edit the size, skew, rotation, and position of the fill image.

Similar Lock Fill options are available when you work with gradients. When this option is toggled on, the gradient is applied relative to the overall Stage; filled areas reveal the relevant area of the gradient. If the option is turned off, the gradient is applied to each object independently.

With the Lock Fill modifier, the same gradient extends across all four squares.

Without the Lock Fill modifier, the gradient is applied individually to each square.

ORGANIZE FINISHED ARTWORK LAYERS

An Animate project can contain dozens of layers representing the various components of the animation or movie. To organize all of these layers into logical groups or categories, you can use layer folders.

1. **With corvette.fla open, select the top layer (Accents) in the Timeline panel.**

2. **Click the New Folder button at the bottom of the Timeline panel.**

New Folder
button

3. **Double-click the new folder name. Type Car Parts as the new folder name and press Return/Enter to finalize the new name.**

   You change the name of a layer folder the same way you change the name of a layer; simply double-click the folder name and type in the new name.

4. **Click the Accents layer to select it, then Shift-click the Shadow layer to add it and all contiguous layers to the selection.**

5. **Click any of the selected layers and drag them into the Car Parts folder.**

   The dragged layers now reside inside the layer folder, which makes it easier to treat the entire group of layers as a single object. This will be helpful later when the artwork is used in programming and interactive development.

Note:

You can rename layer folders in the same way you rename layers, and you can reorder layer folders (and their contents) by dragging the folders into new positions in the layer stack.

Shift-click to
select multiple
adjacent items.

The indented line shows
that the selected layers
will be placed inside the
Car Parts folder.

6. **Click the Lock column for the Car Parts folder.**

   By locking the layer folder, you have effectively locked each layer inside the folder (although you can unlock individual layers in the folder by clicking that layer's Lock icon). The same concept is true of the Visibility and Outline buttons for the layer folder.

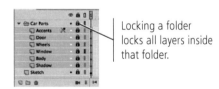

Locking a folder
locks all layers inside
that folder.

Note:

Press Shift to select contiguous layers — that is, layers directly on top of or below one another. To select layers that aren't next to each other, press the Command/Control key while clicking the individual (non-contiguous) layers.

7. **Click the arrow to the left of the Car Parts folder to collapse it.**

   Once collapsed, only the layer folder is visible. This makes it easier to navigate through the Timeline panel, which can grow very large for complex projects.

8. **Select the Sketch layer and click the panel's Delete button.**

Click here to collapse
the Car Parts folder.

Select the Sketch layer
and click here to delete it.

Note:

When you use layer folders, you can lock and hide all the contents in the folder by locking and hiding the entire folder.

9. **Save the file and continue to the final exercise.**

EXPORT ARTWORK AS AN IMAGE

Instead of sending the Animate file to your client, you are going to export a static image that can be easily reviewed by anyone with a Web browser. Animate includes the ability to export a number of static image formats, including JPEG, GIF, and PNG.

1. **With corvette.fla open, choose File>Export>Export Image.**

2. **In the bottom left corner of the resulting dialog box, choose Fit On Screen in the View Percentage menu.**

    You can use the Export Image dialog box to determine what type of file you want to export, as well as the specific settings for the selected file format.

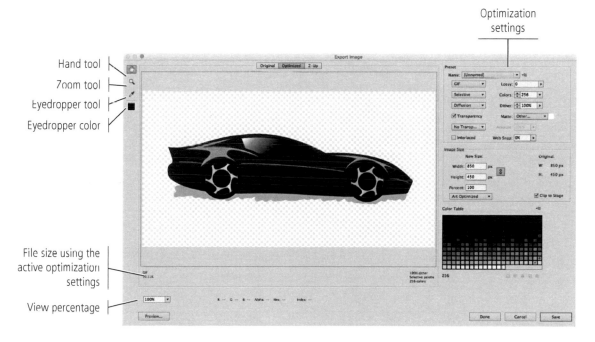

3. **In the right side of the dialog box, choose JPEG in the Format menu and choose Maximum in the Quality menu.**

    Reducing the Quality value will result in a smaller file size, but can significantly decrease the resulting image quality. For review purposes, the highest possible quality setting is a better option.

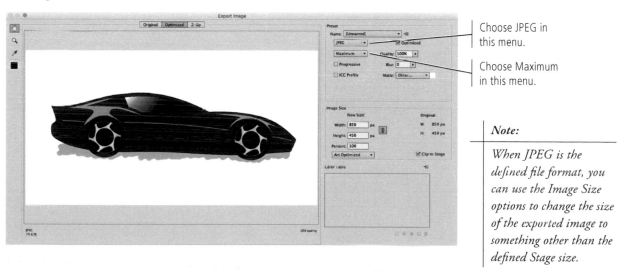

Note:

When JPEG is the defined file format, you can use the Image Size options to change the size of the exported image to something other than the defined Stage size.

4. **Click Save. In the resulting dialog box, navigate to your WIP>Vette folder as the target location.**

5. **Add -drawing to the end of the existing file name (before the file extension).**

   On Windows, the file extension might not be visible in the document window. If this is the case, simply type after the existing file name.

   The original file name is automatically based on the file name of your native Flash file.

   Add the second half of the file name to distinguish this file from the sketch.

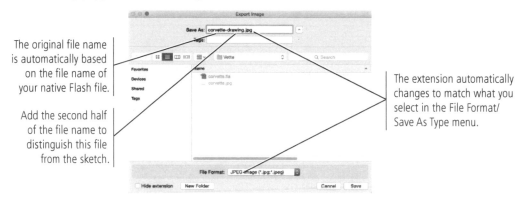

   The extension automatically changes to match what you select in the File Format/ Save As Type menu.

6. **Click Save to export the JPEG file.**

7. **Close the corvette.fla file.**

fill in the blank

1. The _____ can be used to change the size of the Stage.

2. _____ in the Timeline panel can be used to manage the top-to-bottom order of objects on the Stage.

3. When created in _____, the fill and stroke are treated as separate entities; you can individually select each part, and move or modify each part without affecting the other.

4. When you create a shape in _____, it automatically displays the bounding box as soon as you create it; you can't select the fill and stroke independently on the main Stage.

5. A(n) _____ allows multiple objects to be treated as a single entity on the Stage.

6. The _____ tool can be used to select areas of a standard-drawing object, or to bend lines created in either drawing mode.

7. The _____ tool can be used to select individual anchor points and handles that make up a shape.

8. The _____ tool is used to create precise Bézier curves.

9. The _____ tool is used to change the fill color of closed shapes.

10. The _____ tool is used to change the stroke color of any object.

short answer

1. Briefly explain how anchor points and handles control the lines in a vector shape.

2. Briefly explain the difference between the Selection tool and the Subselection tool.

3. Briefly explain what is meant by "destructive editing."

Portfolio Builder Project

Use what you learned in this project to complete the following freeform exercise.
Carefully read the art director and client comments, then create your own design to meet the needs of the project.
Use the space below to sketch ideas; when finished, write a brief explanation of your reasoning behind your final design.

art director comments

Your client is happy with the Corvette, and asked you to create two more illustrations that he can use in different digital projects.

To complete this project, you should:

❑ Search the Internet for photos that you can use as templates for creating the other new illustrations.

❑ Create each illustration in a separate file.

❑ Carefully consider the best approach for each icon and use whichever tool (or tools) are most appropriate to create the icon artwork.

client comments

The cars are a big part of the annual event, but it isn't limited to only cars. Really, the show includes categories for just about anything with a motor. Aside from the American Heavy Metal sports cars, the two most popular parts of the show are Early Antiques and Motorcycles.

I'd like you to create illustrations for both of those categories. For the Early Antiques, the Model T Ford of the 1910s will be a perfect icon for the class. For motorcycles, a 1940s Indian would be ideal for the different projects I want to create.

I really like the Corvette artwork, so I want the two new illustrations to have a similar style. When I look at the three pieces together, I'd like it to be clear that all three were created by the same artist.

project justification

_____

_____

_____

_____

_____

_____

_____

_____

_____

_____

_____

_____

_____

_____

_____

Although Animate is known as an animation program, you can see from this project that the application offers a considerable array of drawing and painting tools. You learned how to import a sketch, control the size of the Animate Stage, and align objects to the Stage. These skills set the groundwork for any type of assignment. You also developed an understanding of layers and how they simplify the construction of complex drawings and artwork.

Animate includes a range of drawing tools — from the basic shape tools, the Line tool for simple lines, and the Pen and Pencil tools for more complex curves. Those tools, combined with the two Animate drawing modes and the unique destructive editing capabilities that are part of the Animate toolset, make it possible to create complex artwork directly on the Stage.

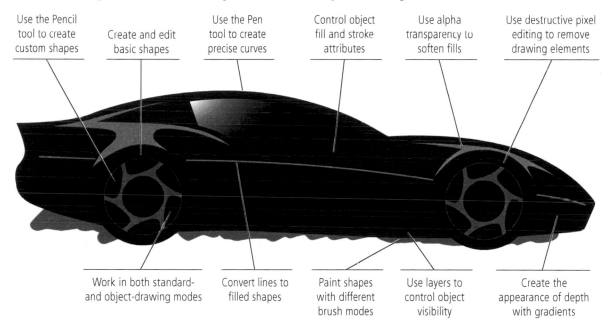

Use the Pencil tool to create custom shapes

Create and edit basic shapes

Use the Pen tool to create precise curves

Control object fill and stroke attributes

Use alpha transparency to soften fills

Use destructive pixel editing to remove drawing elements

Work in both standard- and object-drawing modes

Convert lines to filled shapes

Paint shapes with different brush modes

Use layers to control object visibility

Create the appearance of depth with gradients

Talking Kiosk Interface

You were hired to create an animated introduction for a shopping mall information kiosk. The Animate-based animation must feature a character who offers shoppers assistance in finding various facilities. Each button should also offer audio instructions that explain the link's purpose. As part of the Animate development team, your job is to prepare the interface artwork that will be handed off to the programmer, who will script the interactivity.

This project incorporates the following skills:

❏ Importing and managing artwork from Adobe Illustrator

❏ Using the Library panel to manage a complex file

❏ Building a frame-by-frame animation

❏ Editing various button states

❏ Importing sound files into Animate

❏ Adding event and stream sounds to the Animate timeline

❏ Controlling volume and duration of sound

❏ Applying built-in sound effects

❏ Synchronizing sound to animation

❏ Defining sound compression settings

Project Meeting

client comments

Throughout the facility grounds, we are replacing all of the static "You Are Here" maps with interactive kiosks that will help users more quickly find the shops they are looking for.

I'd like the interface to be personal — a person actually talking to the user. We thought about the video route, but I'm convinced an animated character would be better (plus we won't have to pay an actor to use her image).

The interface should provide a link to four different categories of shops: Shoes & Apparel, Home Furnishings, Music & Electronics, and Casual & Fine Dining. We might break it down into more specific categories later, but the important point for now is to get the first version of this thing into use quickly.

art director comments

I already had all of the kiosk components created. I need you to assemble everything in Animate and prepare the various elements for the programmer, who will create all of the necessary code and links.

The artwork was created in Adobe Illustrator. Our illustrator is fairly knowledgeable about Animate requirements, so you should be able to import the artwork without too many problems. He even created the basic appearance of the navigation buttons, so you'll just need to modify those rather than create them from scratch.

When I reviewed the sound files, it seemed like the background music was very loud compared to the spoken intro. You should fix the music so that the talking is audible above the background.

The lip-syncing part of the interface requires some careful attention to detail, but overall, it isn't a difficult job. Just take your time and try to make the mouths follow the words.

project objectives

To complete this project, you will:

- ❏ Create symbols from imported Illustrator files
- ❏ Place and manage instances of symbols on the Stage
- ❏ Control timing using keyframes
- ❏ Add visual interactivity to button symbols
- ❏ Import sound files into Animate
- ❏ Add event and stream sounds to a movie
- ❏ Use the start and stop sync methods for button sounds
- ❏ Edit a sound envelope to control volume and duration
- ❏ Swap graphics at precise moments in time
- ❏ Define sound compression settings

Stage 1 Working with Symbols

Although Animate can be used to create extraordinary interactive content, the program can also create extremely large files that take a very long time to download. (The size of a file is often referred to as a file's **weight**.) Users will not wait for more than a few seconds to download a file, so you should always try to keep file weight to a minimum — and that's where symbols come into play.

Symbols are objects that can be used repeatedly without increasing file size. The original symbol resides in the Library panel; **symbol instances** are copies of the symbol that you place onto the Stage. Although a regular graphic object adds to the overall file weight every time you use it on the Stage, a symbol counts only once no matter how many times you use it — which can mean dramatically smaller file sizes.

As another benefit, changes made to the content of an original symbol reflect in every placed instance of that symbol. For example, if you have placed 40 instances of a bird symbol, you can simultaneously change all 40 birds from blue jays to cardinals by changing the primary symbol in the Library panel.

A third benefit of symbols is that you can name placed instances, which means those instances can be targeted and affected by programming — one of the keys to animation and interactive development.

Note:

There are three primary types of symbols — graphic, movie clip, and button — and a number of other types of assets, such as audio and video files. In Animate, all of these assets are automatically stored in the Library panel.

The Library Panel in Depth

ANIMATE FOUNDATIONS

Assets in Animate are stored in the Library panel. Additional information about each asset is listed on the right side of the panel, including the name by which an asset can be called using a script (Linkage), the number of instances in the current file (Use Count), the date the asset was last modified (Date Modified), and the type of asset (Type). To show the additional information, you can either make the panel wider or use the scroll bar at the bottom of the panel. In addition to storing and organizing assets, the Library panel has a number of other uses:

- Each type of asset is identified by a unique icon. Double-clicking a symbol icon enters into Symbol-Editing mode, where you can modify the symbol on its own Stage. Double-clicking a non-symbol icon (sounds, bitmaps, etc.) opens the Properties dialog box for that file.

- You can use the Library menu to switch between the libraries of currently open files.

- The Preview pane shows the selected asset. If the asset includes animation, video, or sound, you can use the Play and Stop buttons to preview the file in the panel. (The Stage background color appears in the Preview pane; if you can't see the Play button, move your mouse over the area of the button to reveal it.)

- If a file has a large number of assets (which is common), you can use the Search field to find assets by name.

- Clicking the Pin button to the right of the Library menu attaches the current library to the open Animate file.

- Clicking the New Library Panel button opens a new version of the Library panel, which allows you to view multiple libraries at one time.

- Clicking the New Symbol button opens the Create New Symbol dialog box, where you can define the name and type of the new symbol you want to create.

- Clicking the New Folder button adds a new folder in the current file's library.

- Clicking the Properties button opens a dialog box that shows information about the selected library asset.

- Clicking Delete removes an asset from the library. Placed instances of that symbol are deleted from the file.

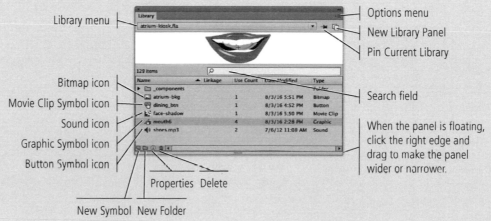

Library menu — Options menu / New Library Panel / Pin Current Library

Bitmap icon / Movie Clip Symbol icon / Sound icon / Graphic Symbol icon / Button Symbol icon — Search field

When the panel is floating, click the right edge and drag to make the panel wider or narrower.

Properties Delete

New Symbol New Folder

When you begin a new Animate project, the first step (obviously) is to create a new file. You can use the options in Welcome Screen to create new files using the default settings, or choose File>New to define a new file using the New Document dialog box.

1. **Download Atrium_ANCC17_RF.zip from the Student Files Web page.**

2. **Expand the ZIP archive in your WIP folder (Macintosh) or copy the archive contents into your WIP folder (Windows).**

   This results in a folder named **Atrium**, which contains the files you need for this project. You should also use this folder to save the files you create in this project.

3. **In Animate, choose File>New. Choose the AIR for Desktop option in the Type list.**

   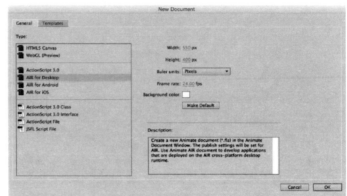

   The Type pane lists the types of documents you can create in Animate. You are creating this file to be a standalone app on a self-contained computer system.

   You can use the options on the right side of the dialog box to define the Stage size, units of measurement, frame rate, and background color of the Stage.

4. **Click OK to create the new file.**

   When you create a new file, the new Stage appears in the document window. The Stage color is determined by the Background color defined in the New Document dialog box (white by default). Every file includes one default layer, named "Layer 1," in the timeline.

   When nothing is selected on the Stage, the Properties panel shows a number of file-specific options, including the target device, type of script being used, and frame rate.

   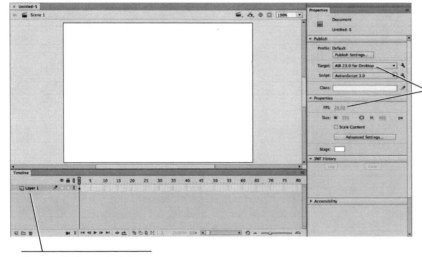

   File-specific options are avaiable in the Properties panel when nothing is selected on the Stage.

   The new file has a single layer, named Layer 1 by default.

5. **Choose File>Save. Navigate to your WIP>Atrium folder as the target location, then change the Save As field to `atrium-kiosk.fla`. Click Save to save the file.**

The File Format menu defaults to Animate Document (*.fla). This option creates a native Animate file, which you can open and edit in Animate as necessary. When you have finished your work, you can export the Animate file to another format that will present the animation on digital media.

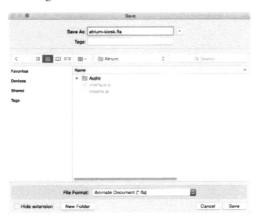

Note:

In this project, you will use the Tools, Properties, Library, Align, and Timeline panels. You should arrange your workspace to best suit your personal preferences.

6. **Continue to the next exercise.**

IMPORT ADOBE ILLUSTRATOR ARTWORK

You can use the built-in Animate tools to draw complex custom artwork. In many cases, however, your work in Animate will incorporate files that were created in other applications. For example, illustrations and other vector graphics for animation are typically created in Adobe Illustrator. This project incorporates a number of external files, which you need to import into your Animate file.

Note:

*Learn more about Adobe Illustrator in the companion book of this series, **Adobe Illustrator CC: The Professional Portfolio**.*

1. **With `atrium-kiosk.fla` open, choose File>Import>Import to Stage.**

2. **At the bottom of the dialog box, choose All Openable Formats in the Enable menu. Navigate to `interface.ai` in the WIP>Atrium folder, and click Open.**

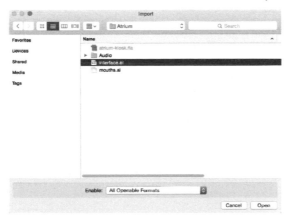

3. **If the button at the bottom of the Import to Stage dialog box shows "Hide Advanced Options," click that button to show only the basic import options.**

When advanced options are visible, you can review the individual layers (and their contents) that will be imported in the Illustrator file. You are importing the entire file in this project, so you don't need to examine each layer and sublayer.

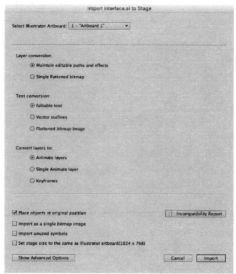

The **Artboard** menu lists all artboards that exist in the Illustrator file you are importing. (An Illustrator artboard is the equivalent of the Animate Stage; it defines the visible area in the final artwork.)

The **Layer Conversion** options determine whether Illustrator objects will be editable after being imported into Animate.

- Maintain Editable Paths and Effects option means you can use the Animate Subselection tool to manipulate the anchor points and handles on the imported paths.

- If you select the Single Flattened Bitmap option, you will not be able to edit the vector paths within Animate.

The **Text Conversion** options determine whether text objects in Illustrator will be editable with the Animate Text tool.

- Editable Text, selected by default, imports text objects that you can edit using the Animate Text tool.

- If you choose Vector Outlines, text objects import as a group of vector shapes; you can't edit the text in these objects (other than manipulating the vector paths).

- If you choose Flattened Bitmap Image, text objects import as raster objects that cannot be edited with either the Text tool or the Subselection tool.

Note:

The Incompatibility Report button tends to disappear and reappear when you make changes in other areas of the dialog box. This is a minor bug in the software.

The **Convert Layers To** options determine how layers in the Illustrator file are managed in the Animate timeline.

- The Animate Layers option maintains the existing layers from the original artwork; each Illustrator layer becomes a layer in the Animate file. This is useful if you aren't sure about what you're importing; you can always change or delete imported layers if you don't need them.

- If you choose Single Animate Layer, all layers in the original artwork are flattened into one layer (named with the imported file name) on the Animate timeline.

- If you choose Keyframes, each layer in the artwork is added as a keyframe on the default Layer 1. (You will learn about keyframes in Stage 2 of this project.)

Many objects created in Illustrator are fully compatible with Animate drawing capabilities, so they are imported as regular drawing objects. Any objects that don't fit the Animate drawing model (primarily, ones with some type of applied transparency) are imported in a way that allows Animate to maintain the overall artwork integrity. If an **Incompatibility Report** button appears in the Import to Stage dialog box, you can click it to see what effects are causing the problem.

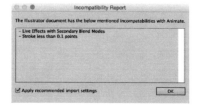

When **Place Objects at Original Position** is checked, the objects imported onto the Animate Stage have the same position relative to one another as they did in the original Illustrator file.

If you check **Import as a Single Bitmap Image**, the entire file is flattened into a raster image; you are not able to access the individual elements that made up the original artwork in Illustrator.

The Illustrator artboard is the area that defines the physical dimensions of the file, just as the Stage defines the physical size of an Animate file. The **Set Stage Size...** option shows the dimensions of the imported file's artboard; if you know the Illustrator file was created to the correct dimensions, you can use this option to automatically change the Stage size to match the imported artwork.

Illustrator can be used to create graphic and movie clip symbols (but not buttons), which are stored in a file's Symbols panel. This can include symbols that are not placed in the file, but which might be necessary for the overall project. If you don't know what a file contains, you can check the **Import Unused Symbols** option to be sure all of the necessary bits are imported; you can always delete unwanted symbols once they have been imported. For this project, we are telling you that all required symbols in the imported artwork are placed on the artboard.

4. **Make the following changes to the default import settings:**

   - **Choose the Vector Outline option in the Text Conversion section.**
   - **Check the Set Stage Size option.**

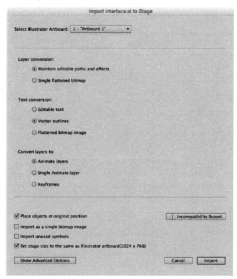

5. **Click Import to import the Illustrator artwork.**

6. **Fit the Stage in the document window, then click away from all objects on the Stage to deselect them.**

   All objects are automatically selected after being imported to the Stage. Deselecting them allows you to review the Animate file's properties.

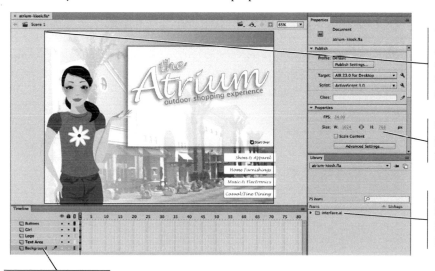

The imported artwork is aligned to the top-left corner of the Stage, matching its relative position on the original Illustrator artboard.

With nothing selected, the Properties panel shows the adjusted Stage size.

A folder (named the same as the imported file) is added to the library, containing all the pieces necessary for the imported artwork.

Five layers are added to the Timeline panel.

7. **In the Library panel, click the arrow to the left of the interface.ai folder to expand it, and then click the arrows to expand all but the Girl folder.**

   Imported assets are sorted by layer; folder names match the imported layer names to help you understand where different pieces are required. A separate folder for Illustrator Symbols is included.

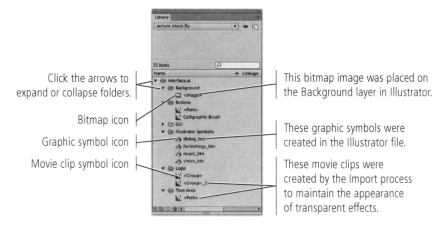

Click the arrows to expand or collapse folders.

Bitmap icon

Graphic symbol icon

Movie clip symbol icon

This bitmap image was placed on the Background layer in Illustrator.

These graphic symbols were created in the Illustrator file.

These movie clips were created by the Import process to maintain the appearance of transparent effects.

Note:

The Girl folder includes a long list of paths and groups that were imported as movie clips to preserve transparency effects that were applied in the Illustrator file. We did not include that folder in this instruction simply because the list is so long.

8. **In the Library panel, collapse the subfolders in the interface.ai folder.**

9. **Save the file and continue to the next exercise.**

IMPORT FILES TO THE LIBRARY

In addition to importing files to the Animate Stage, you can also import external files directly into the Animate file's Library panel. This option is particularly useful when certain objects aren't going to be placed on the main Stage, or if you don't yet know how you will use a particular object.

1. **With atrium-kiosk.fla open, choose File>Import>Import to Library. Navigate to the file mouths.ai in the WIP>Atrium folder and click Open.**

   When you import an Illustrator file directly to the Library panel, most of the options are the same as for importing to the Stage. The Set Stage Size... option is not available because it does not apply to files that only exist (for now) in the file's library.

Note:

Animate defaults to the last-used folder, so you might not have to navigate to the folder you used in the previous exercise.

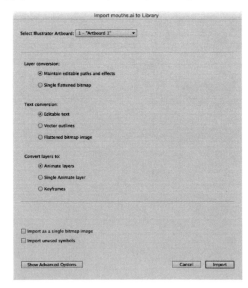

2. **Click Import to import the artwork to the library.**

The Library panel shows that the resulting object was imported as a graphic symbol. Nothing is added to the Stage or the timeline.

3. **In the Library panel, click the mouths.ai item to select it.**

The top portion of the panel shows a preview of the selected item.

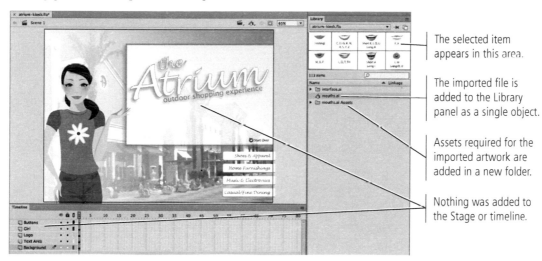

The selected item appears in this area.

The imported file is added to the Library panel as a single object.

Assets required for the imported artwork are added in a new folder.

Nothing was added to the Stage or timeline.

4. **Save the file and continue to the next exercise.**

CONVERT OBJECTS TO SYMBOLS

You now have a number of assets in your file's Library panel. The mouths.ai graphic contains eight groups of graphics — the different mouth shapes that you will use later in this project to synchronize the character to a sound file. For the process to work, you need to separate each mouth shape into a distinct symbol so the correct artwork can be placed at the appropriate point in the file.

1. **With atrium-kiosk.fla open, choose the Selection tool. Double-click the mouths.ai symbol icon to enter into the symbol.**

2. **Zoom as necessary so you can clearly see all the objects on the symbol Stage.**

Every symbol technically has its own Stage, which is theoretically infinite and separate from the main Stage of the base file. When you double-click the symbol icon in the Library panel, you enter **Symbol-Editing mode** for that symbol; other elements of the base file are not visible on the Stage.

The Edit bar shows that you are now working on the mouths.ai Stage (called **Symbol-Editing mode**).

When you first enter into the symbol, all artwork in the symbol is selected.

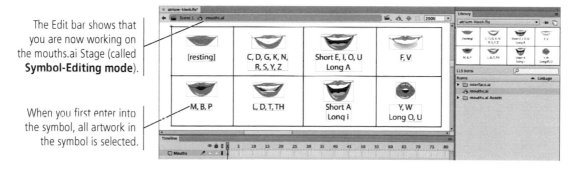

3. **Click away from the artwork to deselect everything, then click the top-left mouth shape to select that group (but not the word "resting").**

   Grouping in the original artwork is maintained in the imported artwork.

4. **Control/right-click the selected artwork and choose Convert to Symbol from the contextual menu.**

Note:

You can also drag an object onto the Library panel to open the Convert to Symbol dialog box for that object.

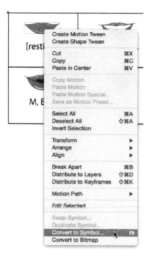

5. **In the resulting dialog box, type `mouth1` in the Name field and choose Graphic in the Type menu.**

   A graphic symbol is the most basic type of symbol. It is typically used for objects that will simply be placed on the Stage. (A graphic symbol can include animation; you will explore these options in Project 4: Ocean Animation.) The type of animation you create in the third stage of this project — simply swapping one symbol with another at various points in time — is ideally suited to graphic symbols.

6. **Select the center point in the registration proxy icon.**

   The registration grid affects the placement of the symbol's registration point, which is the 0,0 point for the symbol. (This will make more sense shortly when you begin editing symbols on their own Stages.)

7. **Click OK to create the new symbol.**

   The Properties panel now shows that the selected object is an instance of the mouth1 symbol, which has been added to the Library panel.

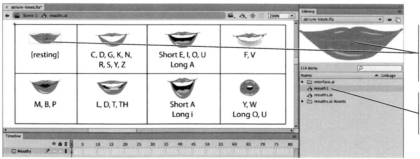

The Properties panel shows that the selected artwork is now an instance of the mouth1 symbol.

The new symbol is added to the file's Library panel.

8. **Click the second mouth shape (to the right) to select it, then press the F8 key.**

   If you are using a laptop or an abbreviated keyboard, you have to press the FN key while you also press the F8 key.

   If you don't have access to function keys, simply Control/right-click the group and choose Convert to Symbol.

9. **Type mouth2 in the Name field and click OK.**

   The Convert to Symbol dialog box remembers the last-used settings. The Type menu is already set to Graphic, and the center registration point is already selected.

10. **Repeat Steps 8–9 to convert the rest of the mouth shapes into symbols, working from left to right across the top row and then left to right across the bottom row.**

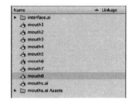

11. **Click Scene 1 in the Edit bar to return to the main Stage.**

12. **Using the Selection tool, click the mouth shape on the Stage to select it.**

   When you select the mouth shape, the layer containing the object (Girl) automatically becomes the active layer.

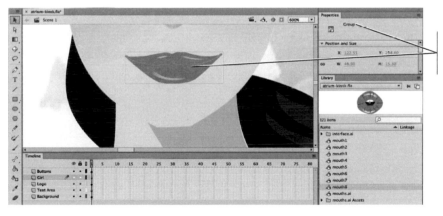

The selected object is a group. It is not an instance of any symbol.

13. **In the Timeline panel, click the New Layer button to add a new layer.**

   When you click the New Layer button, the new layer is automatically added above the previously selected layer. The new layer is also automatically selected as the active layer.

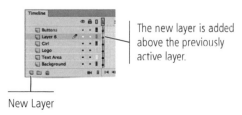

The new layer is added above the previously active layer.

New Layer

14. **Double-click the new layer name to highlight it. Type Mouths, then press Return/Enter to finalize the new layer name.**

15. **Click mouth1 in the Library panel and drag an instance onto the Stage.**

16. **Use the Selection tool to drag the placed instance to the same position as the mouth group on the underlying Girl layer.**

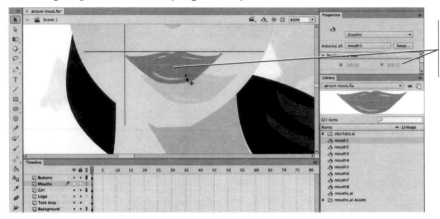

The X and Y fields show the position of the instance's registration point.

Note:

Don't confuse the symbol registration point (the crosshairs) with the transformation point (the hollow circle).

17. **In the Timeline panel, click in the Eye column to the right of the Mouths layer name to hide that layer.**

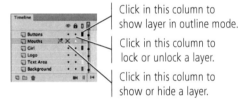

Click in this column to show layer in outline mode.

Click in this column to lock or unlock a layer.

Click in this column to show or hide a layer.

18. **Select the mouth group on the Girl layer and delete it.**

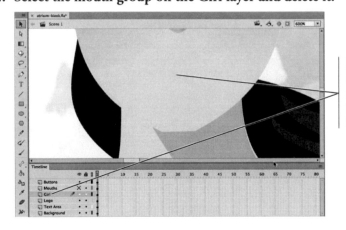

Because the Mouths layer is hidden, you can select and delete the underlying group from the Girl layer.

19. **Show the Mouths layer again, then save the file and continue to the next exercise.**

CREATE A BUTTON SYMBOL

Buttons, one of the three main symbol types in Animate, are interactive assets that change when a user interacts with them. A button symbol has four "states":

- A button's **Up state** (also referred to as the idle or default state) is the basic appearance of a button when a user first loads a file.

- The **Over state** occurs when a mouse pointer rolls over a button. (When a user places a mouse cursor over a rollover area, the cursor often turns into a pointing finger or some other custom shape.)

- The **Down state** occurs when a user clicks a button.

- The **Hit state** defines the size of a rollover area (**hot spot**) of a button.

Note:

Buttons can be both animated and idle at the same time; idle simply means that no one has passed over or clicked the button with the mouse pointer.

This file includes five buttons. Four were created as symbols in the Illustrator artwork, and one was imported onto the Stage as a group.

1. **With atrium-kiosk.fla open, use the Selection tool to select the group containing the words "Start Over".**

2. **Press F8, or Control/right-click the selected group and choose Convert to Symbol in the contextual menu.**

3. **In the resulting dialog box, type start_over in the name field. Choose Button in the Type menu and choose the center registration point (if it is not already selected).**

Choose Button in this menu.

4. **Click OK to create the new symbol.**

Because you created the symbol from objects on the Stage, the Properties panel shows that the selection is automatically an instance of the new symbol.

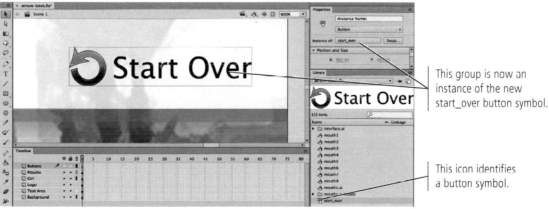

This group is now an instance of the new start_over button symbol.

This icon identifies a button symbol.

5. **Double-click the Start Over button on the Stage to enter into the symbol.**

   This method of editing a symbol is called **editing in place**. Other objects on the Stage are still visible, but they are screened back and cannot be accessed.

   As we explained earlier, a button is a special type of symbol with four distinct states. Each possible state is represented as a frame in the special Button symbol timeline.

The Edit bar shows that you are editing on the start_over button symbol Stage.

Editing a symbol in place means you can see — but not access — the other objects on the Stage.

6. **In the Timeline panel, Control/right-click the Over frame of Layer 1 and choose Insert Keyframe from the contextual menu.**

   A **keyframe** defines a point where something changes. If you want to make something appear different from one frame to the next — whether inside a symbol or on the main Stage — you need to place a keyframe at the point where the change should occur.

Note:

You can also insert a keyframe by choosing Insert> Timeline> Keyframe, or pressing F6.

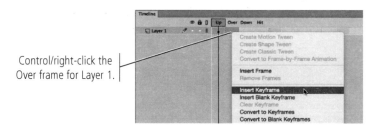

Control/right-click the Over frame for Layer 1.

7. **Make sure the Over frame is selected in the Timeline panel, then double-click the words "Start Over" in the graphic to enter into that group.**

   The contents of the Over frame will appear when the user's mouse moves over the button area. You are going to change the color of the letters in this button.

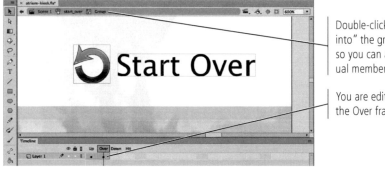

Double-clicking "enters into" the group of objects, so you can access individual members of the group.

You are editing only the Over frame.

8. **Double-click any letter in the group to access the individual letters that make up the group.**

   Remember, Animate remembers the groupings from the original Illustrator file. Depending on how a file was created, you might have to enter into a number of nested groups before you get to the level you need.

9. **With the individual letter shapes selected, click the Fill Color swatch in the Properties panel. Click a medium blue swatch in the color palette to change the fill color of the selected objects.**

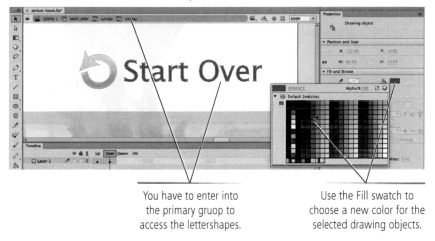

You have to enter into the primary gruop to access the lettershapes.

Use the Fill swatch to choose a new color for the selected drawing objects.

10. **Click Scene 1 in the Edit bar to return to the main Stage.**

Even if you have drilled into multiple levels of Symbol-Editing mode, you can return to the main Stage with a single click on the Edit bar. You can also return to any particular nesting level by clicking a specific item (called "breadcrumbs") in the Edit bar.

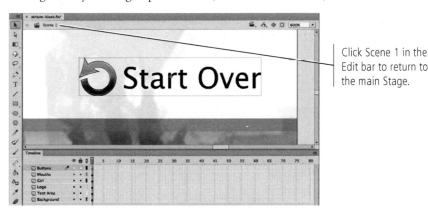

Click Scene 1 in the Edit bar to return to the main Stage.

Note:

You will test the button's functionality in the next exercise.

11. **Save the file and continue to the next exercise.**

DEFINE A HIT FRAME

A button symbol mimics a four-frame Animate animation; it is the basic concept behind all Animate buttons. You add keyframes and modify the content of each frame; the movie displays the appropriate frame when a user hovers over or clicks the object.

In the previous exercise, you changed the color of button text in the Over frame. However, there is still a problem — the button currently works only if the mouse pointer touches the icon or one of the letter shapes. If the pointer lies between two letters, for example, the button fails to activate. All spaces within the button should be active. Moving the pointer close to or on top of the button should trigger the desired action. To resolve the problem, you need to define the Hit frame, which determines where a user can click to activate the button.

1. **With atrium-kiosk.fla open, choose Control>Enable Simple Buttons to toggle that option on.**

This command allows you to test button states directly on the Animate Stage.

2. **Check the current condition of the Start Over button by positioning the pointer between the two words in the button.**

There are "dead" areas within the button that don't cause the color change to occur. (You might need to zoom in to verify this problem.)

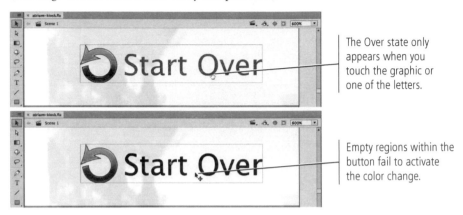

The Over state only appears when you touch the graphic or one of the letters.

Empty regions within the button fail to activate the color change.

3. **Choose Control>Enable Simple Buttons to toggle that option off.**

When this option is active, you can't select a button instance on the Stage — which means you can't double-click the button to edit the symbol in place.

4. **Double-click the Start Over button on the Stage to edit the symbol in place.**

5. **Select the Hit frame in the Timeline and then press the F6 key to insert a new keyframe on the selected frame.**

If you can't use the function keys, Control/right-click the Hit frame and choose Insert Keyframe from the contextual menu.

The **Hit frame** defines the live area of the button, or the area where a user can click to activate the button. Objects on this state do not appear in the movie; you only need to define the general shapes.

Note:

You can use the Insert Blank Keyframe command to add a blank keyframe to the timeline that (as the name suggests) has no content.

Add the new keyframe on the Hit frame.

6. **Choose the Rectangle tool from the Tools panel.**

7. **In the Properties panel, turn off the Object Drawing toggle.**

When this option is turned off (not highlighted), new drawing shapes drop to the back of the stacking order on the active layer.

Because merge-drawing shapes drop to the back of the stacking order, this method allows you to still see the button artwork in front of the "hit" shape.

8. **Set the Stroke color to None, and choose a contrasting color as the Fill color.**

9. Draw a rectangle that covers the entire contents of the button.

We used a red color that contrasted with the blue text, but any color will work because the Hit frame content doesn't appear on the Stage when you play the movie.

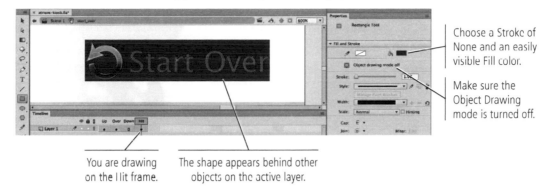

Choose a Stroke of None and an easily visible Fill color.

Make sure the Object Drawing mode is turned off.

You are drawing on the Hit frame.

The shape appears behind other objects on the active layer.

10. Click Scene 1 in the Edit bar to return to the main Stage.

11. Choose Control>Enable Simple Buttons to toggle the option back on, then move the mouse cursor between the words in the button.

The button now works even if you hover over the white areas or between the letters. The Hit frame rectangle determines the live (hit) area of the button.

The button now works even if you hover between the words.

12. Choose Control>Enable Simple Buttons to toggle off that option.

13. Save the file and continue to the next exercise.

EDIT SYMBOL PROPERTIES

The control buttons, which you imported as graphic symbols, are the final pieces of artwork for this movie. Illustrator, does not create button symbols; you need to convert the imported graphic symbols into the necessary button symbols.

1. With atrium-kiosk.fla open, expand the interface.ai>Illustrator Symbols folder in the Library panel (if necessary).

2. Control/right-click the shoes_btn symbol icon in the Library panel and choose Properties from the contextual menu.

3. **In the Symbol Properties dialog box, choose Button in the Type menu, and then click OK.**

   The Symbol Properties dialog box is nearly the same as the Create New Symbol dialog box; it does not have registration options because that has already been defined for the symbol. To move symbol artwork relative to the registration point, edit the symbol on its Stage.

4. **Using the Selection tool, select the Shoes & Apparel button on the Stage.**

5. **In the Properties panel, open the top menu and choose Button.**

   Unlike changing the content of a symbol, changes to the symbol type do not reflect in placed instances. When you change the type of a symbol that has already been placed on the Stage, you also have to change the instance type in the Properties panel.

Choose Button in this menu to change the behavior of the placed instance.

The symbol now shows the button icon instead of the original graphic icon.

6. **Repeat Steps 2–5 to convert the remaining three graphic symbols to buttons.**

7. **Save the file and continue to the next exercise.**

 EXPLORE THE SYMBOL REGISTRATION POINT

Now that the buttons are symbols rather than graphics, you can define the various states of the buttons. You are going to edit the artwork so that the buttons seem to move when the mouse cursor rolls over the hit area.

1. **With atrium-kiosk.fla open, open the Align panel (Window>Align).**

2. **Double-click the Shoes & Apparel button instance to edit the symbol in place. Click the button artwork to select it if necessary.**

   The crosshairs in the middle of the symbol artwork identify the **symbol registration point**; all measurements for placed instances begin at this location.

Symbol registration point

When editing the symbol, the X and Y fields show the position of the top-left corner relative to the symbol's registration point.

3. **In the Align panel, make sure the Align To Stage option is active and then click the Align Right Edge button.**

   The right edge of the symbol artwork is now aligned to the symbol registration point. Because you are editing the symbol in place, you can see the effect of the new alignment relative to the overall file artwork. This illustrates that the registration point is fixed, and the artwork is the thing that moves — not the other way around.

Note:

Use the Align panel with the Align To Stage option active to align the placed object to the symbol's registration point.

4. **Click Scene 1 in the Edit bar to return to the main Stage.**

5. **With the Shoes & Apparel button selected, click the current X value in the Properties panel to access the field.**

On the main Stage, the X and Y fields define the position of the registration point for the instance.

Click the existing value to access the field.

6. **Type 1034 in the highlighted X field and press Return/Enter to apply the change.**

   As we explained earlier, the symbol registration point is the origin of measurements for placed instances. When you change the X position, you are defining the horizontal location of the symbol registration point for the selected instance.

   The Stage for this file is 1024 pixels wide (as defined by the imported Illustrator artboard); you are placing the right edge of the button 10 pixels past the Stage edge.

   In the next few steps, you will use this position as the basis for changing the object's position when a user moves the cursor over the button (i.e., triggers the Over frame).

7. **Double-click the Shoes & Apparel button again to enter back into the symbol Stage.**

8. **Insert a new keyframe on the button's Over frame. With the Over keyframe selected, click the button artwork to select it.**

   The object must be selected to change its properties. Selecting the frame in the timeline also selects the object on that frame.

9. **In the Properties panel, click the current X value in the Properties panel to access the field.**

10. **Place the insertion point after the existing value and type -10 after the existing value. Press Enter to move the selected object.**

    Using mathematical operators makes it easy to move an object a specific distance without manually calculating the change:

    • Subtract from the X position to move an object left.

    • Add to the X position to move an object right.

    • Subtract from the Y position to move an object up.

    • Add to the Y position to move an object down.

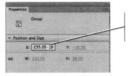

Type **-10** after the current value.

The new X value moves the artwork 10 pixels to the left.

You are editing the Over frame.

11. **Click Scene 1 in the Edit bar to return to the main Stage.**

12. **Repeat Steps 2–11 for the three remaining buttons.**

13. **Choose Control>Enable Simple Buttons to toggle the option back on. Move your mouse cursor over the buttons to test the Over state functionality.**

The buttons should move 10 pixels to the left when the mouse cursor enters the button area.

14. **Save the file and continue to the next exercise.**

Note:

Because this button artwork includes a solid-filled white rectangle, you don't need to define a separate hit frame. The artwork itself is sufficient to trigger the button.

☞ ORGANIZE YOUR LIBRARY WITH FOLDERS

Library folders work the same as layer folders; they help you organize and structure complex files. Movies often contain dozens or even hundreds of assets — and the more complex a movie becomes, the more useful it is to clearly organize those assets. Although this step isn't strictly necessary, it is always a good idea to organize your work so that you can more easily organize your thoughts and processes going forward.

1. **With atrium-kiosk.fla open, expand the interface.ai folder in the Library panel.**

2. **Click the Illustrator Symbols folder (inside the interface.ai folder) and drag down to the empty area at the bottom of the panel.**

    This moves the Illustrator Symbols folder to the first level of the library. The symbols, which are placed on the Stage, are not affected by the move.

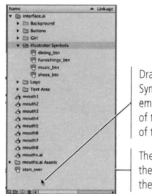

Drag the Illustrator Symbols folder to the empty area at the bottom of the panel to move it out of the interface.ai folder.

The highlight shows that the folder will be moved to the first level of the panel.

Click a column heading to sort library items by that category.

3. **Double-click the Illustrator Symbols folder name to highlight the name. Type Buttons to change the folder name.**

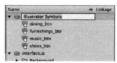 

4. **Click the start_over button symbol icon and drag it into the Buttons folder.**

5. **Double-click the interface.ai folder name to highlight the name. Type Component Artwork to change the folder name.**

Note:

If your Library panel is too short to show an empty area below the current assets, Control/ right-click any of the existing first-level assets and choose Paste. The pasted symbols are pasted at the same level as the asset where you Control/ right-click.

6. **Click the mouths.ai Assets folder and drag it into the Component Artwork folder.**

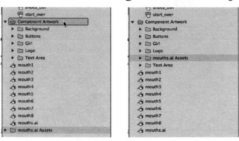

7. **Click the empty area at the bottom of the panel to deselect all assets and folders.**

8. **Click the New Folder button at the bottom of the Library panel. Type Mouth Graphics as the new folder name.**

   The new folder is added at the main level of the library, alphabetized with other items at the same level. If you didn't deselect in Step 7, the new folder would have been created at the same nesting level as the selected item.

   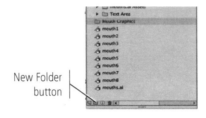

   New Folder button

9. **Click the mouth1 symbol to select it, then Shift-click the mouth8 symbol to select it and all files in between.**

   Press Shift to select multiple contiguous items in the panel, or press Command/Control to select multiple, non-contiguous items.

10. **Click the icon of any selected file and drag into the Mouth Graphics folder.**

    All eight of these files are selected.

11. **Click the mouths.ai graphic symbol and click the panel's Delete button.**

    Although you used this artwork to create the individual mouth symbols, this symbol is not used in the file, so it can be safely deleted from the library. If you delete a symbol that is used in the file, the placed instances will also be deleted from the file.

    Delete button

12. **Collapse all library folders, then save the file and continue to the next stage of the project.**

Stage 2 Working with Sound

Sound files can be categorized into three basic types: uncompressed, compressed (lossless), and compressed (lossy). **Uncompressed sound files** encode all sounds with the same number of bits per unit of time. In an uncompressed format, two sound files of the same duration — whether a symphony or a simple beep — have the same size (which is typically very large). Such files are commonly used for archiving or other situations where file size is not an issue.

Lossless compression sound files lose no data during compression; these files are smaller than uncompressed files, but not as small as lossy compression file formats. **Lossy compression sound files** lose some data but retain good sound quality; a large number of these files can be stored in relatively small amounts of space.

Animate handles most major audio formats, including the ones most commonly used today:

- The **MP3** format is the most commonly used audio format. This format compresses a music file in the most efficient manner, so file size is reduced without compromising quality. MP3 playback does require more processing power than other formats because the data has to be decoded every time the file plays.

- The **WAV** format is an uncompressed format with very high quality. This file type can be used in Animate animations for desktop applications, but should be avoided for Web-based movies because the files are huge and take a long time to download.

- The **AIFF** format (Audio Interchange File Format) is common on Macintosh computers. This format is generally uncompressed, so file sizes are large compared to the MP3 format. AIFF files are suitable for applications specifically targeted for Macintosh computers.

- The **Audio** (AU) file format, developed by Sun Microsystems, transmits sound files over the Internet and can be played in Java programs. These files are smaller than AIFF and WAV formats, but the quality of sound is not as good as regular WAV files.

- The **QuickTime** (MOV) format is technically a video format, but it can also include audio.

 IMPORT SOUND FILES

In general, there are three methods for incorporating sound into an Animate movie. Sounds in a file's library can be placed directly on the timeline, or you can use code to call a library sound based on a particular event. You can also use code to load and play external sound files (those that don't exist in the Animate library).

In this project, you will use the timeline method to add the various sounds that are needed for the kiosk to function properly. The first step is to import the necessary sound files into the Animate library.

1. With **atrium-kiosk.fla** open, choose File>Import>Import to Library. In the resulting dialog box, select all files in the **WIP>Atrium>Audio** folder, then click Open.

2. **Open the Library panel and review the contents.**

   The selected sound files are imported into the file's Library panel.

3. **Click the New Folder button at the bottom of the Library panel. Rename the new folder Audio.**

4. **Command/Control-click all six imported audio files and drag them into the Audio folder.**

5. **Expand the Audio folder so you can see the available files.**

Note:

It's always a good idea to keep your library well organized while developing a file with numerous assets.

6. **Save the file and continue to the next exercise.**

ADD EVENT SOUND

Event sounds are "timeline independent" — they play independently of the movie timeline. They are downloaded completely and stored in the user computer's memory; this means they can be played repeatedly (including continuously looping) without having to redownload the file.

Note:

Because event sounds must be downloaded completely before they can play, they can cause buffering delays in playback.

1. **With the file atrium-kiosk.fla open, click to select the atrium_jazz.mp3 file in the Library panel.**

   This file will be the background music for the entire file. It will play in an infinite loop as long as the kiosk file is open.

2. **Click the Play button in the top-right corner of the Preview area.**

   You can use the Library panel to hear imported sounds before they are used on the Stage.

   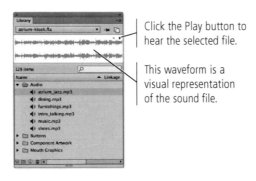

   Click the Play button to hear the selected file.

   This waveform is a visual representation of the sound file.

3. **Select the Frame 1 keyframe on the Background layer.**

4. **In the Sound section of the Properties panel, choose atrium_jazz.mp3 in the Name menu.**

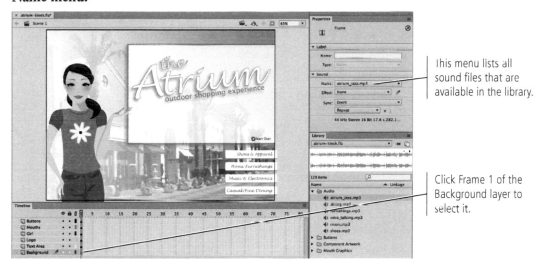

This menu lists all sound files that are available in the library.

Click Frame 1 of the Background layer to select it.

5. **In the Sync menu, choose Event.**

Event sounds default to the Repeat 1 method, which means the sound plays one time. You can change the number in the Repeat field to play the sound a specific number of times.

Choose Event in this menu.

A small line, which is actually part of the sound waveform, crosses the selected frame.

6. **Choose Control>Test.**

Because you created this file targeting AIR for Desktop, this command opens the file in a separate AIR Debug Launcher window. This shows you what the exported file will look and sound like. Although the sound waveform only appears on Frame 1 of the Background layer, the entire sound plays from start to finish when you test the file.

Note:

Press Command-Return/Control-Enter to test the movie in an Animate Player window.

7. **Close the Player window and return to Animate.**

8. **With Frame 1 of the Background layer selected, choose Loop in the menu under the Sync menu (in the Sound area of the Properties panel).**

   Using the Loop method, the event sound plays continuously as long as the movie remains open.

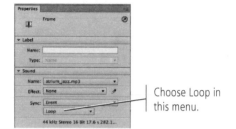

   Choose Loop in this menu.

9. **Press Command-Return/Control-Enter to test the movie again.**

   The background sound now plays from start to finish, and then repeats to create a continuous background sound track.

10. **Close the Player window and return to Animate.**

11. **Save the file and continue to the next exercise.**

 ## EDIT A SOUND ENVELOPE TO CONTROL VOLUME

Although Animate is not intended to be a sound-editing application, you can apply a limited number of effects to control the volume and length of sounds on the Animate timeline. These options are available in the Effect menu of the Properties panel when a sound is attached to a keyframe.

1. **With atrium-kiosk.fla open, click Frame 1 of the Background layer to select the frame where you attached the sound in the previous exercise.**

2. **In the Properties panel, open the Effect menu and choose Custom to open the Edit Envelope dialog box.**

   The Edit Envelope dialog box shows the waveforms for each channel in a sound file. (In many cases, both channels have the same waveform.) You can view the sound waves by seconds or frames, and you can zoom in or out to show various portions of the sound. The left and right channels refer to sound output systems that have more than one speaker — one on the left and one on the right.

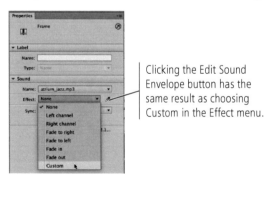

Clicking the Edit Sound Envelope button has the same result as choosing Custom in the Effect menu.

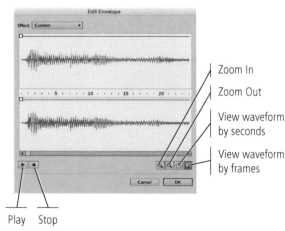

Zoom In

Zoom Out

View waveform by seconds

View waveform by frames

Play   Stop

3. **Click the Frames button to show the sound based on frames (if this isn't already active).**

4. **In the left channel area (the top waveform), click the handle on the left end of the waveform, and drag down to below the existing waveform.**

Click the envelope handle and drag down to this point.

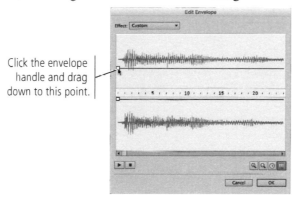

Note:

Click the envelope line to add a new handle to the envelope. Click an existing handle and drag it away from the window to remove a point from the envelope.

5. **Repeat Step 4 for the right channel (the bottom waveform).**

By lowering the envelope handles, you reduced the volume of the sound file.

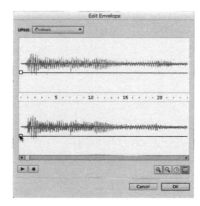

6. **Click OK to close the Edit Envelope dialog box and apply the change.**

7. **Save the file and continue to the next exercise.**

More about Editing Sound Files

ANIMATE FOUNDATIONS

The Effect menu in the Properties panel lists a number of common sound envelope effects built into Animate. These sound effects do not alter the sound in the files; they simply control how the sound data plays.

- **Left Channel** plays only the left channel of the sound.
- **Right Channel** plays only the right channel of the sound.
- **Fade to Right** gradually lowers the sound level of the left channel, and then gradually raises the sound level of the right channel.
- **Fade to Left** gradually lowers the sound level of the right channel, and then gradually raises the sound level of the left channel.
- **Fade In** gradually raises the sound level at the beginning of the sound file.
- **Fade Out** gradually lowers the sound level at the end of the sound file.
- **Custom** opens the Edit Envelope dialog box, where you can define your own sound effects.

USE THE START AND STOP SYNC METHODS FOR BUTTONS

The four category buttons will link to different screens in the kiosk. Each button needs to trigger a sound that plays when the user's mouse rolls over the button. To achieve this result, you can attach the relevant sound to each button using the same technique you applied in the previous exercise. Because of the four-frame nature of button symbols, however, a few extra steps are required to make the sounds play only when you want them to play.

1. **With atrium-kiosk.fla open, choose Control>Enable Simple Buttons to make sure that option is toggled on.**

2. **In the Library panel, double-click the shoes_btn symbol icon to enter Symbol-Editing mode for that symbol.**

   Remember, you can edit a symbol by double-clicking the symbol icon. This is especially useful when the Enable Simple Buttons feature is toggled on because you can't select buttons on the Stage in that mode.

   In Symbol-Editing mode, a discrete Stage appears when you double-click a symbol icon in the Library panel; the name of the symbol appears to the right of the Scene name in the Edit bar, indicating that you're working on the symbol instead of the main scene. You can also access this option by Control/right-clicking a placed instance on the Stage and choosing Edit.

3. **Select the Over frame of Layer 1. In the Properties panel, choose shoes.mp3 in the Sound Name menu and set the Sync menu to Event.**

You are attaching the sound to the button's Over frame.

4. **Click Scene 1 in the Edit bar to return to the main Stage.**

5. **Move your mouse cursor over the Shoes & Apparel button to hear the attached sound.**

Moving the mouse over the button triggers the Over state, including the attached sound file.

6. **Move your mouse cursor away, and then move back over the Shoes & Apparel button to trigger the sound again.**

   When the mouse re-enters the button area — triggering the Over frame — the message plays again. (Because the sound is very short, this might not be apparent unless you move the mouse back into the button area very quickly.)

7. **Double-click the shoes_btn symbol icon in the Library panel to enter back into the button Stage. Select the Over frame, then change the Sound Sync menu to Start.**

   The Start sync option is similar to the Event method. The difference is that the Start method allows only one instance of the same sound to play at a time; this prevents the overlap problem caused by the Event method.

Apply the Start sync method to the Over frame.

8. **Select the Down frame and press F6 to insert a new keyframe, or Control/right-click the Down frame and choose Insert Keyframe from the contextual menu.**

9. **In the Properties panel, choose shoes.mp3 in the Sound menu and choose Stop in the Sync menu.**

   The Stop option stops all instances of the selected sound from playing. When a user clicks the Shoes & Apparel button, the sound triggered on the Over frame will stop playing.

Apply the Stop sync method to a keyframe on the Down frame.

10. **Click Scene 1 to return to the main Stage.**

11. **Repeat the same basic process to add the appropriate event sounds to the other three navigation buttons:**
    - Double-click the button symbol icon to enter the symbol's Stage.
    - Select the Over frame and attach the appropriate sound file using the Start sync option.
      - For the Home Furnishings button, use the furnishings.mp3 sound file.
      - For the Music & Electronics button, use the music.mp3 sound file.
      - For the Casual/Fine Dining button, use the dining.mp3 sound file.
    - Add a keyframe to the Down frame.
    - Attach the same sound you used for the Over frame, and apply the Stop sync option.

12. **If you haven't done so already, click Scene 1 in the Edit bar to return to the main Stage.**

13. **Roll your mouse cursor over the four buttons to test all four sounds. Click each to make sure the sounds stop when they're supposed to.**

14. **Save the file and continue to the next stage of the project.**

Stage 3 Creating Frame Animations

The basic underlying premise of animation is that objects change over time — from complex transitions in color, shape, and opacity to moving a character to a new position. The most basic type of animation is to simply replace one object with another at specific points in time; you will create this type of animation in this stage of the kiosk project to make it seem like the girl is talking.

Repositioning or replacing objects on successive frames results in the appearance of movement when you watch an animation; in reality, your brain is being fooled — you're simply seeing a series of images Animate before your eyes (hence the application's name). Your brain thinks it's seeing movement, when in fact it's simply processing a series of still images displayed in rapid succession.

To make an animation appear to run continuously, you can **loop** it so it starts over at Frame 1 after reaching the last frame. (In fact, as you will see, looping is the default state of an animation; you have to use code to prevent the timeline from automatically looping in the exported file.)

To create animation, you need to understand several terms and concepts:

- The Animate Timeline panel shows a visual depiction of the passage of time. Each fraction of a second is represented by a frame (the rectangles to the right of the layer names). The **playhead** indicates the current point in time, or the frame that is visible on the Stage.

- The number of frames in one second (called **frames per second**, **FPS**, or **frame rate**) determines the length and quality of the overall animation. New Animate files default to 24 fps, which is the standard frame rate of most film movies in the United States (although HD formats range as high as 120 fps). Animations only for the Web are commonly developed at 15 fps.

- A **keyframe** indicates the point in time at which something changes. If you want to change something, you need to insert a keyframe at the appropriate moment on the timeline.

- Regular frames between keyframes have the same content as the preceding keyframe.

Note:

*The term **playhead** is a throwback to the days when animation and video were shown on physical tape-reading machines. The playhead is the component under which the tape moves, and the tape is read by the player. By sliding the tape back and forth underneath the playhead, an animator could make a movie run forward and backward.*

ADD STREAMING SOUND

Unlike the event sounds that you used in the previous exercises, **stream sounds** play as soon as enough data is downloaded (called **progressive downloading**) to the user's computer. Stream sounds cannot be saved on a user's computer; the sound file must be redownloaded every time it is played. Stream sounds are linked to the timeline, which means they stop playing if the timeline stops (i.e., they are "timeline dependent").

1. **With atrium-kiosk.fla open, add a new layer named Talking immediately above the Mouths layer.**

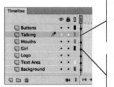

The empty circle indicates that no content currently resides on the keyframe.

The filled circle indicates that some content exists on the keyframe.

2. **Select the Frame 1 keyframe of the Talking layer.**

By default, the first frame of every layer is a keyframe.

3. **In the Properties panel, choose intro_talking.mp3 from the Sound menu and choose Stream in the Sync menu.**

Frame 1 of the Talking layer is selected.

Note:

Because stream sounds are typically larger files (longer sounds equal more data and larger file size), the quality of these sounds might be poor for users who have slow Internet connections.

4. **Choose Control>Test to test the movie.**

The background sound plays as expected, but the intro_talking sound does not. Remember, stream sounds are related to the position of the playhead on the timeline (they are timeline dependent). Because this file currently has only one frame, the playhead has nowhere to move, so the sound file does not play in the Player window.

5. **Close the external window and return to Animate.**

6. **In the timeline, Control/right-click Frame 95 of the Talking layer and choose Insert Frame from the contextual menu.**

Frame numbers appear in the frame ruler at the top of the timeline.

Control/right-click Frame 95 of the Talking layer to open the contextual menu.

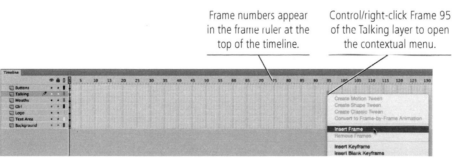

When you add a new frame, you extend the layer's timeline to the point where you place the new frame. The red playhead above the timeline shows the currently active frame.

You can now see the entire waveform of the sound that is attached to Frame 1 of the Talking layer. As you can see, however, none of the graphics are visible on the Stage because you have not added frames to the other layers. In other words, objects on those layers don't yet exist at Frame 95.

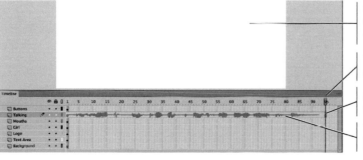

Other layers are not yet extended to Frame 95, so the graphics on those layers are not visible.

The playhead shows the currently active frame.

Adding a frame extends the layer's timeline.

The waveform on the Talking layer is now entirely visible.

7. Click Frame 95 of the Buttons layer to select it, then press F5.

This keyboard shortcut inserts a new frame at the selected location on the timeline; it is the same as choosing Insert Frame from the contextual menu.

If you are using a laptop or keyboard that has system-specific functions assigned to the Function keys, you can either press FN plus the required function key, or use the Insert>Timeline menu commands to insert frames and keyframes.

After adding the new frame to the Buttons layer, objects on that layer are now visible at Frame 95. The other graphics are still not visible because those layers do not yet have frames at Frame 95.

Note:

You can also insert a frame, keyframe, or blank keyframe by Control/right-clicking a specific frame in the Timeline panel and choosing from the contextual menu.

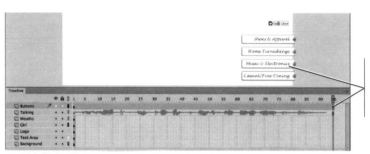

Objects on the Buttons layer are visible once that layer has been extended to Frame 95.

8. Click Frame 95 of the Mouths layer, then Shift-click Frame 95 of the Background layer.

9. Press F5 to add new frames to all five selected layers.

Because all of the layers now "exist" on Frame 95, all of the kiosk graphics are now visible on the Stage.

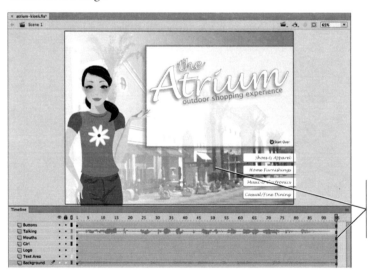

Because all layers now extend to Frame 95, all graphics in the interface are visible on the Stage.

10. Click Frame 1 of any layer to move the playhead to the beginning of the timeline.

The playhead identifies the current point in time on the Animate timeline. If you don't move the playhead back to Frame 1, the background sound will not play.

11. Press Return/Enter to test the movie on the Animate Stage.

You should now hear two sounds: the character talking and the background music.

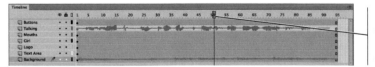

Pressing Return/Enter causes the playhead to move, playing the movie directly on the Stage.

12. **Choose Control>Test to test the movie in the external debugger window.**

The movie plays entirely through and then starts over again (**loops**) — this is what would happen in the actual exported file.

To make the timeline play only once, you have to use code to intentionally stop the playhead from looping. This code will be implemented by your developer partner after you are finished creating the lip-syncing animation.

Note:

You can choose Control>Loop Playback to allow the playhead to loop on the Animate Stage.

13. **Close the external window and return to Animate.**

14. **Save the file and continue to the next exercise.**

PREPARE FOR LIP SYNCING

If you have ever watched cartoons, you have probably seen the results of the time-consuming and painstaking work involved in synchronizing a character's movements to sounds. Realistic lip syncing is an extremely complex art that requires precise attention to detail, as well as in-depth study of behavioral movement. Other projects, such as this one, do not call for the precision and detail required for lifelike animation; rather, they use representative movements to create the effect of a character talking.

1. **Sit or stand in front of a mirror. Say the following sentence slowly, paying careful attention to the shape of your mouth for each syllable:**

Need help? Use the buttons to find exactly what you're looking for.

Note:

To better understand how to sync lip movements to sounds, you should study the different facial movements that are involved in spoken sound (called phonology).

2. **With atrium-kiosk.fla open in Animate, expand the mouth graphics folder in the Library panel.**

3. **Click each mouth symbol in the Library panel and review the shapes.**

The illustrator for this project created eight different mouth shapes to represent the various "talking" sounds. Note that each symbol was created with the registration point at the center.

Symbol	Use for:	Symbol	Use for:	Symbol	Use for:	Symbol	Use for:
mouth1	Silent, M, B, P	mouth2	C, D, G, J, K, N, R, S, Y, Z	mouth3	Short E, I, O, U Long A	mouth4	F, V
mouth5	M, B, P	mouth6	L, D, T, Th	mouth7	Short A, E Long I	mouth8	Ch, Sh, Qu, W Long O, U

4. **In the timeline layers area, double-click the icon to the left of the Talking layer name to open the Layer Properties dialog box.**

5. **Choose 300% in the Layer Height menu and click OK.**

Double-click the layer
icon to open the Layer
Properties dialog box.

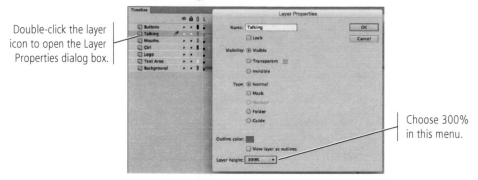

Choose 300%
in this menu.

It's easier to sync movement to sound when you can see the variations in the sound file. By enlarging the layer height, you can see the peaks and valleys of the waveform directly on the timeline.

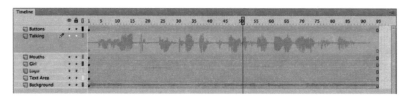

6. **Continue to the next exercise.**

 CREATE LIP SYNC ANIMATION

While lip syncing might seem complicated, it's actually quite simple — you show the graphic that supports the sound heard at a particular frame on the timeline. Because the different mouth shapes for this project have already been created, the most difficult part of the process is determining which shape to place at which point on the timeline.

1. **Click Frame 1 above the timeline to reset the playhead to the beginning of the movie.**

2. **Click the playhead and drag quickly to the right.**

   Dragging the playhead, a technique called **scrubbing the timeline**, allows you to manually preview portions of an animation. Because the sound on the Talking layer is a stream sound, you hear the sound as you drag the playhead. The background music — an event sound — is not related to the playhead, so scrubbing the playhead does not play the background music.

   As you drag the playhead from Frame 1, you hear the first sound in the spoken message beginning at Frame 4 (also indicated by the rise in the waveform).

Click the playhead
and drag right to find
the first spoken sound.

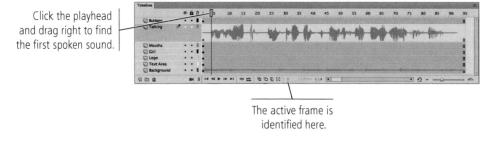

The active frame is
identified here.

3. **Select Frame 3 of the Mouths layer, then press F6 to insert a new keyframe.**

   Remember, a keyframe is the point at which something changes. In this case, you are going to change the mouth shape, so you need to add a keyframe at the appropriate point in time (when the mouth begins to move to make the spoken sound).

   Content on the preceding frame is automatically duplicated on the new keyframe.

   Although the sound begins at Frame 4, people's mouths usually start moving before actual words are spoken. You are adding a keyframe one frame earlier than the sound to accommodate for this behavior.

4. **Click the mouth symbol on the Stage to show its properties in the Properties panel.**

The object on the selected keyframe is selected on the Stage.

The Properties panel shows the name of the symbol being used.

The new keyframe is selected.

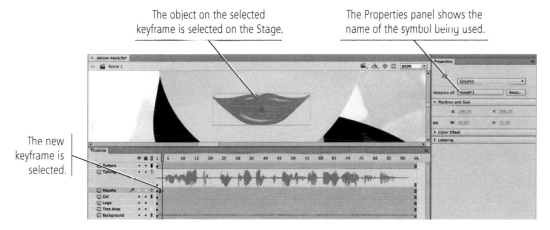

5. **With the mouth shape on the Frame 3 keyframe selected, click the Swap button in the Properties panel.**

   Lip syncing requires one primary task: swapping symbols to show the graphics that correlate to the sound at that particular moment.

6. **In the Swap Symbol dialog box, choose the mouth2 graphic symbol.**

   This is the mouth that correlates to the "N" sound at the beginning of the word "Need".

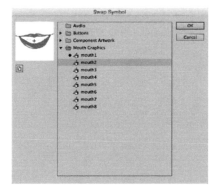

7. **Click OK to close the Swap Symbol dialog box.**

The new mouth now appears on Frame 3. The mouth symbol (mouth1) on the previous keyframe will remain visible until the playhead reaches Frame 3.

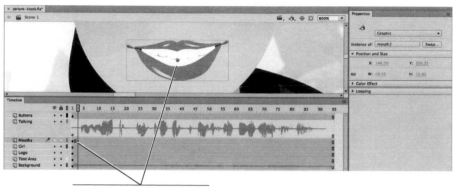

The new mouth shape appears,
starting at Frame 3.

8. **Drag the playhead right to find the next significant change in sound.**

The brief pause between the words "need" and "help" suggests a change in the speaker's mouth position at Frame 8.

9. **Select Frame 8 on the Mouths layer, then add a new keyframe to the selected frame.**

10. **With the mouth on the Frame 8 keyframe selected, click to select the mouth shape on the Stage, then click the Swap button in the Properties panel. In the Swap Symbol dialog box, choose the mouth5 symbol and click OK.**

This mouth shape is nearly closed, so it works well for the brief pause between words. It correlates to the short "I" sound, but it also works well as a good transition shape between a wide-open mouth and a closed mouth.

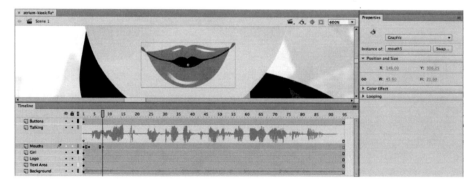

11. **Insert a new keyframe at Frame 10 of the Mouths layer. Select the mouth shape on the Stage, open the Swap Symbol dialog box, and replace the mouth shape with the mouth3 symbol.**

This shape correlates to the "short e" sound in "help". (The "h" sound typically blends into the vowel sound.)

12. **Return the playhead to Frame 1 and press Return/Enter to play the movie on the Stage.**

So far you have only three changes in the character's mouth, but you should begin to see how the different symbols appear at the appropriate points in the playback. In general, lip syncing in Animate is a relatively simple process. The hardest parts are determining when to change the graphics in relation to the sound, and deciding which shape best suits the animation at any given point.

13. **Applying the same process you used to create the first three mouth changes, continue scrubbing the playhead to identify points of change. Insert keyframes and swap symbols on the Mouths layer at the appropriate locations. In our example, we used the following locations and symbols:**

Frame	Symbol	Frame	Symbol	Frame	Symbol
15	mouth1	43	mouth4	64	mouth3
23	mouth8	46	mouth3	66	mouth2
27	mouth2	48	mouth2	68	mouth8
30	mouth6	50	mouth3	70	mouth2
31	mouth1	52	mouth2	72	mouth6
33	mouth3	55	mouth7	74	mouth2
36	mouth6	57	mouth2	79	mouth4
39	mouth2	60	mouth6	82	mouth8
41	mouth8	62	mouth2	84	mouth2

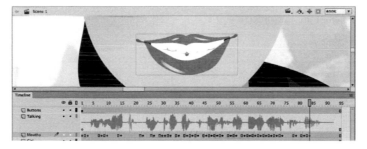

14. **Return the playhead to Frame 1, then press Return/Enter test the animation.**

By swapping the mouth symbol at various points on the timeline in relation to the sounds on the Talking layer, you now have a character who appears to be talking.

15. **Save the file and continue to the next exercise.**

DEFINE SOUND COMPRESSION SETTINGS

Before you export the final movie file, you should optimize the sounds to produce the smallest possible files while still maintaining the best possible quality. You can define default export settings for all stream sounds and all event sounds, but you can also experiment with different compression settings for individual sound files in the library.

1. **With `atrium-kiosk.fla` open, Control/right-click the atrium_jazz.mp3 file in the Audio folder of the Library panel. Choose Properties from the contextual menu.**

2. **In the resulting Sound Properties dialog box, make sure the Options tab is active at the top of the dialog box.**

3. **Choose MP3 in the Compression menu. If available, uncheck the Use Imported MP3 Quality option.**

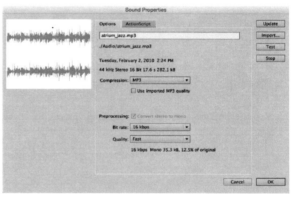

   Animate supports five sound compression options:

   - **Default.** This option uses the global compression settings (mp3, 16kbps, mono) defined in the Publish Settings dialog box when you export your SWF file. If you select Default, no additional export settings are available.

   - **ADPCM.** This option converts sounds into binary data. ADPCM encoding is not as efficient as MP3 compression, but it is useful if you need to export a file to be compatible with older versions of Animate.

   - **MP3.** Over the past few years, this format has become a *de facto* standard for audio on the Web. MP3 compression produces small files with very good quality, but it can cause problems for older computers with limited processing power.

   - **Raw.** This option does not compress the audio data, which results in very large file sizes. This option should only be used for files that will be delivered on the desktop instead of over the Internet.

     ADPCM and Raw use less processing power on each playback than MP3. They are recommended for very short (small) sounds that are played back rapidly. A shooting game in which guns fire many times a second, for example, might benefit from encoding the gun sound in ADPCM or Raw; the cost in file size would probably be less than 1k, and processor performance would be significantly enhanced.

   - **Speech.** This option uses a compression algorithm designed specifically for compressing spoken sounds. Sounds compressed with this option are converted to mono sounds (instead of stereo). Speech-compressed sounds require Animate Player 6 or higher.

Note:

The Preprocessing check box, enabled by default, converts stereo sounds to mono sounds.

4. Choose 48 kbps in the Bit Rate menu.

Depending on the selected compression option, you can also change the bit rate or the sample rate to affect the quality of the exported sound.

- The **Sample Rate** menu is available for ADPCM, Raw, and Speech compression; lower sample rates decrease file size, but can also decrease sound quality. The 22 kHz setting is recommended for reasonably good quality of most sounds.

- The **Bit Rate** menu is available for MP3 compression. This option determines the bits per second in the exported sound. Higher bit rates result in better sound quality. Most experts recommend at least 20 kbps for speech, and 48 kbps for reasonably good quality of complex sounds such as music.

Note:

Animate cannot increase the sample rate or bit rate of an imported sound above its original settings.

5. Choose Best in the Quality menu.

Three quality options — in order of file size (from small to large) and quality (from low to high) — are available for MP3 sounds: Fast, Medium, and Best.

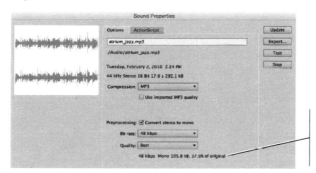

The dialog box provides feedback regarding the size of the file using the selected settings.

6. Click OK to change the export settings for the selected sound file.

7. Open the Sound Properties dialog box for the intro_talking sound file.

8. Choose Speech in the Compression menu.

9. Choose 11 kHz in the Sample Rate menu, and then click the Test button.

When the sound plays, you might notice some popping or hissing noises behind the spoken message.

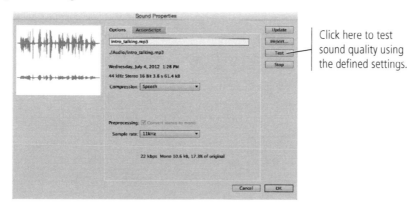

Click here to test sound quality using the defined settings.

Note:

You can change the default sound export settings in the Publish Settings dialog box.

10. Choose 44 kHz in the Sample Rate menu, and then click the Test button.

This sample rate results in much better quality. Because this kiosk will not be downloaded over the Internet, the larger file size is not a problem.

11. Click OK to apply the new compression settings for this sound file.

12. Save the Animate file and close it.

1. In a Button symbol, the _____ defines the area where a user can click to trigger the button.

2. _____ to edit a symbol in place on the Stage.

3. The _____ marks the location of the defined X and Y values of a placed instance.

4. A(n) _____ defines the point in time when a change occurs.

5. _____ is the number of animation frames that occur in a second.

6. _____ sounds are timeline independent; they must download completely before they play.

7. _____ sounds are timeline dependent; they play as soon as enough of the data has downloaded to the user's computer.

8. The _____ sync method prevents more than one instance of the same sound from playing at the same time.

9. You can use the _____ dialog box to change the length of a specific sound file.

10. Use the _____ option to replace one symbol with another at a specific frame.

1. Briefly describe at least three uses of the Library panel.

2. Briefly explain the difference between event sounds and stream sounds.

3. Briefly explain the concept of lip syncing, as it relates to symbols and the Animate timeline.

Portfolio Builder Project

Use what you learned in this project to complete the following freeform exercise.
Carefully read the art director and client comments, then create your own design to meet the needs of the project.
Use the space below to sketch ideas; when finished, write a brief explanation of your reasoning behind your final design.

art director comments

Your client is a company that provides technical support for children's online video games. The owner wants an introduction page for that site similar to the kiosk interface with a talking character that identifies the options.

To complete this project, you should:

❏ Download the client's supplied files in the **Robot_ANCC17_PB.zip** archive on the Student Files Web page.

❏ Review the client-supplied sound and artwork files.

❏ Develop a site intro page with a talking robot and two different buttons.

❏ If you use the client's artwork, import the file into Animate and create movie clips as necessary from the different elements.

❏ If you don't use the supplied file, create or find artwork as appropriate.

client comments

We want to build a new introduction page to our video game site. We're using a robot avatar throughout the video game site, and want that character to be featured on the intro page — I even recorded the intro message with a "mechanical" sounding voice. (Feel free to re-record the audio if you want to, as long as the message stays the same.)

I found a robot illustration that I like, but I'm not an artist; I'd be happy to review other artwork if you have a better idea. I also want you to develop some kind of background artwork that makes the piece look like a cohesive user interface.

You need to include two buttons: one that links to online technical support and one that links to a telephone support page.

In the final file, I want the robot to look like it's talking, but I also want the robot to point to the related buttons when the appropriate part of the intro sound plays.

project justification

_____

_____

_____

_____

_____

_____

_____

_____

_____

_____

_____

_____

_____

Project Summary

This project introduced many of the basic concepts and techniques of animating objects in Animate. You learned about frames and keyframes, as well as two different types of symbols that will be used in many Animate projects, both throughout this book and in your professional career. You also learned how to import artwork that was created in Adobe Illustrator — a very common workflow in the graphic design/animation market.

You should understand how frames on the Animate timeline relate to the passage of actual time, and how keyframes are used to make changes at specific points in an animation. You should also understand the basic concept of symbols and instances, including the different ways to edit the conent of a specific symbol. You will build on these skills as you complete the rest of the projects in this book.

This project also showed you how to add audio content to a movie — placing a looped sound in the background of a file, triggering specific sounds with a button's Over state, and even synchronizing graphics to a spoken message.

Import artwork from
Adobe Illustrator files

Add a streaming
sound as the
interface introduction

Create symbols from
imported artwork

Synchronize graphics
to sound to create a
"talking" effect

Add an event sound
that loops continuously
in the background

Edit a sound envelope to
control the sound volume

Attach and control
button sounds

Edit button symbols
to change different
button states

Animated Internet Ads

Your client wants to create a series of ads to place on Web sites that are used by existing and potential customers. They have asked you to create a short animation rather than just a static image in hopes of attracting more attention when the ad appears in a browser with other content.

This project incorporates the following skills:

❑ Creating shape tweens to animate changes in shape and color

❑ Creating classic tweens to animate changes in position and opacity

❑ Adding text to an Animate movie

❑ Adapting file content to match different file dimensions

❑ Publishing a file to SWF for distribution

client comments

We've provided you with our logo and an image that we want to use in the ads. Since these are going to be placed into a variety of Web sites, we want some kind of animation that might help catch a user's eye.

Most of the sites where we're planning on advertising use standard ad sizes. I'm not sure exactly which sizes we're going to purchase, but we do like the rectangle and square shapes better than the narrow banners.

We might decide on some of the other options later, but we'd like to get started with three common sizes:

- 300 × 250 pixels
- 336 × 280 pixels
- 250 × 250 pixels

art director comments

Animate includes predefined templates for most of the common ad sizes, so that's the easiest way to start the first file.

I want you to animate different aspects of the client's logo over the course of the animation. The kayaker is ideally suited to move across the stage. He should paddle across the stage while the sun rises. Halfway through, he should pause and wait until the tagline appears, then move the rest of the way across while the image gradually appears in place of the sunrise.

After you create the initial ad, you can use several built-in techniques to repurpose the content for other sizes.

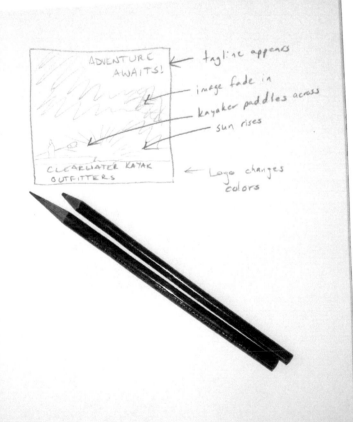

project objectives

To complete this project, you will:

- ❏ Create a file based on a template
- ❏ Create a shape tween
- ❏ Tween an object's color
- ❏ Create a classic tween
- ❏ Tween an object's opacity
- ❏ Stop the animation timeline
- ❏ Create and control a text object
- ❏ Define font embedding
- ❏ Control object stacking order
- ❏ Scale content to document properties
- ❏ Publish files to SWF

Stage 1 Animating Symbols

Animation — the true heart of Animate — can be created in a number of different ways. To create the animated ads for this project, you will use **shape tweening** and **classic tweening**.

In this project, you work with movie clip symbols. Both graphic symbols and movie clip symbols can include animation, but movie clips offer a number of advantages over graphic symbols.

Movie clips are **timeline independent**; the animation contained in a movie clip requires only a single frame on the timeline where it is placed (called the **parent timeline**). A movie clip timeline might include 500 frames, but the entire animation will play on a single frame of the parent timeline.

An animated graphic symbol, on the other hand, is **timeline dependent**; it requires the same number of frames on the parent timeline that are present inside the symbol's timeline. In other words, a 500-frame animation inside the graphic symbol requires 500 corresponding frames on the timeline where the symbol is placed.

Because movie clip timelines function independently of the parent timeline, you can more easily incorporate animations of different duration onto the same parent timeline.

Note:

Another advantage of movie clips is that placed instances can be named, which means they can be addressed — and controlled — using code. You will learn more about this option in Project 4: Ocean Animation.

Planning a movie

When you start any new project, you should begin by analyzing what you need to accomplish. A bit of advance planning can help you avoid unnecessary rework and frustration — in the project planning phase, you can determine, for example, that an independent movie clip is a better option than animating an object directly on the main timeline.

The ad that you are going to create in this project has the following plan or **storyboard**:

- The entire animation should last four seconds.

- The logotype will change from white to dark blue throughout the entire four-second animation.

- The kayaker will move across the Stage throughout the entire four-second duration, pausing halfway until the client's tagline appears.

- The sun is going to rise while the kayaker moves across the Stage. The sunrise animation should be finished when the kayaker gets halfway across the Stage.

- An image will gradually appear to replace the sunrise.

This information tells you a number of things about what you need to do:

- The finished ad requires four separate animations — the logo changing colors, the moving kayaker, the sunrise, and the image fading in.

- Each animation requires different timing. The sunrise and the image fade-in each occupy only half the time of the moving kayaker.

- The animations also require different starting points. The sunrise and the moving kayaker need to start as soon as the file opens. The image fade-in doesn't start until the sunrise animation is complete.

As you complete this project, you are going to use movie clip symbols and timeline frames to achieve the stated goals.

The final goal of this project is three separate ads that can be placed on Web sites where your client has decided to advertise. Because Internet ads typically use standard sizes, Animate includes those sizes as templates in the New Document dialog box.

In the first stage of this project, you are going to create the initial ad using one of the defined templates. Later you will use Animate's built-in tools to repurpose the existing content into the other required ad sizes.

1. **Download Kayaks_ANCC17_RF.zip from the Student Files Web page.**

2. **Expand the ZIP archive in your WIP folder (Macintosh) or copy the archive contents into your WIP folder (Windows).**

    This results in a folder named **Kayaks**, which contains the files you need for this project. You should also use this folder to save the files you create in this project.

3. **Choose File>New. In the General tab of the New Document dialog box, choose ActionScript 3.0 in the Type list.**

4. **Click the Templates tab to display those options. Select Advertising in the left pane, then select 300 × 250 Medium Rectangle in the right pane.**

    Animate includes templates for a number of standard file sizes, including the most common ads that are placed on the Internet.

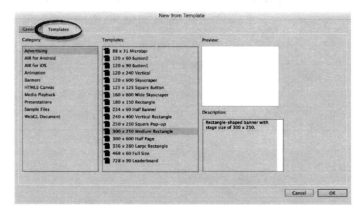

5. **Click OK to create the new file.**

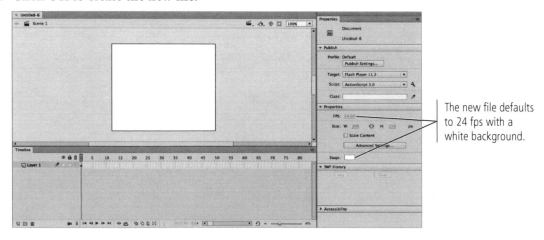

The new file defaults to 24 fps with a white background.

6. **Choose File>Import>Import to Stage. Select `cko_logo.ai` (in the WIP>Kayaks folder) and click Open.**

7. **In the Import to Stage dialog box, hide the advanced options if necessary. Define the following settings:**

Layer Conversion	Maintain Editable Paths and Effects
Convert Layers To	Animate Layers
Import as a Single Bitmap Image	Unchecked
Import Unused Symbols	Unchecked
Set Stage Size...	Unchecked

You created this Animate file at a specific file size to meet specific needs, so you are not converting the Stage to match the imported artwork.

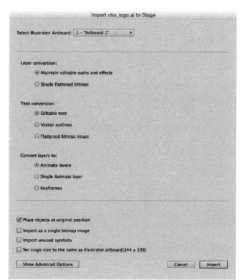

Note:

Refer to Project 2: Talking Internet Kiosk for an explanation of these options.

8. **Click Import to import the artwork to the Stage.**

The imported Illustrator file was created with four layers, each containing a different element of the logo. The Animate file now includes four layers, matching the layers in the original Illustrator file. All the imported artwork is automatically selected. As you complete this project, you will use several techniques to animate different parts of the logo artwork.

The imported artwork is centered in the document window.

Each separate object has its own bounding box.

Four layers were added to the file.

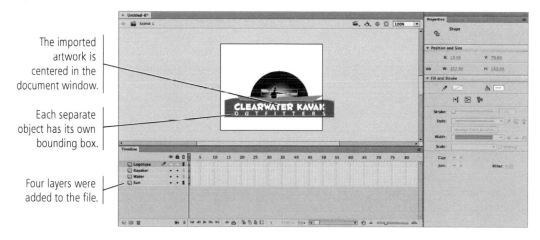

9. **Using the Selection tool, drag the selected artwork until the bottom edge snaps to the bottom edge of the Stage, and the artwork appears to be centered horizontally.**

   Each logo component, identified by the various bounding boxes, is an individual object (or group). If you tried to use the Align panel to align the artwork to the bottom and center of the Stage, each individual component would be aligned to the bottom of the Stage; the objects' positions relative to one another would not be maintained.

Note:

Because these objects all reside on different layers, you can't use the Group command to treat them as a single object for positioning purposes.

Use the Selection tool to move all selected objects at one time without changing their positions relative to one another.

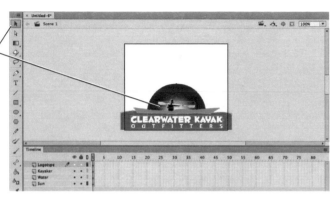

10. **Click away from everything on the Stage to deselect everything.**

11. **In the Properties panel, click the Stage swatch and choose Black from the pop-up color panel.**

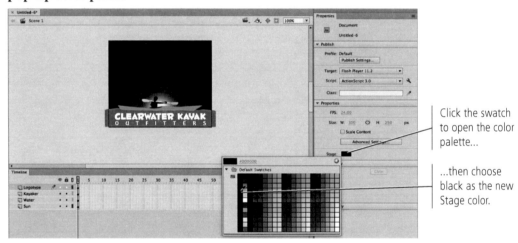

Click the swatch to open the color palette...

...then choose black as the new Stage color.

12. **Click the FPS hot text to access the field. Type 15 as the new FPS value, then press Return/Enter to finalize the change.**

   The ads you are creating are only going to be distributed over the Internet; 15 fps is high enough for good-quality display. (Higher frame rate would result in larger file sizes that are unnecessary for this type of file and could be problematic for users with slower download speeds.)

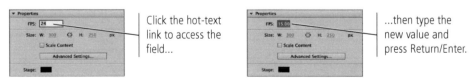

Click the hot-text link to access the field...

...then type the new value and press Return/Enter.

13. **Save the file as `cko-med-rect.fla` in your WIP>Kayaks folder, then continue to the next exercise.**

CREATE A SHAPE TWEEN

A **shape tween** allows you to convert one shape into another over time. You define the starting and ending shape, then Animate creates the in-between frames (hence the name "tween") that create the appearance of continuous movement when the finished animation plays.

You will use this type of tween to create the sunrise animation, as well as change the colors of the logotype.

1. **With `cko-med-rect.fla` open, use the Selection tool to select the sun object on the Stage.**

2. **Open the Color panel.**

   This object was created with a gradient fill. You are going to edit the gradient so the edge of the shape blends smoothly into the Stage background color.

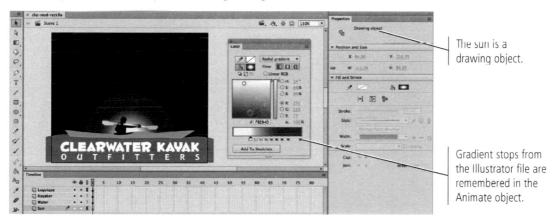

The sun is a drawing object.

Gradient stops from the Illustrator file are remembered in the Animate object.

3. **Click the right gradient stop to select it, then change the Alpha value of the selected stop to 0.**

   Alpha refers to transparency; a value of 0 means something is entirely transparent.

   This step makes the last gradient stop entirely transparent. Colors between the next-to-last and last stop will now transition from entirely opaque (100% Alpha) to entirely transparent (0% Alpha), which allows the object to blend into the background without a harsh edge.

Change the Alpha value of the last stop on the gradient.

4. **With the sun object selected, press F8 to convert the object to a symbol, or Control/right-click the selected object and choose Convert to Symbol.**

5. **Define the following settings in the Convert to Symbol dialog box:**

   Name: **sun_mc**

   Type: **Movie Clip**

   Registration: **Bottom center**

   You are using the bottom-center registration point because you want the sun object to grow out from that point.

6. **Click OK to create the new symbol.**

   When you create a symbol from existing artwork, the original object is automatically converted to an instance of that symbol.

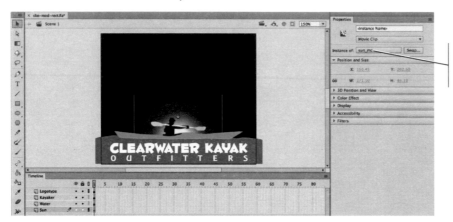

The selected object is now an instance of the new symbol.

7. **Double-click the instance on the Stage to enter into Symbol-Editing mode.**

   You are editing this symbol in place because you need to be able to see the shape's size relative to the Stage on which it is placed.

8. **Select Frame 30 in the timeline, then press F6 to add a new keyframe.**

   The completed ad needs to last four seconds. At 15 fps, the entire ad will require 60 frames; the sunrise should take half that time to complete, so this movie clip needs 30 frames.

   When you add a keyframe to a layer, the contents of the previous keyframe are automatically copied to the new keyframe. You can edit the contents on each keyframe independently without affecting the same contents on other keyframes.

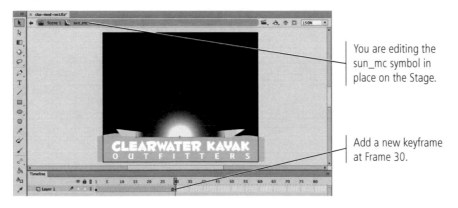

You are editing the sun_mc symbol in place on the Stage.

Add a new keyframe at Frame 30.

Note:

If you can't use, or don't have, Function keys, you can use the Insert> Timeline submenu, or the frame's contextual menu, to insert a frame, keyframe, or blank keyframe.

Note:

Remember, keyframes are required when an object needs to change in some way at a given point in time.

9. Choose the Free Transform tool.

When the Free Transform tool is active, a solid white circle on the selected object identifies the transformation point, or the point around which transformations will be made. Think of the transformation point as a pin that keeps that spot in place when you apply specific transformations.

Free
Transform
tool

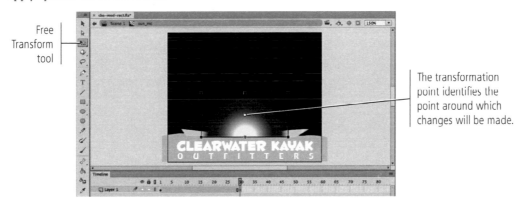

The transformation point identifies the point around which changes will be made.

10. With Frame 30 selected in the timeline and the sun object selected on the Stage, move the transformation point to the object's bottom-center bounding-box handle.

When you create the animation, you want the sun to appear as if it is growing out from the horizon. To accomplish this, you are going to make the sun shape larger, using the bottom-center point as the anchor.

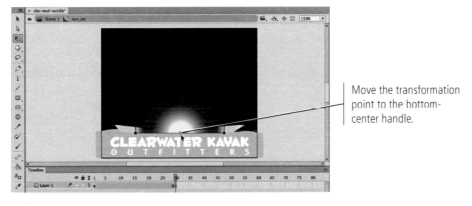

Move the transformation point to the bottom-center handle.

11. Zoom out so you can see the area around the Stage on all four sides.

Feel free to zoom in and out as necessary while you complete the projects in this book.

12. Open the Transform panel. At the top of the panel, make sure the Constrain icon is active.

The Transform panel can be used to make precise numerical changes or simply to monitor the changes you make with the Free Transform tool.

When the Constrain icon appears as two connected chain links, the object's width and height are linked to maintain object's original aspect ratio. If this icon is a broken chain, you can change one value without affecting the other.

13. **Place the cursor over the existing Width value. When you see the scrubby-slider cursor, click and drag right to enlarge the object until none of the black background color is visible.**

   Although you can use the Properties panel to change an object's height and/or width, those changes apply from the top-left corner of the selection instead of the defined transformation point that you set in Step 10. Changes made through the Transform panel respect the defined transformation point, so this is a better option for making this type of change.

Note:

*This technique of dragging to change a property value is called **scrubbing**.*

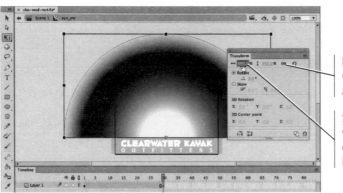

Make sure the Constrain icon appears as a linked chain.

Scrub the Width value until the object obscures the entire black background.

14. **Control/right-click any frame between Frame 1 and Frame 30, and choose Create Shape Tween from the contextual menu.**

   In the timeline, Animate identifies the shape tween with green frames and an arrow between keyframes.

Control/right-click between the keyframes to create the tween.

Note:

You can't create a shape tween for a group.

15. **Click Frame 1 in the timeline to move the playhead back to the beginning of the animation.**

16. **Press Return/Enter to play the animation on the Stage.**

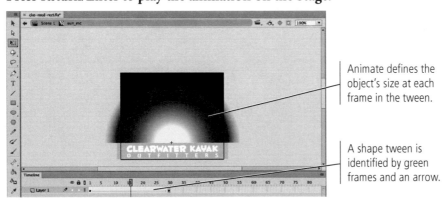

Animate defines the object's size at each frame in the tween.

A shape tween is identified by green frames and an arrow.

ANIMATE FOUNDATIONS

The Transform Panel

At times, you might need to apply very specific numeric transformations, such as scaling an object by a specific percentage. Rather than manually calculating new dimensions and defining the new dimensions in the Properties panel, you can use the Transform panel to make this type of change.

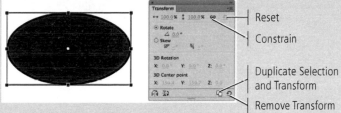

Reset

Constrain

Duplicate Selection and Transform

Remove Transform

When you change a value in the Transform panel, press Return/Enter to apply the change, or click the Duplicate Selection and Transform button to make a copy of the object and apply the change to the copy.

Keep in mind that all transformations made in the Transform panel apply around the defined transformation point.

The Modify>Transform Submenu

The Modify>Transform submenu has a number of valuable options for transforming objects.

Free Transform displays a set of eight bounding box handles, which you can drag horizontally or vertically to scale, stretch, skew, and rotate an object. During a free transform, an object's overall shape is maintained (an oval remains an oval, a square remains a square, and so on).

Distort displays a set of eight bounding box handles. If you drag one of the corner handles, you can "stretch" the object out of its original shape. For example, you can drag one corner of a rectangle to create a polygon with odd angles.

Envelope adds control handles to the object's anchor points, which you can use to warp the shape. You can drag the handles to reshape the connecting curves, and/or drag the anchor points to new positions to create an entirely different shape than the original.

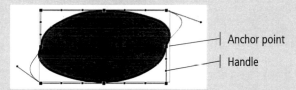

Anchor point

Handle

Scale is a subset of Free Transform. You can see the eight bounding box handles, but you can only scale or stretch the object; you can't rotate or skew it.

Rotate and Skew are also subsets of Free Transform. You can see the eight bounding box handles, but you can only skew or rotate the object; you can't scale or stretch it.

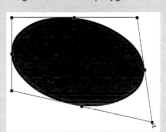

Scale and Rotate opens a dialog box where you can define specific scale percentages or rotation angles. You can also use the **Rotate 90°** (Clockwise and Counterclockwise) options for a selected object.

Flip Horizontal or **Flip Vertical** options allow you to flip objects on either axis.

Even though you can transform objects, Animate remembers the object's original size and shape. You can remove any transformation — except envelope distortion — from drawing objects and symbol instances using the **Remove Transform** option. (You can't remove a transformation from a merge-drawing object after you have deselected the object.)

To remove an envelope distortion, you have to choose Modify>Combine Objects>Delete Envelope.

17. **Click Scene 1 in the Edit bar to return to the main Stage.**

Remember, pressing Return/Enter plays the *current* timeline on the Stage. Because the main timeline has only one frame, this command would have no effect. Testing a movie on the Stage does not initiate the timeline of movie clips that are placed on the Stage.

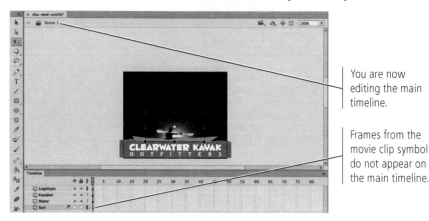

You are now editing the main timeline.

Frames from the movie clip symbol do not appear on the main timeline.

18. **Save the file and continue to the next exercise.**

 TWEEN AN OBJECT'S COLOR

Changing an object from one color to another is a common animation task. This is simply accomplished using a shape tween, using the same method you used to change the size of the sun symbol.

1. **With cko-med-rect.fla open, use the Selection tool to select the logotype on the Stage.**

The logotype group is selected.

2. **With the logotype object selected, press F8 to convert the object to a symbol, or Control/right-click the selected object and choose Convert to Symbol.**

As we continue through this project, remember your options for converting an object to a symbol. We will no longer repeat the entire instruction for accomplishing this task.

3. **Define the following settings in the Convert to Symbol dialog box:**

        Name: **logo_mc**

        Type: **Movie Clip**

        Registration: **Leave at default**

You will only change the color of the logotype, so the registration point is not important for this symbol.

4. **Click OK to create the new symbol.**

5. **Double-click the symbol instance on the Stage to enter into it.**

6. **With the logotype selected on the Stage, choose Modify>Ungroup.**

   You can't create a shape tween with a group, so you first have to ungroup the letters. After ungrouping, you can see that each letter is a separate drawing object.

Note:

You could also choose Modify>Break Apart (or press Command/Control-B) to accomplish the same general effect.

You are editing the logo_mc symbol in place on the Stage.

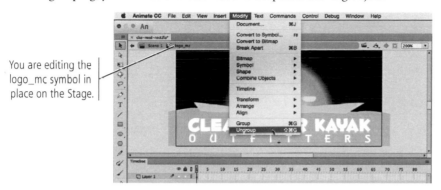

7. **Click Frame 60 in the timeline to select it, then press F6 to add a new keyframe.**

   When you add or select a frame on the timeline, the frame becomes the active selection.

   This is deceptive because the objects' bounding boxes are still visible, suggesting that they are selected — even though they are not.

8. **Click the filled area of any of the drawing objects on the Stage to make them the active selection.**

   To edit an object's properties, you first have to remember to intentionally reselect the object(s) on the Stage. If you aren't sure what is actually selected, look at the top of the Properties panel.

After adding the keyframe, the Properties panel shows that the frame is selected.

The individual objects on the selected frame are visible.

Click any filled area to make the drawing objects the active selection.

Creating and Controlling Shape Tweens

In addition to changing object properties in a shape tween, you can also create a **shape tween** to change one shape into another over time (as the name suggests). A shape tween requires two existing keyframes — one with the starting shape and one with the ending shape.

If you Control/right-click between two keyframes, choosing Create Shape Tween generates the shape tween; the tween frames automatically change the shape of the object as necessary to convert Shape A into Shape B. The following illustrations show a simple shape tween that changes a blue square into a green circle.

The blue square exists on the Frame 1 keyframe.

The green circle exists on the Frame 50 keyframe.

Control/right-click between the two keyframes and choose Create Shape Tween.

Because the two keyframe objects are different colors, the tween also calculates the required change in color for each frame.

Playing the animation shows the object twisting from a square to a circle.

9. **Using the Fill swatch in the Properties panel, change the objects' fill color to #000033.**

After ungrouping, click any of the active objects to select them.

Use the Properties panel to change the fill color to #000033 with 100% Alpha.

10. **Control/right-click any frame between Frame 1 and Frame 60, and choose Create Shape Tween from the contextual menu.**

Although you did not change the objects' shapes, a shape tween is still an appropriate method for changing an object's color over time.

11. **Move the playhead to Frame 1, then press Return/Enter to test the animation on the Stage.**

12. **Click Scene 1 in the Edit bar to return to the main Stage.**

Again, there is only one frame on the main timeline, so there is nothing to play. Remember, a movie clip symbol operates independently of the main timeline; you can't view the movie clip's animation directly on the Animate stage.

13. **Save the file and continue to the next exercise.**

Reducing and Enlarging the Timeline View

At the bottom-right corner of the Timeline panel, you have several options for adjusting the size of frames that are visible in the panel.

Two buttons can be used to show more or less frames in the panel, effectively reducing or enlarging (respectively) the size of the visible frames. You can also use the slider between the two buttons to manually resize the visible frames.

You can click the Reset button (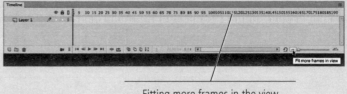) to restore the frames to their default size in the panel.

Fitting more frames in the view reduces the size of frames in the panel.

Fitting less frames in the view enlarges the size of frames in the panel.

Adding Frames to the Timeline

If you create animations with very long timelines, you might need to extend the timeline beyond what is available by default. To accomplish this, scroll the timeline all the way to the right and then add a regular frame to the layer near the end of the visible timeline.

When you add a frame after the last visible frame, the timeline scroll bar moves to the middle of the panel, indicating that more frames are now available in the timeline. You can then scroll again to the new end of the timeline and add another frame, which again extends the length of the available timeline. Continue this process until you have the number of frames you need.

The default timeline only goes up to a certain frame number.

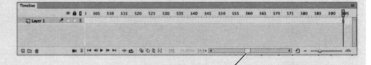

After adding a regular frame near the end of the default timeline, the scroll bar indicates that more frames are available.

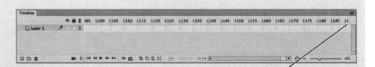

Continue adding regular frames and scrolling the timeline until you have the number of frames you need.

CREATE A CLASSIC TWEEN

As you can probably guess, there is much more to animation than changing an object's shape or color. In this exercise, you will create very simple classic tweens that move the kayaker across the Stage, using keyframes to control the movement's timing.

1. **With cko-med-rect.fla open, click the Kayaker layer in the timeline to select all objects on the layer.**

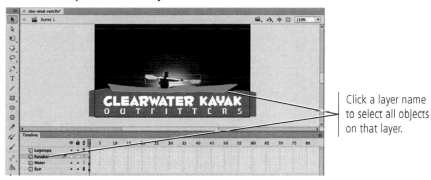

Click a layer name to select all objects on that layer.

2. **Convert the selected object to a symbol. Define the following settings in the Convert to Symbol dialog box:**

Name:	kayaker_mc
Type:	Movie Clip
Registration:	Right center

3. **Click OK to create the new symbol.**

4. **With the new symbol instance selected on the Stage, change the X value in the Properties panel to 0.**

   Remember, the X and Y properties define the position of a symbol's registration point. Because you chose the right-center registration point, changing the X value to 0 moves the kayaker entirely off the Stage.

You are editing the symbol instance on the main timeline.

The X property defines the position of the symbol's registration point.

5. **Click Frame 30 of the Kayaker layer and press F6 to add a new keyframe.**

6. **Click the kayaker symbol instance to select it, then scrub the X property in the Property panel until the instance is approximately centered on the Stage (as shown here).**

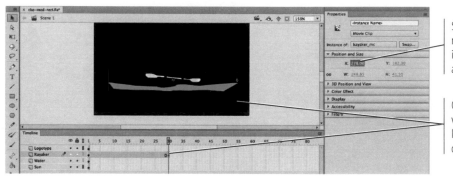

Scrub the X value to move the selected instance horizontally across the stage.

Other objects are not visible because those layers don't yet exist on Frame 30.

7. **Control/right-click any frame between Frame 1 and 30 of the Kayaker layer and choose Create Classic Tween from the contextual menu.**

A classic tween is one method for creating motion in an Animate animation. Like the shape tweens you created already, you have to define the starting and ending keyframes, then create the tween; Animate automatically determines the instance's position on the in-between frames.

In Project 4: Ocean Animation, you will learn about Motion Tweens, which provide far more control over numerous aspects of a tween. You should understand what a classic tween is, though, so you can recognize one if you find one in a file — especially files created in older versions of the software.

Note:

This is called a "classic" tween because this technique was available in previous versions of the application.

In the timeline, Animate identifies the classic tween with blue frames and an arrow between keyframes.

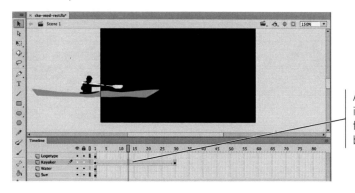

A classic tween is identified by blue frames and an arrow between keyframes.

8. **Select Frame 38 on the Kayaker layer, then press F6 to add another keyframe.**

Remember: when you add a new keyframe, Animate duplicates the content on the previous keyframe. By adding this keyframe at Frame 38, you are holding the symbol instance in place for approximately half a second.

(We say "approximately half a second" because the frame rate in this file is 15 fps, which is not equally divisible by 2. Because you can't have half a frame, you are using slightly more than half a second for the pause in animation.)

9. **Select Frame 60 of the Kayaker layer and add a new keyframe.**

10. **Select the symbol instance on the Stage, then change the X property in the Properties panel until the instance is entirely past the right edge of the Stage.**

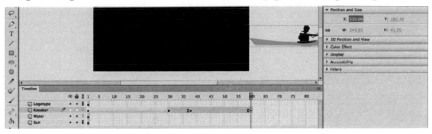

11. **Control/right-click any frame between Frame 38 and 60 of the Kayaker layer and choose Create Classic Tween from the contextual menu.**

The new tween occupies the entire range of frames between the keyframes that you defined on Frames 38 and 60.

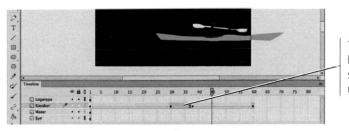

There is no tween between these keyframes, so the instance will remain in place.

12. **Select Frame 60 of the Logotype layer. Press Command/Control, then click Frame 60 of the Water and Sun layers to add them to the active selection.**

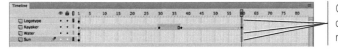

Command/Control-click to select non-contiguous frames.

Note:

You can press Shift to select contiguous frames, or press Command/Control to select non-contiguous layers.

Although two of these layers contain animated movie clips, those movie clips' timelines do not transfer to the main movie timeline. They will not exist in the main movie beyond Frame 1 unless you extend those layers' timelines on the main Stage.

13. **Press F5 to add regular frames to the three selected layers.**

This extends all three layers to Frame 60, so their content will be visible throughout the entire animation.

14. **Click Frame 1 to select it, then press Return/Enter to test the animation on the timeline.**

Remember, you can't see the sunrise and logotype animations because those are created inside the individual symbols. To see all three animations together, you have to test the movie in the Player window. (You will do this after you create the final required animation in the next exercise.)

The sunrise and logotype animations do not play on the main Stage.

15. **Save the file and continue to the next exercise.**

The last required animation for this movie is an image that fades in after the sun finishes rising. In this exercise you will create a new layer on the timeline and use a blank keyframe to prevent the image from appearing too early.

1. **With `cko-med-rect.fla` open, create a new layer named `Photo` directly above the Sun layer.**

2. **Control/right-click Frame 30 on the new layer and choose Insert Blank Keyframe.**

    You are inserting a blank keyframe before placing the image onto the Stage at Frame 30, so the preceding frames (1–29) will remain blank — preventing the image from appearing until halfway through the movie.

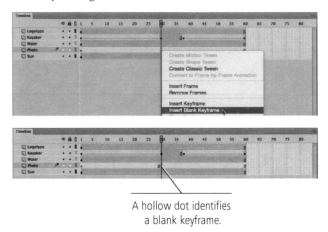

A hollow dot identifies
a blank keyframe.

3. **With the blank keyframe on Frame 30 selected, choose File>Import>Import to Stage.**

4. **Choose the file `kayaks.jpg` in your WIP>Kayaks folder, then click Open.**

5. **Align the image to the top of the Stage, centered horizontally.**

    Unlike the imported Illustrator artwork, you can use the Align panel to move the image into the correct position.

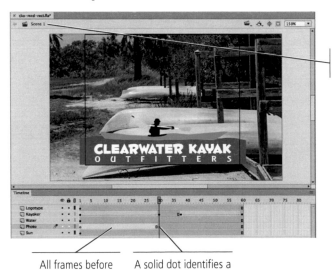

You are working
on the main Stage.

All frames before
Frame 30 are empty.

A solid dot identifies a
keyframe with content.

6. **Choose the Free Transform tool, then move the image's transformation point to the top-center bounding-box handle.**

7. **Using the Transform panel, reduce the image scale (proportionally) until the bottom edge is just hidden by the blue shape that makes up the water.**

   You can't animate a bitmap object; to cause this image to appear gradually over time, you first need to convert it to a symbol.

Because you moved the transformation point, the top-center point of the image remains in place when you scale it.

8. **Convert the selected object to a symbol. Define the following settings in the Convert to Symbol dialog box:**

Name:	**photo_mc**
Type:	**Movie Clip**
Registration:	**Top center**

9. **Click OK to create the new symbol.**

   Symbols have a number of properties that are not available for bitmap or drawing objects. In this case you are going to edit and animate the Color Effect property to change the alpha (transparency) value of the symbol over time.

10. **In the Properties panel, expand the Color Effect options, then choose Alpha in the Style menu. In the secondary Alpha field that appears, change the Alpha value to 0.**

    Remember, the Alpha value controls an object's opacity; a value of 0 means the object is not visible.

The placed image is a symbol instance.

Alpha is related to color, so you can change an instance's Alpha value in the Color Effect properties.

Changing the Alpha value to 0 makes the instance entirely transparent on the Stage.

11. **Add a new keyframe to Frame 60 of the Photo layer.**

12. **Using the Selection tool, click inside the area of the photo to select the instance on the Stage.**

   The symbol instance is not visible because its Alpha value is currently 0; you can still click inside the image area to select it.

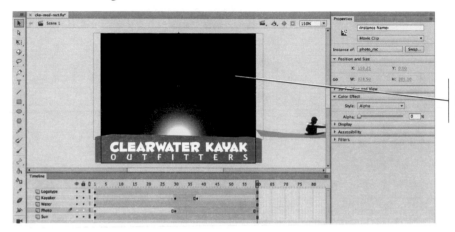

Click inside the image area to select the symbol instance.

13. **In the Properties panel, change the Alpha value to 100%.**

Change the Alpha value to 100%.

The Frame 60 keyframe is active.

14. **Control/right-click anywhere between Frames 30 and 60 in the Photo layer and choose Create Classic Tween.**

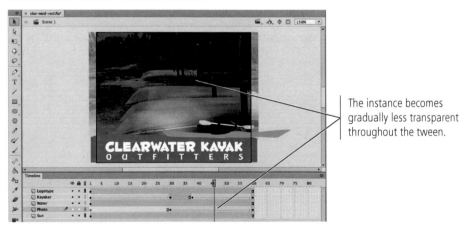

The instance becomes gradually less transparent throughout the tween.

15. **Save the file and continue to the next exercise.**

STOP THE ANIMATION TIMELINE

Remember, movie clips each have their own timelines, which are independent of other movie clips and of the main movie timeline. As soon as the playhead reaches the end of the timeline in each symbol, it automatically returns to the beginning and plays again (called **looping**). To prevent this, you have to add the Stop command to the timeline.

1. **With cko-med-rect.fla open, press Command-Return/Control-Enter to test the movie in the Player window.**

   As you can see, the four animations in your movie play repeatedly. You should also notice that the sun rises twice in the time it takes the logotype to change colors and the kayaker to move out of the movie area.

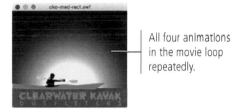

All four animations in the movie loop repeatedly.

2. **Close the Player window and return to Animate.**

3. **In the timeline, select Frame 60 of the Kayaker layer.**

   It really doesn't matter what layer you selected because the Stop command applies to the entire timeline. Any animation on this timeline — the main movie timeline — will be stopped when the playhead reaches Frame 60.

4. **Open the Code Snippets panel. Expand the ActionScript folder, then expand the Timeline Navigation subfolder.**

   The Code Snippets panel is intended to make it easier for non-programmers to add a certain level of interactivity to an Animate movie. Different types of common commands are available, grouped into logical sets or folders. Each snippet includes a plain-English name; if you move your mouse over a snippet, more information about that item appears in a tool tip.

Expand the various folders to find the available commands.

Move your mouse over a snippet to get more information about that item.

5. **Double-click Stop at this Frame in the Code Snippets panel.**

The Actions panel opens and shows the code that is required to stop the timeline from playing more than once.

A new Actions layer is added at the top of the layer stack on the main timeline. A small "a" in the selected keyframe (Frame 60) indicates that code exists on that frame.

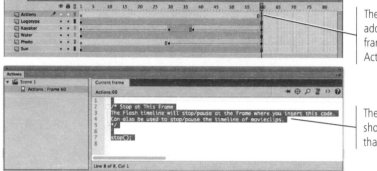

The code was added to the active frame on a new Actions layer.

The Actions panel shows the code that was added.

6. **Press Command-Return/Control-Enter to test the animation in the Player window.**

The kayaker and photo animations play once and stop; however, the two movie clip animations continue to loop. It is important to note that the stop command does not stop movie clip animations that are placed on the current timeline.

The two animations on the main timeline stop after playing once.

The sunrise and logotype movie clip animations still loop.

Remember, movie clip timelines are independent of other movie clips and of the main timeline; you have to add the stop command to each symbol timeline to prevent them from looping.

7. **Close the Player window and return to Animate.**

8. **In the Library panel, double-click the sun_mc icon to enter into the symbol.**

9. **Select Frame 30 in the timeline, then double-click Stop at this Frame in the Code Snippets panel.**

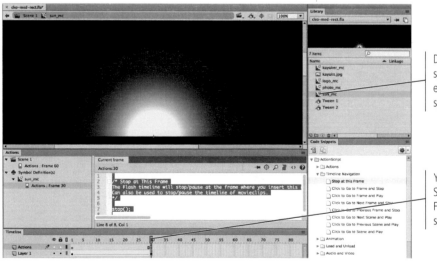

Double-click the symbol icon to enter into the symbol Stage.

You are adding the Stop command to Frame 30 of the sun_mc symbol.

10. **In the Library panel, double-click the logo_mc symbol icon to enter into that symbol.**

    When you use the Library panel to enter into a symbol, you don't need to return to the main movie Stage before entering into a different symbol. You can simply double-click the symbol icons to navigate from one symbol to another.

11. **Select Frame 60 in the timeline, then double-click Stop at this Frame in the Code Snippets panel.**

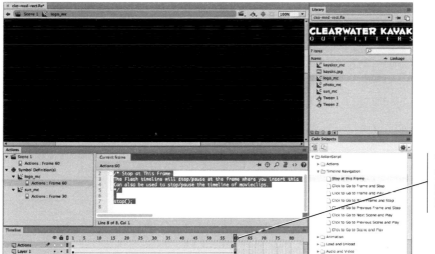

You are adding the Stop command to Frame 60 of the logo_mc symbol.

12. **Click Scene 1 in the Edit bar to return to the main Stage.**

13. **Press Command-Return/Control-Enter to test the movie in the Player window.**

    All four animations now play once and stop.

14. **Close the Player window and return to Animate.**

15. **Save the file and continue to the next stage of the project.**

Stage 2 Working with Text

One of the more frustrating aspects of Web design is working with text elements; this is because the appearance of type is dependent on the available fonts on a user's computer. Animate movies are not subject to this limitation because used fonts are embedded in the exported SWF file, which means you can use any font you like in an Animate file, and it will appear exactly as expected in the movie.

The Text tool is used to add text elements to movies; the tool includes options that tie text fields to variables using ActionScript. This added functionality means text fields can automatically update from formulas and databases, or they can take user input from online forms.

Animate allows you to create three types of text:

- **Static text** is placed, kerned, aligned, and manually edited with the Text tool. To create static text, simply select the Text tool, click the Stage, and type.

- **Dynamic text** is basically an area into which a separate file (such as text-only or XML) can be read.

- **Input text** is a field in which users can type to submit information (as you would find in an online form).

Note:

The words "static" and "dynamic" do not, in this context, indicate movement. In the case of text in an Animate file, these terms refer instead to whether the text is manually placed with the Text tool (static text) or is data-driven with variables (dynamic text).

CREATE A NEW TEXT OBJECT

Your client wants a very simple text message added to the top of the ad. The message shouldn't appear until halfway through the animation, so you will again use blank keyframes to prevent the message from appearing until it should.

1. **With `cko-med-rect.fla` open, choose View>Magnification>Fit in Window.**

   You are going to create a heading across the top of the entire movie, so it will help to see the entire Stage.

2. **Add a new layer at the top of the layer stack named `Text`.**

3. **Create a new keyframe at Frame 37 of the Text layer, then select that frame as the active one.**

4. **Choose the Text tool in the Tools panel. At the top of the Properties panel, choose Static Text in the Text Type menu.**

5. **In the Character section of the Properties panel, change the Family menu to a sans-serif font such as Arial or Helvetica. Choose a Black, Heavy, or Bold variation of the selected font in the Style menu.**

   Any formatting you define before clicking with the Text tool will be applied in the new text area.

Note:

You might need to choose a different tool and then rechoose the Text tool to show the appropriate options in the Properties panel.

6. **Click the current Size link to access the field. Type 24 in the field and press Return/Enter.**

7. **Click the Color swatch to open the Color palette, and choose white (#FFFFFF) as the text color.**

8. **In the Paragraph section of the Properties panel, click the Align Right format option.**

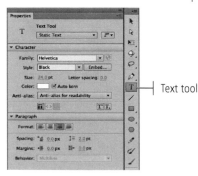

 Text tool

Controlling Text Properties

A number of options for controlling text appear in the Properties panel when the Text tool or an existing text element is selected.

- **Text Type menu.** This menu defines a text field as static, dynamic, or input text.
- **Orientation menu.** When creating a static text object, you can use this menu to orient text horizontally, vertically, or vertically left-to-right within the text object.

Character Options

- **Family and Style menus.** As with any computer application, the font defines the appearance of the text. The entire list of fonts installed on your machine appears in the Family menu. The Style menu lists available variants of the selected font (Bold, Italic, etc.).
- **Embed button.** This button allows you to embed selected fonts or specific characters to ensure that text will appear on users' computers in the font you define.
- **Size.** The size of the text (in points) can be changed in the Font Size field or selected from the menu.
- **Letter Spacing (Tracking) field.** This option is used to increase or decrease the spacing between a selected range of characters.
- **Color.** This swatch changes the fill color of selected characters.
- **Auto Kern check box.** You can uncheck this option to prevent Animate from applying a font's default kerning values in static text.
- **Anti-aliasing menu.** This menu determines the level of anti-aliasing applied (if any).
- **Selectable button.** When you create static or dynamic text, you can activate this option to allow users to select the text within the Player window. (If you are adding text to a button, you should make sure this option is turned off so the text does not interfere with the click properties of the button.)
- **Render Text as HTML button.** When you create dynamic or input text fields, you can activate this option to show text in the field using default HTML settings instead of your specific fonts. This is usually a good choice, but when you choose it, you won't have ultimate control over the appearance of text in these areas.

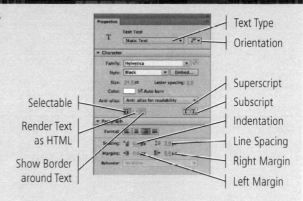

Text Type
Orientation
Superscript
Subscript
Indentation
Line Spacing
Right Margin
Left Margin
Selectable
Render Text as HTML
Show Border around Text

- **Show Border Around Text button.** For dynamic or input text areas, you can use this option to add a visible black line around the text area, so users can more easily identify the area. This option is particularly useful for input text fields when the background is not sufficient to differentiate the field area.
- **Type Style buttons.** These buttons change the style of text to (from left) superscript (such as the TH in 4th) or subscript (the 2 in H_2O).

Paragraph Options

- **Paragraph Format buttons.** Text can be aligned to the left, center, or right of its containing area, or it can be justified so that all lines fill the available horizontal space.
- **Spacing: Indentation.** This option defines how far the first line of the paragraph is indented from the left edge of the remaining text in the same paragraph.
- **Spacing: Line Spacing.** This option defines the distance between the bottoms of lines in the same type area (basically, this is the type leading).
- **Margins.** These options define how far text is moved from the left and right edges of the containing area.
- **Behavior.** This menu is only available when you are creating dynamic or input text areas. A text area can be a single line, multiple lines, or multiple lines with no wrap. If you are creating an input text field, you can also define the field as a password field.

9. **Click near the top-left corner of the Stage and drag to create a rectangular text area about the width of the movie.**

   To include text in a movie, you have to first create an area to hold the text characters. As you drag, notice that dragging affects only the width of the rectangle. The area's height is determined by the current type settings defined in the Properties panel.

   When you release the mouse button, the text area appears as a white box. When the insertion point is flashing, you can type in the box to add text.

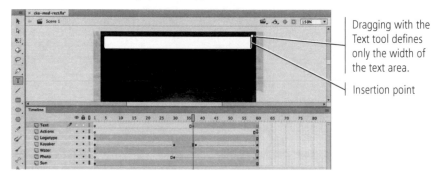

Dragging with the Text tool defines only the width of the text area.

Insertion point

Note:

You can't define the height of a static text area; it automatically changes to accommodate the text in the area.

10. **Type Adventure Awaits!.**

    The text appears in the text area you just created, using the character and paragraph formatting options that you already defined. (Because you chose white as the text color, the text appears gray in the area so you can see it as you type.)

Note:

The insertion point appears on the right side of the area because you chose the Align Right paragraph formatting option in Step 8.

11. **Choose the Selection tool, and then expand the Position and Size options in the Properties panel. Change the properties of the selected text area to:**

    X: 0   Y: 10
    W: 280

When the Selection tool is active, you can drag the area handles but you can't change the text content in the area.

Use these fields to change the area width and position.

Using the Position and Size properties, you can define specific numeric parameters for the area. You can also reposition a text area by clicking inside the area with the Selection tool and dragging to a new location, or resize the area by dragging any of the handles that appear on the outside edges of the object.

Note:

When the insertion point is flashing in a text area, you can't use the one-key shortcuts to choose other tools.

Note:

Depending on how wide you create a text area, the height of a text area might enlarge if the text you type requires a second line.

Note:

Using the Free Transform tool on a text area stretches or condenses type inside the area.

12. **With the text area still selected, change the Size value (in the Character section of the Properties panel) to 40.**

When a text area is selected, changes to character and paragraph formatting apply to all text inside the area. You can change the formatting of only certain characters by highlighting the target characters with the Text tool before making changes in the Properties panel.

The text area automatically expands to accommodate the new text formatting; in this case, it is high enough to show two lines of text.

13. **If necessary, adjust the Line Spacing in the Paragraph option so that only a small amount of space appears between the two lines of text.**

Required line spacing will be different depending on the specific font you use. In our example, using the Helvetica Black font on a Macintosh, the default options are fine.

When the entire text object is selected, formatting changes affect all text in the area.

The text object height expands to accommodate the new formatting.

14. **Click away from the text area to deselect it.**

15. **Save the file and continue to the next exercise.**

DEFINE FONT EMBEDDING

When you use text in a movie, the fonts you use must be available to other users who open your file. If not, the users' systems will substitute some font that is available — which can significantly change the appearance of your movie. To solve this potential problem, you can embed fonts into your movies so the required fonts are always available.

1. **With cko-med-rect.fla open, select the Text tool.**

2. **Click inside the heading text area to place the insertion point and reveal the formatting for that area.**

The insertion point is placed in the text.

3. **In the Character section of the Properties panel, click the Embed button.**

This button opens the Font Embedding dialog box. The currently applied font is automatically selected in the Family and Style menus.

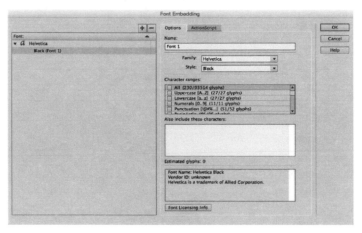

4. **Change the Name field to Heading Font.**

5. **In the Character Ranges list, check the Uppercase, Lowercase, and Punctuation options.**

Remember, embedding characters from fonts increases the resulting file size. You know only letters and punctuation were used in this document, so you can limit the embedded characters to only these ranges rather than embedding every possible character of the font.

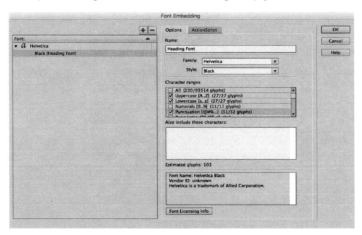

6. **Click OK to close the dialog box.**

7. **Review the Library panel.**

When you embed a font into the file, it is added to the file's library.

The embedded font is added to the file's library.

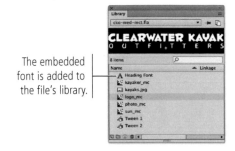

Note:

Keep in mind that embedding fonts adds to the resulting file size and increases download time. The font outline (embedded character) is stored as part of the SWF file, so repeatedly using the same character of the same font in the movie does not increase the file size (the same theory as using instances of symbols). Keeping the number of fonts in a movie to a minimum ensures a faster-loading movie.

Note:

The item on the left side of the dialog box won't reflect the new name until you click away from the Name field.

8. **Press Command-Return/Control-Enter to test the file in the Player window.**

When the movie ends, you might notice a problem — the white text is difficult to read when the image is entirely opaque. You will solve this problem in the next exercise.

9. **Close the Player window and return to Animate.**

10. **Save the file and continue to the next exercise.**

CONTROL OBJECT STACKING ORDER

It is not uncommon for designers to use individual layers for each object in the file — which makes things much easier to find as long as you use descriptive layer names.

You should also understand, however, that stacking order applies to multiple objects that are created on the same layer. Drawing objects and symbols exist from bottom to top in the order they were created *on a single layer*. It is easy to create something in the wrong order, but fortunately, Animate makes it relatively easy to rearrange the stack.

1. **With cko-med-rect.fla open, select Frame 37 of the Text layer.**

2. **Using the Selection tool, click an empty area around the Stage to deselect the text object.**

3. **Choose the Rectangle tool, and make sure Object-Drawing mode is active.**

4. **In the Color panel, change the Stroke color to None.**

5. **Click the Fill button to make it the active attribute, then open the Color Type menu and chose Linear Gradient.**

6. **Open the Fill color palette and choose the white-to-black linear gradient swatch.**

7. **Click the left gradient stop to select it, then change the Alpha value to 0%.**

8. **Click the right gradient stop to select it, and drag it to the 50% point along the gradient. Change the stop color to #000033, and change the Alpha value to 50%.**

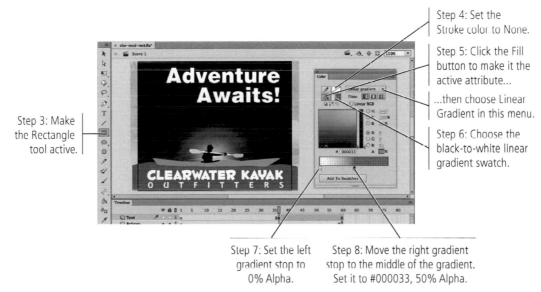

Step 3: Make the Rectangle tool active.

Step 4: Set the Stroke color to None.

Step 5: Click the Fill button to make it the active attribute... ...then choose Linear Gradient in this menu.

Step 6: Choose the black-to-white linear gradient swatch.

Step 7: Set the left gradient stop to 0% Alpha.

Step 8: Move the right gradient stop to the middle of the gradient. Set it to #000033, 50% Alpha.

9. **With Frame 37 of the Text layer selected, click and drag to create an object that fills the top half of the Stage.**

The gradient defaults to fill the object from left to right.

The gradient goes from entirely transparent to 50% transparent (the Alpha value of each stop on the gradient).

10. **Choose the Gradient Transform tool in the Tools panel. If necessary, click the gradient-filled rectangle to reveal the gradient-editing handles.**

Rotation handle

Width handle

11. **Rotate the gradient 90° counterclockwise, then use the gradient width handle to make the gradient the same size as the object's height.**

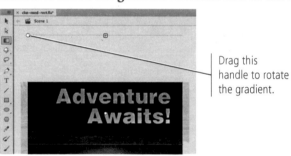

Drag this handle to rotate the gradient.

Drag this handle to change the gradient width.

12. **Using the Selection tool, select the gradient-filled rectangle.**

The gradient-filled shape is currently on top of the text object. You want the text to appear on top of the gradient, so you need to rearrange the object stacking order.

13. **Choose Modify>Arrange>Send to Back.**

Options in the Modify>Arrange submenu control the stacking order of objects on the active layer. These options have no effect on the relative stacking of objects on different layers.

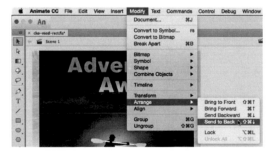

Note:

Merge-drawing shapes, which result when the object-drawing mode is not toggled on, are always created at the back of the stacking order, behind any other objects on the layer (symbol instances, object-drawing shapes, type areas, etc.).

By placing the gradient-filled rectangle behind the text object but in front of the underlying layers, the white text will be more easily visible when the background photo is entirely visible at the end of the animation.

14. **Save the file and continue to the next stage of the project.**

Stage 3 **Repurposing Animate Content**

The first ad required for this project is now complete. However, the entire job calls for three versions of the same ad, using different standard ad sizes but the same content in each ad. Rather than simply creating a new file and then copying the existing content into it, you will use two different techniques to scale the existing content to suit the alternate file sizes.

SCALE CONTENT TO DOCUMENT PROPERTIES

To complete the entire assignment, you need two more versions of the ad: one is a slightly larger rectangle size (336 × 280 px), and one is a 250 × 250-pixel square.

You could use the New Document dialog box to create the file using the built-in templates, then copy and paste all of the necessary content from one file to another. However, that process is time-consuming and introduces the potential for error since you need to copy the entire timeline as well as the objects on the Stage.

1. **With cko-med-rect.fla open, make sure nothing is selected on the Stage and the Selection tool is active.**

2. **In the Properties panel, click the Advanced Settings button.**

With nothing selected on the Stage, click here to open the Document Settings dialog box.

3. **In the resulting dialog box, change the Width dimension to 336 px and change the Height dimension to 280 px.**

4. **Check the Scale Content option, then click OK to apply the change.**

   Because the new file dimensions have the same width-to-height aspect ratio (6:5), the objects in the new file are easily scaled up and require no further manipulation to function properly. By using the existing file as the basis of the new one, the Scale Content option made the entire process possible in only a few clicks.

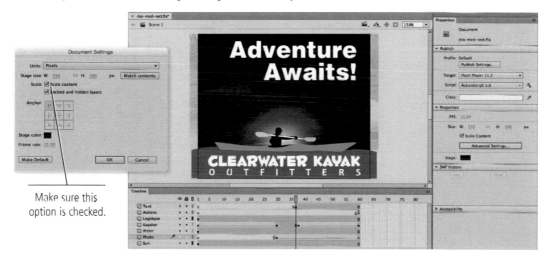

Make sure this option is checked.

5. **Choose File>Save As. Make sure your WIP>Kayaks folder is the target destination, change the Save As/File Name field to `cko-lg-rect.fla`, then click Save.**

6. **Close the active Animate file, then continue to the next exercise.**

MANUALLY ADJUST CONTENT TO DOCUMENT PROPERTIES

Because the new file size in the previous exercise had the same aspect ratio as the original, you did not need to make any further changes other than saving the file with a new name. In many cases, the new file size will not have the same aspect ratio as the original; you will have to make some manual adjustments to keep the content in the same general position as in the original.

1. **Choose File>Open. Select `cko-med-rect.fla` in your WIP>Kayaks folder and click Open.**

2. **Deselect everything on the Stage, then click the Advanced Settings button in the Properties panel.**

3. **In the resulting dialog box, change the Width and Height dimensions to 250 px. Choose the top-center anchor, then check the Scale Content with Stage option.**

   For some reason, the anchor options are unavailable when Scale Content with Stage is active. You have to select the appropriate anchor first.

4. **Click OK to finalize the change.**

   In this case, the new file does not use the same aspect ratio as the original. As you can see, Animate is not able to interpret the necessary positions of all elements in the file. Although this is a good start, you still need to make some adjustments manually.

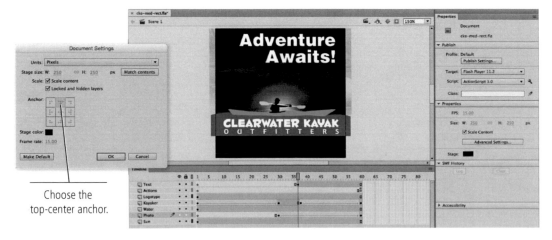

Choose the
top-center anchor.

4. **Save the file as `cko-square.fla` in your WIP>Kayaks folder.**

   By immediately saving the new file with a different name, you avoid accidentally changing something in the wrong file.

5. **Click Frame 1 in the timeline to move the playhead to the beginning of the movie.**

6. **In the Timeline panel, Command/Control-click to select the Logotype, Kayaker, Water, and Sun layers.**

   You need to move the content on all four of these layers down to the bottom of the adjusted Stage. You don't want to move the Photo layer content because you want it to remain attached to the top of the Stage.

7. **Using the Selection tool, click any of the selected objects on the Stage, press Shift, and drag down until the water aligns with the bottom of the Stage.**

   By moving the content on all four layers at once, you maintain the same relative positions between the selected objects.

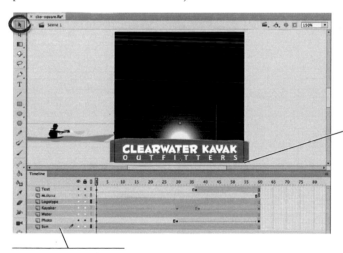

Shift-drag the selected objects until they align to the bottom of the Stage.

Command/Control-click each layer to select the content on all four layers.

8. Press Return/Enter to play the movie on the Stage.

You should notice the kayaker symbol instance moves up and away from the water as the playhead progresses. If you review the timeline, remember that this layer has four separate keyframes, each of which define a specific position in a classic tween. To keep the kayaker paddling straight across the Stage, you have to change the instance's position on each keyframe in the layer.

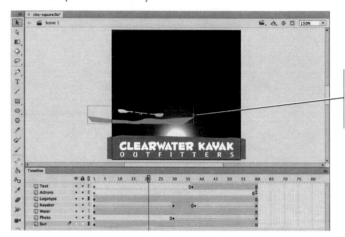

As the playhead moves, the kayaker moves back to its original position on Frame 30.

9. Return the playhead to Frame 1 on the timeline, then click the kayaker symbol instance to select it.

10. In the Properties panel, note the instance's Y position.

In our example, the Y position is 193.60. If yours is different, you should use the exact value from your file in the following steps. The point is to make the instance's Y (vertical) position consistent in all keyframes.

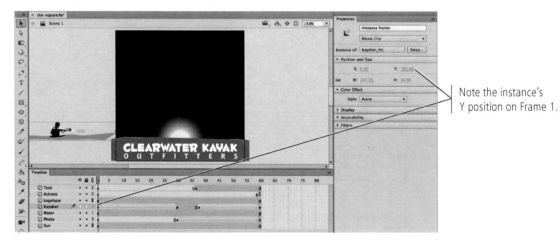

Note the instance's Y position on Frame 1.

11. **Click Frame 30 of the Kayaker layer, then click the symbol instance on the Stage to select it.**

12. **In the Properties panel, change the Y position to the same value you noted in Step 10.**

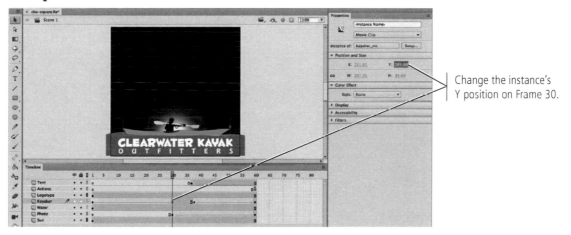

Change the instance's Y position on Frame 30.

13. **Repeat Steps 11–12 for the two remaining keyframes on the Kayaker layer.**

    When you get to Frame 60, you should notice another problem — the photo no longer fills the background area. (This was harder to see when the image was entirely or semitransparent). You now need to adjust the photo to fill the space.

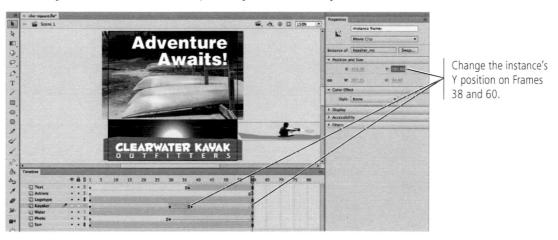

Change the instance's Y position on Frames 38 and 60.

14. **Select Frame 30 on the Photo layer.**

    The first keyframe (Frame 1) on the Photo layer is blank; the image doesn't exist on that frame, so you don't need to edit that keyframe.

    Remember, this image is actually an instance of a symbol, which you created from the original bitmap image.

15. **If necessary, use the Selection tool to nudge the photo up to cover the top of the Stage.**

16. **Choose the Free Transform tool, then move the transformation point of the selected object to the top center handle.**

17. **Using the Transform panel, scale the instance proportionally until the bottom edge is just hidden by the top edge of the water shape.**

    Be careful when you scale bitmap images, especially making them larger. Bitmap images have a fixed resolution, which means enlarging them can significantly reduce the quality.

    If you remember the first part of this project, you actually reduced the image before creating the symbol instance. Enlarging this particular instance above 100% still keeps the image smaller than the original bitmap's physical dimensions, so you should not see any significant lack of quality in this case.

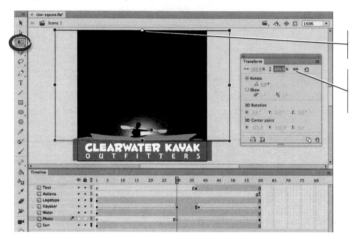

Move the transformation point to this handle.

Make sure this chain is linked to scale the instance proportionally.

18. **Repeat Steps 14–17 for the instance on the Frame 60 keyframe.**

    You should apply the exact same transformation on Frame 60 as you did on Frame 30. Rather than scrubbing the values in the Transform panel, you can click one of the existing values to enter the field, constrain the two dimensions, and then type the exact same value that you applied in Step 16.

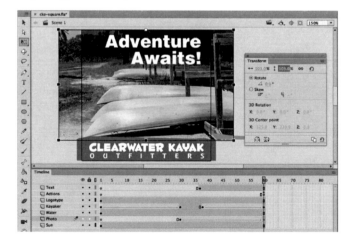

19. **Save the file and continue to the final exercise.**

PUBLISH THE AD FILES

Exporting a document refers to publishing it in a form that can be viewed in another application. The File>Export menu has three options: Export Image, Export Movie, and Export Video.

- If you choose **Export Image**, you can save your file as a static graphic (with no animation) in formats such as GIF or JPEG.

- **Export Movie** allows you to create a file (or sequence of files) that includes animation, which can be placed into an HTML document created in another application. A number of formats are available in the File Format/Save As Type menu. Each format has distinct uses, advantages, and disadvantages.

  SWF Movie. A Animate movie file can be placed into an HTML file, or it can be used in another Animate application.

  – **JPEG Sequence.** Selecting this option allows the file to be exported in the JPEG format. The Match Movie option matches the size of the exported file with that of the original document. When you use any of the sequence options, each frame of the movie is exported as a separate image.

  – **GIF Sequence.** This format exports the files in GIF format, except the files are generated in a sequence for each frame animation. The animated GIF format exports a single file that contains all of the animations; this option generates a sequence of files.

  – **PNG Sequence.** This option saves the files in the Portable Network Graphics (PNG) format, which supports transparency for objects that might need to be placed on various backgrounds. You can specify options such as dimension, resolution, colors, and filters.

- If you choose **Export Video**, you will export the active file as a MOV video file, which is a QuickTime file. (The format was created by Apple Computer to work with multimedia files.)

You can also use the Publish option (File>Publish) to generate a SWF file, as well as a number of other formats. When you publish a file, the resulting output is based on the active options in the Publish Settings dialog box.

1. **With cko-square.fla open, choose File>Publish Settings.**

   Rather than simply choose File>Publish, you are using this dialog box to first review the settings that will apply when you publish the files.

2. **In the Publish options on the left side of the Publish Settings dialog box, make sure the Flash (.swf) option is selected.**

3. **Uncheck all other options in the left side of the dialog box.**

   If the HTML Wrapper option is checked, the publish process also generates an HTML file that includes the necessary code for opening the SWF file in a browser window. Because these ads will be distributed for insertion into other sites, the HTML option is not necessary.

4. **Click Publish at the bottom of the dialog box.**

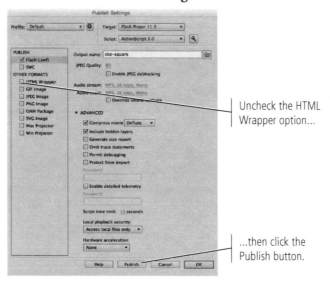

Uncheck the HTML Wrapper option...

...then click the Publish button.

5. **When the publish process is complete, click OK to close the Publish Settings dialog box.**

6. **Save the open file (cko-square.fla) and close it.**

7. **Repeat Steps 1–6 for the other two ad files in the project.**

   Publish settings are file-specific, so you have to define these options for each file that will be published.

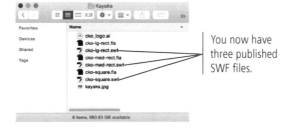

You now have three published SWF files.

The Publish Settings dialog box (File>Publish Settings) contains all the necessary settings for publishing files from Animate.

- The **Profile** menu lists all available saved profiles, which save defined publish settings for easier access. You can use the attached Profile Options button to create, import, export, and manage saved profiles.

- The **Target** menu allows you to export the Animate movie to be compatible with an earlier version of Player, or different versions Adobe AIR.

- **Script** specifies which version of ActionScript is or will be used in the file. (ActionScript 3.0 is the default and only option in Animate CC.) Clicking the ActionScript Settings button opens a dialog box where you can specify the path of an external ActionScript file.

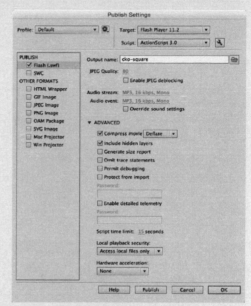

The **Publish** list on the left side of the dialog box lists the available formats that can be exported; the Flash (.swf) and the HTML Wrapper formats are selected by default. When you click a specific format in the Publish list, options related to that format appear on the right side of the dialog box.

When **Flash (.swf)** is selected in the Publish list, options on the right side of the dialog box determine how the animation is exported.

- The **Output File** field shows the default file name, based on the FLA file name, that will be used for the exported file. By default, exported files are created in the same location as the FLA file you are exporting; you can click the folder icon next to a file name to specify a different publishing location. (This is available for all publishing formats.)

- **JPEG Quality** specifies the quality of exported JPEG images. Lower values result in smaller file sizes, but also lower image quality; as the quality increases, so does the size of the file. The **Enable JPEG Deblocking** option helps smooth the appearance of JPEG files with very high levels of compression.

- The **Audio Stream** and **Audio Event** options show the current sound export settings for stream and event sounds (respectively). Clicking either link opens the Sound Settings dialog box, where you can change the compression format, quality, and bit rate options for each type of sound.

  (A streaming sound plays as soon as enough data is downloaded; the sound stops playing as soon as the movie stops. An event sound does not play until it downloads completely, and it continues to play until explicitly stopped.)

- If **Override Sound Settings** is checked, the default options in the Audio Stream and Audio Event settings override any settings that are defined for individual sound files in the file's library.

- **Compress Movie** reduces the size of the exported file, which also reduces download time. Compressed files can only be played in Player 6 or later.

- **Include Hidden Layers** allows you to export hidden layer information in the exported file.

- **Generate Size Report** creates a text file with information about the amount of data in the final Animate content.

- **Omit Trace Statements** allows Animate to ignore trace options, which are ActionScript functions that display the results of certain code in the Output panel.

- **Permit Debugging** allows you to debug your SWF file and allows other users to debug your SWF file remotely. You can also define a password, which other users will have to enter in order to debug the file.

- **Protect from Import** prevents others from importing your SWF file. This option also allows you to protect your SWF file with a password. (**Password** is activated if you select the Protect from Import or the Permit Debugging option. You can specify a password that other users must enter to import the file or debug the movie.)

- **Local Playback Security** options provide security for your application. If you select Access Local Files Only, your SWF file can interact only on the local machine. If you choose Access Network Only, your SWF file can communicate with resources only on the network and not on the local machine.

- **Hardware Acceleration** options can be used to speed up the graphics performance of the exported movie.

ANIMATE FOUNDATIONS

HTML Wrapper options relate to publishing an Animate document on the Web. In this case, you might need an HTML file that will embed your SWF file.

- The **Template** menu contains various templates in which an HTML file can be published. Selecting a template and then clicking the Info button shows a dialog box with information about the selected template.

- If you select **Detect Flash Version**, you can use the Version fields to define which is required. Detection code is embedded in the resulting file to determine if a user has the required version. If not, a link is provided to download the latest version of the player plug-in. (Some templates do not support this code.)

- The **Size** options define the dimensions of the resulting HTML file. You can choose Match Movie to use the size of the Animate Stage, or define specific width and height (in pixels or percent).

- The **Paused at Start** option keeps the SWF file from being played unless the user clicks to initiate the movie.

- The **Loop** option causes the Animate content to repeat after it reaches the final frame, so the movie plays in a continuous loop.

- The **Display Menu** option enables a shortcut when the user Control/right-clicks the SWF file in the browser. Deselecting this option shows only About Animate in the shortcut menu.

- Selecting the **Device Font** option displays users' system fonts instead of the fonts used in the SWF file, if those fonts are unavailable in the user's system.

- **Quality** specifies the quality of the SWF content embedded in the HTML file. Auto Low gives preference to document loading rather than quality, but also tries to improve the quality of the SWF file. Auto High treats loading and quality equally; when the loading speed is reduced, quality is compromised. The remaining three options are self-explanatory; lower quality settings mean higher compression, smaller file sizes, and faster download times.

- **Window Mode** sets the value of the wmode attribute in the object and embed HTML tags. Window does not embed window-related attributes in the HTML tags; the background of the Animate content is opaque. Opaque Windowless sets the background of the Animate content to opaque, which allows HTML content to appear on top of Animate content. Transparent Windowless sets the background of the Animate content to transparent.

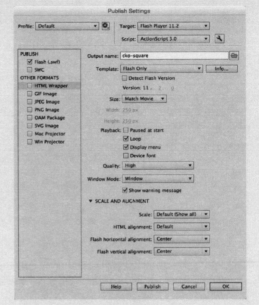

- The **Show Warning Message** option displays all warning and error messages whenever a setting for publishing the content is incorrect.

- **Scale** controls the display of Animate content when you change the dimension of the Animate content in the HTML file. Default (Show All) displays the entire document in the specified area. No Border fits the document in the specified area and maintains the quality of the SWF file by avoiding distortion. Exact Fit fits the entire SWF file in the specified area, but compromises the quality of the SWF file. No Scale prevents the Animate content from being scaled in the HTML file.

- **HTML Alignment** aligns the Animate content in the browser window. The Default option displays the SWF file in the center of the browser; you can also choose Left, Right, Top, or Bottom.

- **Animate Horizontal and Vertical Alignment** set the alignment of Animate content within the HTML file.

fill in the blank

1. A(n) _____ timeline functions independently of other symbols in the same file.

2. _____ are required when an object needs to change in some way at a given point in time.

3. The _____ can be used to scale an object proportionally with respect to the object's defined transformation point.

4. A(n) _____ can be used if you need to change an object's color over time.

5. A(n) _____ is identified by blue frames and an arrow in the timeline.

6. _____ is simple text that does not change.

7. _____ is essentially a text area that can be populated with the contents of an external file.

8. _____ solves the potential problem of used fonts not being available on a user's computer.

9. The _____ option allows you to change objects' size based on the edited document settings.

10. _____ is the default extension for exported file movies.

short answer

1. Briefly explain how a movie clip symbol relates to the primary timeline of a file.

2. Briefly explain the process of creating a shape tween.

3. Briefly explain why embedding fonts in an Animate file is important.

Portfolio Builder Project

Use what you learned in this project to complete the following freeform exercise.
Carefully read the art director and client comments, then create your own design to meet the needs of the project.
Use the space below to sketch ideas; when finished, write a brief explanation of your reasoning behind your final design.

art director comments

Our agency has been hired to create a series of animated videos explaining scientific principles for children.

To complete this project, you should:

❏ Research the topics you are going to model and determine what (if any) data will be required to create a scientifically accurate illustration.

❏ Create or locate images or graphics that will result in a "kid-friendly" learning experience.

❏ Develop the animations so they can be placed into an existing Web site, using a 600 × 800 file size.

client comments

We would like you to create a series of videos over the next year (as the grant funds become available). The first one we want is an illustration of gravity. We're not entirely sure how it should look or function. We kind of like the legend of Isaac Newton sitting under an apple tree, when an apple fell on his head. If you could figure out how to make that work, great. If not, we're happy to consider other solutions.

As more funds become available, we're also going to want movies to illustrate other scientific principles. Our current list includes tectonic plate movement, tidal patterns, volcanic eruptions, and friction.

It will be easier to secure the secondary grants for later projects if we can include a specific plan for the different programs. Once you finish the gravity illustration (which we already have the money for), can you sketch out plans for at least two others?

project justification

_____

_____

_____

_____

_____

_____

_____

_____

_____

_____

_____

_____

_____

_____

The ability to control object shape and movement is one of the most important functions in designing animations. In this project, you used a number of basic techniques for animating object properties, including size, color, and position. As you complete the next projects in this book, you will expand on the knowledge from this chapter, learning new ways to animate multiple properties at once. The skills and knowledge from this project, however, apply to any animation — understanding frame rate, keyframes, and timeline independence are essential to being a successful animator.

This project also introduced the concept of adding text to a movie. Many Animate projects will involve some text, even if that text is eventually converted into drawing objects; you now know how to create and format text to communicate a client's message directly within an Animate file.

Finally, you learned about issues you will encounter if you need to create multiple variations of the same file —whether you need to create multiple different-sized ads or different versions for various mobile device sizes.

Create a shape tween to animate a change in object size

Create a classic tween to animate a change in object position

Use keyframes to control animation timing

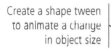

Place and format text on the Flash Stage

Define font embedding for an SWF file

Create a shape tween to animate a change in object color

Create a classic tween to animate a change in object opacity

Use blank keyframes to prevent an object from appearing too early

Scale and adjust content to match different file dimensions

Ocean Animation

Your client, Bay Ocean Preserve, wants to add an interactive animation to the kids' side of its Web site. As part of the Animate development team, your job is to build the required animations, and then add the necessary controls to make the buttons function as expected.

This project incorporates the following skills:

- ❏ Importing and managing artwork from Adobe Photoshop
- ❏ Importing symbols from external Animate file libraries
- ❏ Understanding the different types of Animate symbols
- ❏ Building frame-by-frame animations
- ❏ Creating motion tweens to animate various object properties
- ❏ Animating in three dimensions
- ❏ Preparing symbol instances for scripting
- ❏ Adding basic button controls to instances on the Stage

Project Meeting

client comments

Our organization focuses on natural resource conservation and habitat preservation on the central California coast. This area is home to a number of endangered species, and we work to educate people about observing those creatures without interacting and interfering with them.

We've been told that some kind of interactivity will be an important part of capturing a younger audience. Although we think cartoon fish dancing across the screen would minimize the seriousness of our message, we understand that we have to do something to make the site more interesting for children.

We were thinking about an "aquarium" screen saver we used to have, and we thought that kind of thing would be a good balance between user interactivity and pointless arcade games.

art director comments

Since the client clearly wants to avoid a cartoon look, I had the staff artist create some fish and other illustrations that are fairly realistic. I also found a good photo of a turtle that will work well with the other elements.

One of the animations — the swaying kelp forest — should play constantly, and will not be controlled by buttons.

Two animations will be controlled by the buttons. First, a fish hiding in a cave will blow bubbles. Second, a turtle will swim across the scene and get bigger, to create the effect of swimming closer.

One other animation — the organization's logo — will play as soon as the file opens, and then not again until the entire file is reset.

The programming for this isn't very complicated, so you should be able to create it with Animate's built-in Code Snippets.

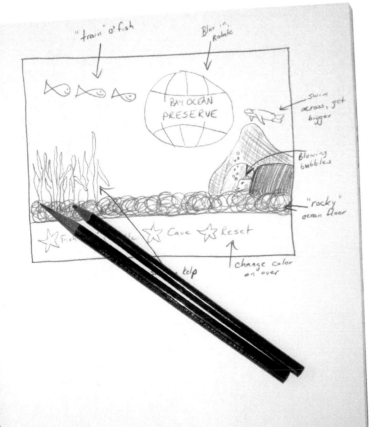

project objectives

To complete this project, you will:

- ❑ Create symbols from imported Photoshop artwork
- ❑ Import symbols from other Animate files
- ❑ Place and manage instances of symbols on the Stage, and control the visual properties of those symbols
- ❑ Control timing using keyframes
- ❑ Create animated movie clip symbols
- ❑ Generate motion tweens to animate changes in object properties
- ❑ Use the Transform panel to numerically control properties at specific points in time
- ❑ Add interactivity to button symbols

Stage 1   Importing Bitmaps and Symbols

In this project, much of the artwork was created in Adobe Photoshop — a common workflow. It's important to understand that artwork from a Photoshop file is imported into Animate as bitmap objects, which are raster images that can result in large file sizes. Fortunately, the Animate symbol infrastructure means that objects in a file's library are downloaded only once; you can use multiple instances of a symbol without increasing overall file size.

You should also keep in mind that the quality of a bitmap object is defined by its resolution. Bitmap objects can typically be reduced in size, but enlarging them much beyond 100% could significantly reduce the image quality.

Finally, it's important to realize that Animate is designed to create files that will be viewed on a digital screen. Animate recognizes the actual number of pixels in a bitmap image rather than the defined pixels per inch (ppi). If you import a 3" × 3" bitmap image that is saved at 300 ppi (typical of print-quality images), that image is 900 pixels × 900 pixels high. In Animate, the image is still 900 pixels × 900 pixels, but those same pixels occupy 12.5" at a typical screen resolution of 72 ppi.

Import Adobe Photoshop Artwork

Importing a Photoshop file to the Animate Stage is very similar to importing an Illustrator file. Because of the different nature of the two applications, however, you have fewer options when you work with Photoshop files.

1. **Download Aquarium_ANCC17_RF.zip from the Student Files Web page.**

2. **Expand the ZIP archive in your WIP folder (Macintosh) or copy the archive contents into your WIP folder (Windows).**

    This results in a folder named **Aquarium**, which contains the files you need for this project. You should also use this folder to save the files you create in this project.

3. **In Animate, create a new Animate document for ActionScript 3.0.**

    Use the default settings for the new file.

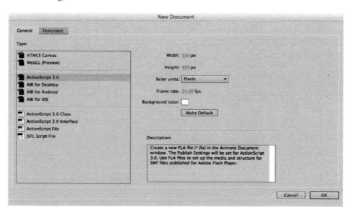

4. **Choose File>Save. Save the file in your WIP>Aquarium folder as an Animate file named ocean.fla.**

5. **Choose File>Import>Import to Stage. Navigate to the file ocean.psd in your WIP>Aquarium folder and click Open/Import.**

Note:

*Learn more about Adobe Photoshop in the companion book of this series, **Adobe Photoshop CC: The Professional Portfolio**.*

6. **If the button at the bottom of the resulting dialog box shows "Hide Advanced Options," click that button to show only the basic import options. Review the available options.**

   As with Illustrator, Animate recognizes individual layers in the native Photoshop file; objects on each individual layer will be imported as separate bitmap objects. Most of the options in this dialog box are the same as those for importing an Illustrator file.

7. **Check the Place Objects at Original Position and Set Stage Size... options, then click OK to complete the import process.**

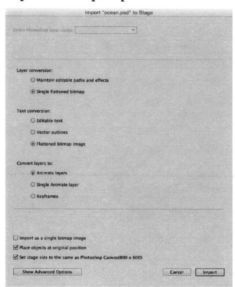

Note:

The Photoshop document area is called the canvas; the Illustrator document area is an artboard.

Note:

When artwork is created in Photoshop, each object that needs to be managed separately in Animate should be created on a separate Photoshop layer.

8. **Expand the Timeline panel until you can see all layers in the file, then choose View>Magnification>Fit in Window.**

   Layers and layer groups in the Photoshop file were imported as separate Animate layers and layer groups, as you defined in the Import to Stage dialog box. The default Layer 1 from the original file is also maintained at the bottom of the layer stack.

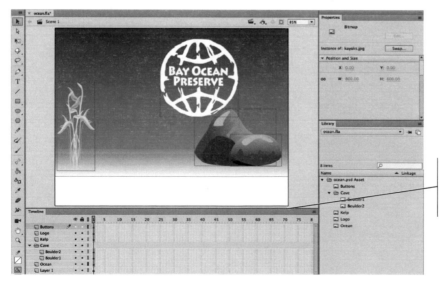

Click this line and drag up to make the panel higher (and show more layers).

9. **Select Layer 1 and click the Delete button at the bottom of the Timeline panel.**

10. **Save the file and continue to the next exercise.**

Copy Assets from External Libraries

When objects already exist in an Animate file, it is a fairly simple process to copy them from one file to another. If both files are open, you can simply copy a symbol instance from the Stage of one file and paste it into the Stage of the other file; the necessary assets are automatically pasted into the library of the second file. You can also simply open the Library panel of an external file, which enables you to access the assets in that library without opening the second file's Stage.

1. **With `ocean.fla` open, choose File>Open. Navigate to `creatures.fla` (in the WIP>Aquarium folder) and click Open.**

   When more than one file is open, each file is represented by a tab at the top of the document window. You can click any document tab to make that file active.

Note:

Press Shift to select multiple consecutive items in a dialog box or panel. Press Command/ Control to select multiple non-contiguous items.

2. **In the Library panel, Shift-click to select the Fish and Turtle items in the library. Control/right-click one of the selected items and choose Copy from the contextual menu.**

The document tabs show that there are two open files.

The Library panel shows the library for the currently active file.

3. **Click the Library menu at the top of the Library panel and choose `ocean.fla` to display that file's library.**

Use this menu to switch between the libraries of all open files.

4. **Control/right-click the empty area at the bottom of the Library panel (below the existing assets) and choose Paste from the contextual menu.**

   The Air bitmap item is also pasted because it is used in the Fish movie clip.

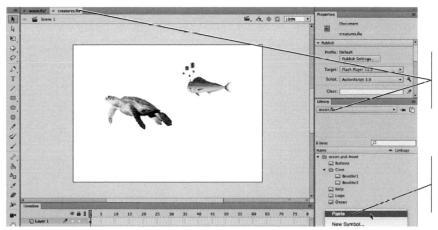

Although creatures.fla is active, the Library panel now shows the library of the ocean.fla file.

Control/right-click the empty area at the bottom of the Library panel to paste the copied items.

5. **Click the Close button on the creatures.fla document tab to close that file.**

   None of the pasted symbols is added to the Stage; they are only placed in the ocean.fla file's library.

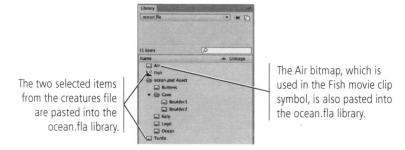

The two selected items from the creatures file are pasted into the ocean.fla library.

The Air bitmap, which is used in the Fish movie clip symbol, is also pasted into the ocean.fla library.

6. **With ocean.fla still open, choose File>Import>Open External Library.**

7. **Select buttons.fla (in the WIP>Aquarium folder) and click Open.**

   You can use this option to open the library of another file without opening the external FLA file. The external library opens as a separate panel; the file name is included in the panel tab.

Note:

The keyboard command for opening an external library is Command/Control-Shift-O.

8. **Shift-click the Reset, Showcave, and Showturtle button symbols.**

9. **Click any of the selected items and drag to the ocean.fla Library panel.**

   The files don't disappear from the external library; they're simply duplicated in the ocean.fla Library panel. The Starfish bitmap object is also copied because it is used in the four button symbols.

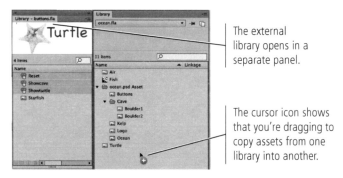

The external library opens in a separate panel.

The cursor icon shows that you're dragging to copy assets from one library into another.

10. **Click the Close button of the buttons.fla Library panel to close the external file's library.**

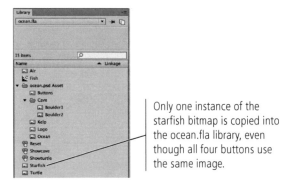

Only one instance of the starfish bitmap is copied into the ocean.fla library, even though all four buttons use the same image.

11. **Save the ocean.fla file and continue to the next exercise.**

ALIGN OBJECTS ON THE STAGE

The four buttons for this project need to be placed across the bottom of the Stage, aligned to appear equally distributed across the Stage area. The Align panel makes it very easy to position multiple selected objects relative to one another.

1. With `ocean.fla` open, select the Buttons layer to make it active.

2. Drag instances of the three button symbols to the middle of the Stage, arranged so they do not overlap.

3. Select the placed Showturtle button instance. Using the Properties panel, position the instance at X: 40, Y: 510.

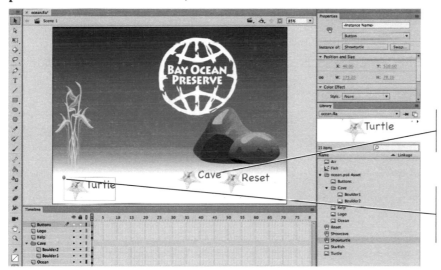

Place all three button symbols anywhere on the Stage.

Use the Properties panel to precisely position the Showturtle button instance.

4. Using the Selection tool, Shift-click to select all three button instances on the Stage.

5. In the Align panel, turn off the Align To Stage option and then click the Align Bottom Edge button.

   The Align options position objects based on the selected edge. Because you used the Align Bottom Edge button, the selected objects are all moved to the bottom edge of the bottommost object in the selection.

Align Bottom Edge button

Align To Stage should not be checked.

The selected objects move to align with the bottom edge of the bottommost selected object.

6. Select only the Reset button and set the X position to 585.

7. Select the three placed button instances.

8. **In the Align panel, click the Space Evenly Horizontally button.**

This option calculates the overall space across the selection, then shifts the objects so that the same amount of space appears between each object in the selection. Because the buttons are different widths, this option creates a better result than the distribution options.

Space Evenly Horizontally button

The middle object is moved to create equal space between all objects in the selection.

9. **Save the file and continue to the next exercise.**

TRANSFORM SYMBOLS AND INSTANCES

Placed instances of a symbol are unique objects, which means they can be manipulated separately without affecting other instances of the symbol. Each instance remains linked to the primary symbol, however, so transforming the actual symbol affects all placed instances of that symbol.

1. **With ocean.fla open, use the Selection tool to select the Kelp object on the stage. Press the F8 key to convert the object to a symbol.**

Remember, you can also Control/right-click the object on the Stage and choose Convert to Symbol from the contextual menu.

2. **Define the following settings in the Convert to Symbol dialog box:**

Name:	**Seaweed**
Type:	**Movie Clip**
Registration:	**Bottom center**

Remember, the name of the actual symbol is only used internally while you develop the file. The specific names of instances on the Stage are more important, as you will see later when you add ActionScript to control the various pieces of this movie.

3. **Click OK to create the new symbol.**

The Properties panel now shows that the selected object is an instance of the Seaweed symbol, which has been added to the Library panel.

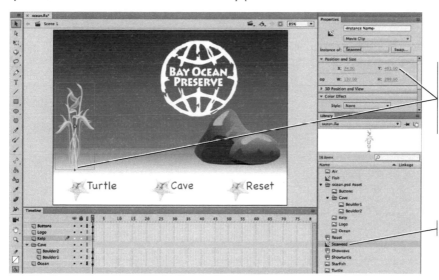

You defined bottom-center registration for this symbol, so measurements are based on the bottom-center point of the instance.

There's the new symbol.

4. **Using the Selection tool, Option/Alt-click the existing instance and drag right to clone a second instance of the Seaweed symbol.**

5. **Repeat Step 4 to clone one more instance.**

6. **Deselect everything on the Stage. Choose the Free Transform tool in the Tools panel and click the middle Seaweed instance to select it.**

The Free Transform tool is used to change the size or shape of an object. Remember, all transformations are applied around the transformation point.

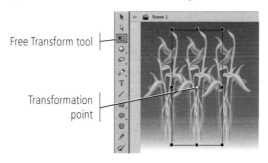

Free Transform tool

Transformation point

Note:

If the Free Transform tool is active when you click and drag to move an object, make sure you don't click the object's transformation point before you drag the object.

7. **Drag the transformation point until it snaps to the bottom-center bounding box handle.**

8. **Click the top-center bounding box handle and drag down to make the selected instance shorter.**

Transformations applied to individual instances have no effect on the original symbol or on other placed instances.

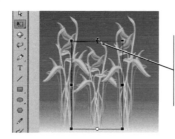

Because the bottom-center is the transformation point, dragging the top-center handle makes the instance shorter without moving the bottom of the instance.

Note:

You can also press Option/Alt and drag a center handle to transform the object around the opposite bounding-box handle, without moving the transformation point.

9. **In the Library panel, double-click the Seaweed symbol icon to enter into the symbol.**

   The crosshairs in the bottom center identify the **symbol registration point**, or the location of X:0, Y:0 for placed instances; all measurements for placed instances begin at this location.

   Even though you changed the transformation point of one placed instance on the main Stage, the transformation point remains in the center of the object on the symbol Stage. The transformation point is specific to each placed object or instance.

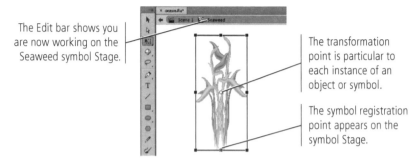

The Edit bar shows you are now working on the Seaweed symbol Stage.

The transformation point is particular to each instance of an object or symbol.

The symbol registration point appears on the symbol Stage.

10. **With the Free Transform tool still selected, drag the transformation point until it snaps to the bottom-center bounding box handle of the object on the symbol's Stage.**

11. **Show the Transform panel (Window>Transform).**

12. **In the Transform panel, make sure the Link icon is not active and then change the Scale Height value to 80%.**

   If the Link icon shows two solid chain links, changing the height of the object would proportionally affect the width of the object (and vice versa). Because you only want to change the height, you need to break the Link icon.

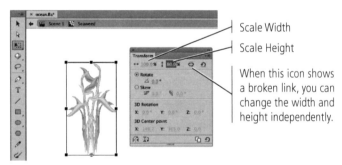

Scale Width

Scale Height

When this icon shows a broken link, you can change the width and height independently.

13. **In the Edit bar, click Scene 1 to return to the main Stage.**

   When you modify the original symbol, the changes ripple through all placed instances.

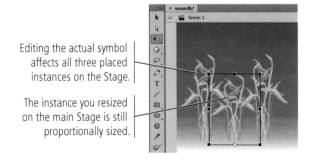

Editing the actual symbol affects all three placed instances on the Stage.

The instance you resized on the main Stage is still proportionally sized.

14. **Save the file and continue to the next exercise.**

CREATE A MOVIE CLIP FROM OBJECTS ON DIFFERENT LAYERS

When you imported the project artwork, the two pieces of the cave were created on separate layers — in a layer group — because you need to place a fish inside the cave, stacked between the two boulders. If the two boulders had existed on a single layer, the result would have been a single bitmap object, which could not be broken apart in Animate to accomplish the desired effect.

1. **With ocean.fla open, use the Selection tool to click both boulders in the right side of the Stage.**

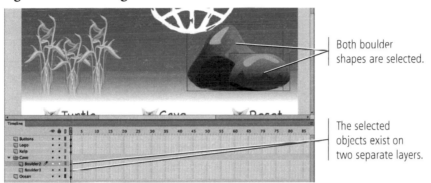

Both boulder shapes are selected.

The selected objects exist on two separate layers.

Note:

Remember, the symbol registration point marks the location of the defined X and Y values on the main Stage.

2. **Press the F8 key to convert the two selected objects to a symbol.**

3. **Define the following settings in the Convert to Symbol dialog box:**

Name:	**cave**
Type:	**Movie Clip**
Registration:	**Bottom right**

4. **Click OK to create the new symbol.**

   The original selected objects were on two separate layers. After converting those objects into a single symbol, the new symbol instance appears on the higher layer in the layer stack (in this case, the Boulder2 layer).

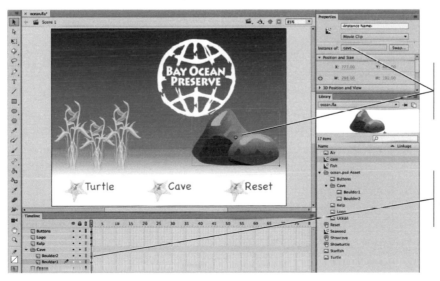

The selected objects are now a single symbol instance.

The instance exists on the highest of the previously selected layers.

5. **In the Timeline panel, change the Boulder2 layer name to Cave.**

6. **Drag the Cave layer above the Cave layer group.**

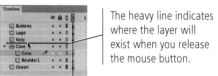 The heavy line indicates where the layer will exist when you release the mouse button.

7. **Select the Cave layer group (not the layer) and then click the Delete button at the bottom of the Timeline panel.**

8. **Read the resulting message, then click Yes.**

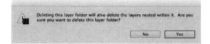

Although Steps 5–8 are not technically necessary, it is a good idea to keep your files clean by deleting unnecessary layers.

9. **Select the cave instance on the Stage. In the Properties panel, change the X position of the selected instance to 850.**

If the cave objects had been placed in the correct position in the Photoshop file, the imported bitmap objects would have been clipped at the Stage edge. If you create artwork in Photoshop, make sure pieces are entirely inside the Canvas edge if you don't want them clipped when they are imported into Animate.

 The symbol's registration point is positioned at X: 850.

10. **Double-click the cave movie clip instance on the Stage to edit the symbol in place on the Stage.**

Although this movie clip was created based on a layer group in the imported artwork, the layers that made up the group are not maintained in the symbol timeline.

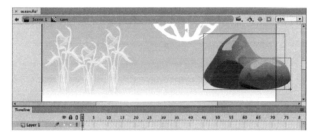

11. **Drag an instance of the Fish movie clip symbol onto the Stage, so only the head appears to the left of the front rock.**

12. **With the Fish instance still selected, choose Modify>Arrange>Send Backward.**

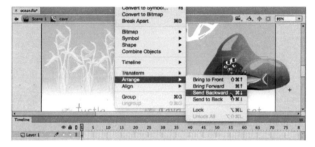

This command moves the selected object back one step in the stacking order. The Fish instance now appears between the two boulder objects that comprise the cave symbol.

In the second stage of this project, you will learn a number of techniques for creating animations — including making this fish blow bubbles that rise up and off the Stage.

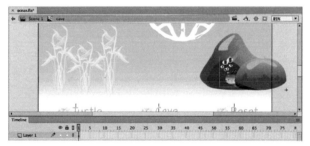

13. **Click Scene 1 in the Edit bar to return to the main Stage.**

14. **Save the file and continue to the next exercise.**

Folders make it easy to organize the assets that make up a movie, and easy to find the assets you need.

1. **With ocean.fla open, click the Library panel to activate it.**

2. **In the Library panel, change the name of the ocean.psd Assets folder to Bitmaps.**

    Changing a library folder name has no effect on placed instances of the symbols inside that folder.

3. **Select the two bitmap objects in the nested Cave folder and move them into the first-level Bitmaps folder.**

    Moving symbols to a new location in the Library panel has no effect on placed instances of the moved symbols.

4. **Select the three bitmap objects in the first level of the library and drag them into the Bitmaps folder.**

5. **Delete the nested Cave folder from the Bitmaps folder.**

6. **Click the New Folder button at the bottom of the Library panel.**

    New folders are created at the same nesting level as the current selection. (If a nested symbol is already selected and you want to create a new folder at the first level of the library, click the empty area at the bottom of the panel to deselect any files before clicking the New Folder button.)

7. **Change the name of the new folder to Movie Clips, then drag the three movie clip symbols from the main level of the Library into the Movie Clips folder.**

Note:

In this case, we're using simple names for the symbol folders. The names you assign to symbol (or layer) folders aren't functional; they just need to make sense to you (or other people working with your files).

8. Create a new folder named **Buttons** at the first level of the library. Drag the three button symbols into the new folder.

8. Collapse the Bitmaps and Buttons folders in the Library panel

9. Save the file, and then continue to the next stage of the project.

Stage 2 Animating Symbols

In Project 2: Talking Kiosk Interface, you created simple animation by swapping symbols at specific points in time; although nothing technically changed position, replacing one object with another is still considered "animation." In Project 3: Animated Internet Ads, you used classic tweening to move objects across the Stage; this technique creates smooth motion by defining the start point keyframe, end point keyframe, and path shape. In this project, you learn several different techniques for creating various types of animation, including animating specific properties of an object.

CREATE A BASIC FRAME ANIMATION IN A MOVIE CLIP SYMBOL

Movie clips are animated symbols that reside on a single frame of the timeline. In its simplest form, a movie clip can include a solitary fish swimming across the ocean; at its most complex, a movie clip can include fully interactive elements in a video game. In this exercise, you create the most basic type of animation — a frame animation.

1. With **ocean.fla** open, choose the Selection tool and make sure nothing is selected on the Stage.

2. In the Properties panel, change the FPS hot text to 15 frames per second.

Using 15 fps for a movie — especially one that's going to run on the Web — provides decent quality. The default 24 fps is not necessary for standard computer viewing and could create files that require too much processing power for some users.

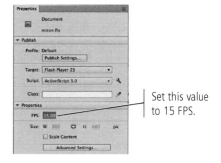

Set this value to 15 FPS.

3. **On the Stage, double-click the cave symbol instance to enter into the symbol Stage (edit in place).**

4. **Double-click the placed Fish instance to enter into the nested symbol.**

    You are going to move only the bubbles, which are an instance of the Air bitmap object that is placed inside the Fish symbol. You are editing in place on the main Stage so that you can see when the bubbles are entirely outside the Stage area.

Note:

If you change an object on a regular frame in the middle of a movie, all frames between the two surrounding keyframes (or the nearest preceding keyframe and the final frame) reflect that change.

5. **In the timeline, click Frame 7 to select it, then press the F6 key to insert a new keyframe.**

    You can also Control/right-click a frame in the timeline and choose Insert Keyframe from the contextual menu, or choose Insert>Timeline> Keyframe.

    As you already know, **keyframes** are special frames where something happens to an object: it appears or disappears, changes size, moves to another position, changes color, and so on. When you add a new keyframe, regular frames are automatically added immediately before the previous keyframe; objects on the preceding keyframe will remain in place until the playhead reaches the new keyframe.

You are working on the Fish symbol, which is nested inside the cave symbol.

When you add a keyframe, regular frames are automatically added directly before it.

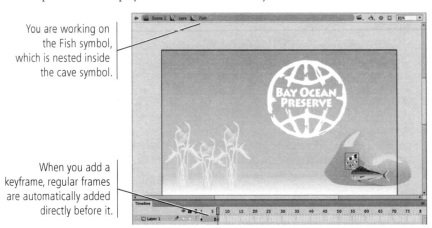

6. **With Frame 7 selected in the timeline, select only the air bubbles graphic object. Using the Selection tool, drag to reposition that graphic directly above the original position.**

    When you create or select a keyframe, all objects on that keyframe are automatically selected. You can Shift-click the fish to deselect that object, leaving only the air bubbles object selected.

With the Frame 7 keyframe active, move the bubbles up from their previous position.

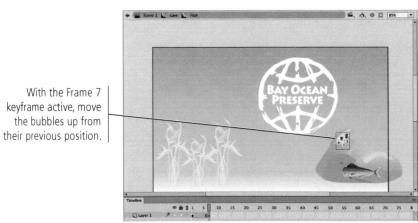

7. **Repeat Steps 5–6 six more times, adding a new keyframe every seven frames and moving the air bubbles up until they are outside the top edge of the Stage.**

Because you're editing the symbol in place, you can see how far you need to move the bubbles until they are outside the Stage area. If you edited this symbol on its own Stage, you would have to guess about positioning, return to the main Stage to test your guess, return to the symbol to add more frames, return to the main Stage to test again, and so on.

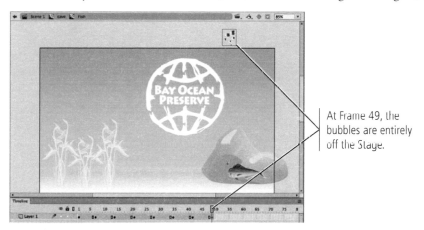

At Frame 49, the bubbles are entirely off the Stage.

8. **Select Frame 56 on the timeline and press F5 to add a regular frame.**

This regular frame at Frame 56 extends the timeline by half a second, which prevents the bubbles from reappearing in the fish's mouth (Frame 1) immediately after they move past the top of the Stage (Frame 49).

9. **Click the playhead above the timeline and drag left and right.**

Scrubbing the playhead allows you to look at specific sections of a movie over time, so you can see if they work the way you expect.

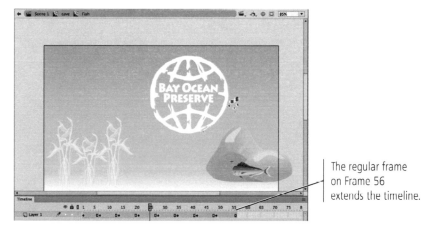

The regular frame on Frame 56 extends the timeline.

10. **Click Scene 1 in the Edit bar to return to the main Stage.**

11. Press Command-Return/Control-Enter to test the movie.

You can see the air bubbles moving up in a continuous loop. Even though the primary Stage has only one frame, the movie clip's timeline continues to play as long as the movie remains open.

The animation plays in the Flash Player window.

Note:

Remember from Project 3: Animated Internet Ads, you can't preview the animation inside a movie clip on the main Stage. You have to test the file in the Animate Player window to see the animation.

12. Close the Animate Player window and return to Animate.

13. Save the file and continue to the next exercise.

CREATE A MOTION TWEEN

Creating the appearance of continuous, fluid movement requires a slightly different position or shape (depending on what you are animating) on every frame in an animation. Rather than defining each individual frame manually — which could take days, depending on the length of your animation — you can let Animate define the frames that are in between two keyframes (the tween frames).

   Animate incorporates technology that makes it very easy to define smooth animations by simply moving a symbol object around on the Stage.

1. With ocean.fla open, create a new layer named Turtle immediately above the Logo layer. Select the Turtle layer as the active layer.

2. Drag an instance of the turtle bitmap image from the Library panel onto the Stage. Use the Transform panel to scale the instance uniformly to 50%, and then position it beyond the right edge of the Stage, higher than the Cave instance.

3. Press the F8 key to convert the turtle instance to a symbol.

4. Define the following settings in the Convert to Symbol dialog box:

   Name: **Swimmer**

   Type: **Movie Clip**

   Registration: **Center**

5. Click the Folder:Library Root link. Select the Existing Folder radio button and choose Movie Clips in the list. Click Select to return to the Convert to Symbol dialog box, and then click OK to create the new symbol.

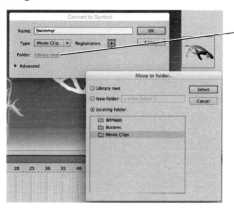

Click this link to open the Move to Folder dialog box.

6. Click Frame 90 on the Turtle layer and press F5 to add a new regular frame.

   Other objects on the Stage are not visible because you have not yet extended the other layers' timelines.

Note:

You can also select the frame and then choose Insert>Timeline>Frame.

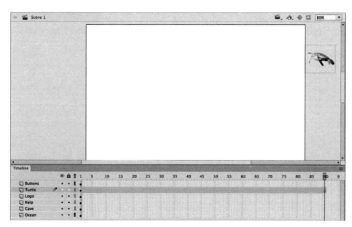

7. Control/right-click any frame on the Turtle layer and choose Create Motion Tween.

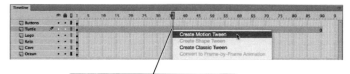

Control/right-click between keyframes to add a motion tween between keyframes (or between a keyframe and the final frame on that layer).

8. **Click Frame 90 of the Turtle layer to select that frame.**

   Animate creates a motion tween in the frames between keyframes. Because Frame 1 is the only keyframe on this layer, the motion tween is created between Frame 1 and the last frame on the layer.

   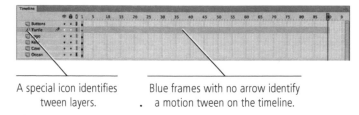

   A special icon identifies tween layers.

   Blue frames with no arrow identify a motion tween on the timeline.

9. **Select the Turtle image located at the right of the Stage, and drag it off the left edge of the Stage.**

   A new keyframe is automatically added on Frame 90 to mark the new position of the Swimmer symbol. A line — the motion path — shows the path of movement from the symbol's position on Frame 1 to its position on Frame 90. The small dots along the motion path correspond to the frames within the tween.

   When you edit symbols on a tween layer, the position of the playhead is crucial. When you change any property of an object on a tween layer, a property keyframe is automatically inserted at the current frame. Animate generates the tween frames based on the change in the property value between the active keyframe and the previous one.

   Note:

   The motion path line corresponds to the color of the layer containing the path.

   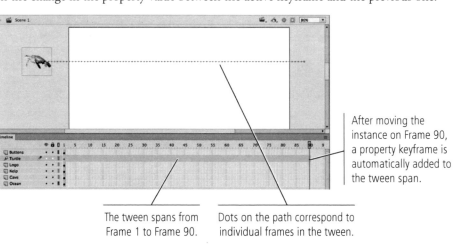

   After moving the instance on Frame 90, a property keyframe is automatically added to the tween span.

   The tween spans from Frame 1 to Frame 90.

   Dots on the path correspond to individual frames in the tween.

10. **Click Frame 1 to move the playhead back to the beginning of the timeline, and then press Return/Enter to play the timeline on the Stage.**

    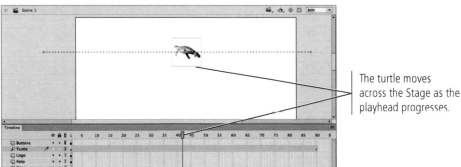

    The turtle moves across the Stage as the playhead progresses.

Using Onion Skins

Onion skinning, accessed through a set of buttons at the bottom of the timeline, is a technique that allows you to view more than one frame of an animation at a time.

- Clicking the **Onion Skin** button toggles the feature on or off.
- Clicking the **Onion Skin Outlines** button turns all visible skins to outlines (or wire frames). Combining outlines and onion skins allows you to clearly see the components of your animations without fills or (true-weight) strokes.
- Clicking the **Edit Multiple Frames** button allows you to edit multiple frames at the same time: moving an entire animation, for example, or simply changing single frames within a tween. Without this feature, you would have to move objects one frame at a time. With the feature, you can see previous or subsequent frames, which often helps when you're fine-tuning an animation and you need to move an object in one frame relative to its position in other frames.
- Clicking the **Modify Markers** button allows you to select from a range of predefined skins, or turn onion skinning off. You can choose to have onion skins span two frames, five frames, or all frames. You can also manually adjust the onion skin markers and bypass these presets.

The following illustrations show a simple motion tween that moves the oval symbol across the Stage, from left to right.

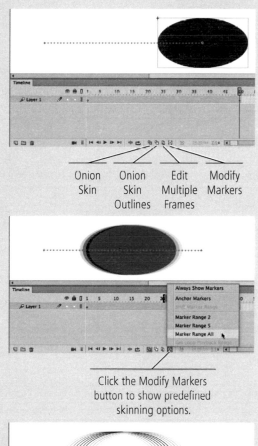

Onion Skin | Onion Skin Outlines | Edit Multiple Frames | Modify Markers

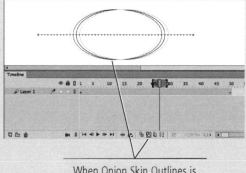

When the Onion Skin feature is active, you can see multiple frames at once (around the playhead).

These markers show the range of frames that is visible on the Stage.

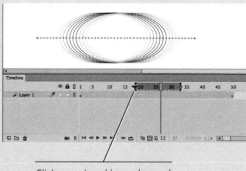

Click the Modify Markers button to show predefined skinning options.

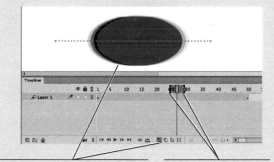

When Onion Skin Outlines is active, frames within the visible onion skin display as wireframes.

Click an onion skin marker and drag to manually change the number of visible frames.

ANIMATE FOUNDATIONS

11. **Move the playhead to Frame 90, then click the turtle instance to select it. Scale the selected instance to 200% of its current size. If necessary, use the Selection tool to reposition the resized turtle so that it is entirely outside the edge of the Stage.**

The term "motion path" is deceptive because you can animate much more than just motion when you apply a motion tween. By scaling the object on Frame 90, you told Animate to change both the symbol size and position as the timeline progresses.

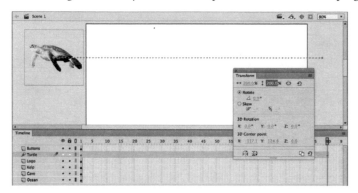

Note:

Because you scaled the object to 50% before you created the Swimmer symbol, resizing this instance to 200% restores the bitmap to its original size.

12. **Return the playhead to Frame 1, and then press Return/Enter to play the timeline on the Stage.**

Now the turtle gets larger as it moves across the stage, creating the effect of the turtle swimming closer. Animate automatically calculates the appropriate position and size of the symbol for all frames between the Frame 1 and Frame 90 keyframes.

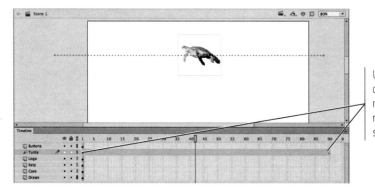

Using a motion tween, only two keyframes are required to smoothly move and resize the symbol instance.

13. **Save the file and continue to the next exercise.**

Controlling Animation Speed with Easing

Physical objects are subject to physical laws; in the real world, friction, momentum, and mass (among other things) affect how an object moves. A bouncing ball is a good example of these laws. If you throw a ball at the ground, how hard you throw the ball determines its beginning speed. When the ball hits the ground, it transfers energy to the ground and then rebounds, causing the ball to move away from the ground (its first bounce), at which point it is moving slightly faster than when you threw it. As the ball arcs through the bounce it slows down, then starts to drop and hits the ground again, repeating the process in ever-decreasing arcs until it finally gives up its energy and then stops. The speed of the ball changes when the energy behind the ball changes.

In animation terms, these changes in speed are called **easing**. In Animate, you can control easing in the Properties panel when a tween is selected in the timeline.

- Positive Ease values decrease the distance of movement on subsequent frames, causing the object to slow down as it moves through the tween.
- Negative Ease values increase the distance of movement on subsequent frames, causing a moving object to speed up through the tween.
- Ease values closer to 100 or −100 result in greater apparent changes in speed.

The accompanying illustrations show a simple 50-frame motion tween that moves a circle symbol across the Stage.

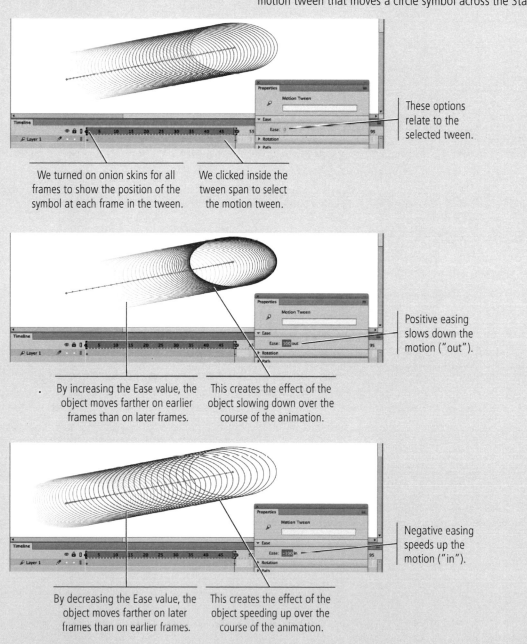

These options relate to the selected tween.

We turned on onion skins for all frames to show the position of the symbol at each frame in the tween.

We clicked inside the tween span to select the motion tween.

Positive easing slows down the motion ("out").

By increasing the Ease value, the object moves farther on earlier frames than on later frames.

This creates the effect of the object slowing down over the course of the animation.

Negative easing speeds up the motion ("in").

By decreasing the Ease value, the object moves farther on later frames than on earlier frames.

This creates the effect of the object speeding up over the course of the animation.

As you learned in the previous exercise, moving an object and changing its size (or other properties) can be as simple as creating a motion tween and adjusting the symbol at specific frames on the timeline. You don't need to manually create keyframes because Animate adds them for you whenever you change the symbol at a particular point in the timeline. In this exercise, you work with the motion path line, which can be edited like any other line in Animate — giving you precise control over the course of a tween.

1. **With ocean.fla open, click the Swimmer symbol on the Stage to select it and reveal the related motion path.**

2. **Move the Selection tool cursor near the center of the motion path until you see a curved line in the cursor icon. Click near the path and drag up to bend the motion path.**

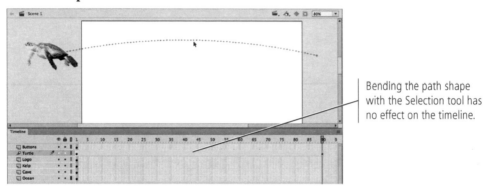

Bending the path shape with the Selection tool has no effect on the timeline.

3. **Return the playhead to Frame 1 on the timeline, and then press Return/Enter to play the timeline.**

The turtle now follows the new shape of the motion path.

4. **Click Frame 45 of the Turtle layer to select that frame. Using the Selection tool, click the Swimmer symbol instance and drag down.**

Animate automatically adds another keyframe to the motion tween to mark the instance's position at that point; the motion path bends again to reflect the defined position for the turtle at the selected frame. Animate adds an anchor point to the path at the new keyframe.

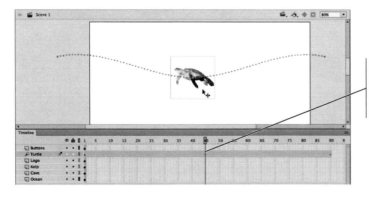

Moving the object affects the shape of the path by adding a new position keyframe to the timeline.

5. **Choose the Subselection tool in the Tools panel, and then click the new anchor point in the middle of the path.**

The Selection tool selects entire paths. The Subselection tool selects the anchor points and handles that make up a shape.

6. Click the selected anchor point and drag left.

Moving the anchor point changes the shape of the motion path, just as it does when you edit a regular Bézier curve. You can also adjust the handles of the point to change the shape of the motion path between the two connecting anchor points (the selected point and the point at the left end of the path).

When you change the position of the anchor point, notice that the number of dots (representing frames in the tween) on either side of the point remains unchanged. Because you effectively shortened the left half of the path, the same number of frames display over a shorter distance than the same number of frames to the right of the selected point. In effect, you made the turtle swim faster in the first half of the animation (moving a longer distance) and slower in the second half (moving a shorter distance).

Note:

You can use the Convert Anchor Point tool to convert a smooth anchor point on a motion path to a corner anchor point, allowing you to change directions in the tween.

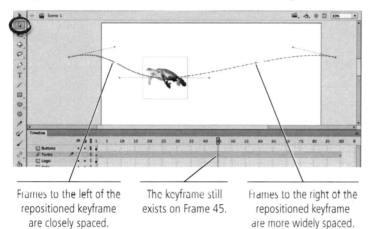

Note:

By default, motion paths are created with a non-roving keyframe property, which means the anchor points along the path are attached to specific keyframes in the timeline.

Frames to the left of the repositioned keyframe are closely spaced.

The keyframe still exists on Frame 45.

Frames to the right of the repositioned keyframe are more widely spaced.

7. Control/right-click anywhere within the motion tween (in the timeline), and then choose Motion Path>Switch Keyframes to Roving in the contextual menu.

When you choose this option, the dots along the path redistribute to equal spacing across the entire length of the tween, and the keyframe from Frame 45 is removed from the layer timeline. The shape of the path is not affected.

Note:

If you convert keyframes to roving, frames are redistributed along the entire span of the tween. If you then convert the frames back to non-roving, the location of keyframes added to the tween is determined by the location of anchor points on the path.

A roving-property keyframe is not attached to any particular frame in the tween. This type of keyframe allows you to create a custom-shaped motion path with consistent speed throughout the tween.

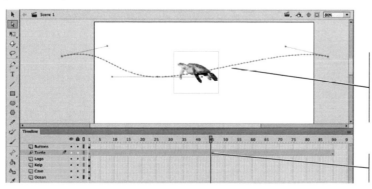

After choosing the Roving option, the frames along the path are redistributed to be equally spaced across the entire path.

The property keyframe is removed from the timeline.

8. Save the file and continue to the next exercise.

ANIMATE FOUNDATIONS

In Animate, the motion tween includes all information for the animation, including the length of the animation and specific object properties at various points along the path. A motion path is actually a specific type of object rather than simply a guide; the Properties panel shows a number of options that relate to the selected motion tween.

Because a motion tween is an actual object, you can attach any symbol to the path by simply dragging a new symbol onto the Stage when the motion tween layer is selected.

Use this field to define a name for the motion path instance.

Use Ease values to speed up or slow down an animation over time.

Use this option to rotate a symbol X number of times as it moves along the motion path.

Check this option to rotate the object so its bottom edge follows the contour of the path.

Use these options to change the position and size of the overall path.

Check this option to synchronize the number of frames in a tween within a graphic symbol to match the number of frames on the timeline where the graphic symbol is placed.

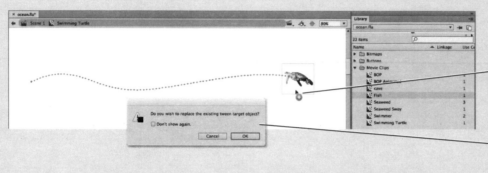

We dragged the Fish symbol onto the Stage while the motion path layer was active.

A warning asks if you want to replace the current symbol on the selected motion path.

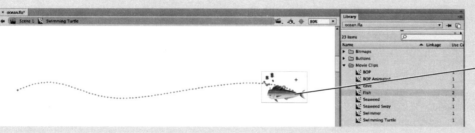

After clicking OK in the warning, the Fish symbol follows the same motion path.

Animate includes a number of predefined motion presets (Window>Motion Presets), which you can use to add common animations to your files. You can also save your own motion presets by Control/right-clicking an existing motion path and choosing Save as Motion Preset from the contextual menu. (User-defined presets are stored and accessed in a Custom folder in the Motion Presets panel. Custom presets do not include previews.)

COPY AND PASTE FRAMES

Your turtle currently swims from right to left across the Stage. When the animation loops, however, it would seem to miraculously jump back to the right and swim across again. For a more realistic effect, you are going to make a copy of the motion path animation and reverse it so the turtle swims back across the Stage before the animation loops.

1. **With ocean.fla open, Control/right-click anywhere in the Turtle layer motion tween and choose Copy Frames from the contextual menu.**

   You could also use the options in the Edit>Timeline submenu, but the standard Edit menu commands (and the related keyboard shortcuts) do not work when you want to copy or paste frames in the timeline.

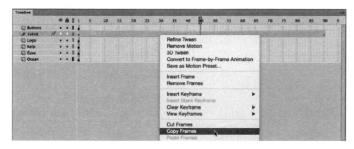

2. **Control/right-click Frame 95 of the Turtle layer and choose Paste Frames.**

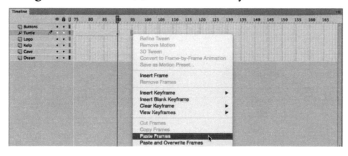

   You pasted an exact copy of the selected frames (the motion tween) — including the position of the symbol at various keyframes. In other words, the turtle is on the right at Frame 95 and on the left at Frame 184 (the end of the pasted animation).

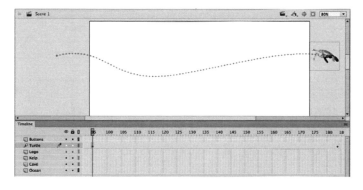

Note:

You are allowing five extra frames between the time the turtle leaves and then re-enters the Stage area (ostensibly enough time for it to turn around before it swims back).

3. **Control/right-click anywhere between Frame 95 and Frame 184 and choose Reverse Keyframes.**

   Reversing the keyframes moves the turtle to the left at Frame 95 and the right at Frame 184.

4. **Select the Frame 95 keyframe in the timeline. Click the turtle instance with the Selection tool, then choose Modify>Transform>Flip Horizontal.**

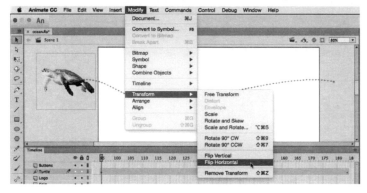

   For the turtle to realistically swim back across the Stage, you have to flip the symbol instance to face in the correct direction.

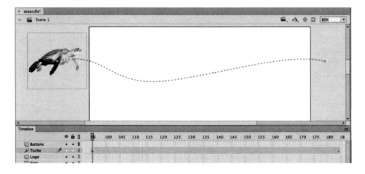

5. **Click Frame 184 to make that the active frame. With the turtle on the Frame 184 keyframe selected, choose Modify>Transform>Flip Horizontal again.**

   The turtle now faces to the right throughout the entire second half of the animation.

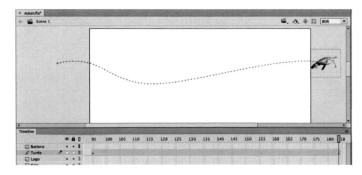

6. **Add new regular frames to Frame 184 of the remaining layers on the timeline.**

   Remember, you have to manually extend each layer so that they will all exist throughout the length of the entire animation.

7. **Click Frame 1 to reposition the playhead, then press Return/Enter to play the movie on the Stage.**

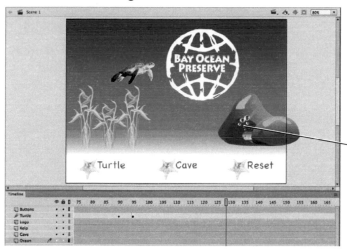

The air bubbles in the Cave movie clip instance do not move because that animation exists only inside the movie clip timeline.

8. **Save the file and continue to the next exercise.**

DEFINE NUMERIC TRANSFORMATIONS IN A TWEEN

In addition to making changes on the Stage, you can also use various panels to define specific changes to specific properties at specific points in time. In this exercise, you use the Transform panel to animate the seaweed with a tween that creates the effect of a smooth, swaying motion.

1. **With ocean.fla open, double-click the Seaweed movie clip icon in the Library panel to enter into the symbol Stage.**

2. **In the timeline, select Frame 40 and press F5 to insert a new regular frame.**

   You can also Control/right-click the frame and choose Insert Frame from the contextual menu.

3. **Control/right-click anywhere between Frame 1 and Frame 40 and choose Create Motion Tween.**

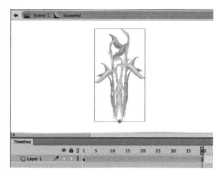

4. **Read the resulting message.**

   You created the Seaweed movie clip symbol by converting the bitmap instance on the main Stage to a symbol. However, the artwork on the symbol Stage is still a regular bitmap object. Motion tweens only work with symbol instances. As you see in the warning dialog box, Animate can automatically convert the placed bitmap instance to a movie clip symbol.

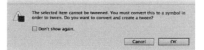

5. **Click OK in the message to create a symbol from the selected object.**

   You are not creating this tween on the main Stage because you want the animation to loop continuously regardless of the position of the playhead on the main timeline. Even though you are already inside of a symbol, you need to create a nested symbol structure for the motion tween to work properly.

6. **In the Library panel, change the name of Symbol 1 to Seaweed Sway, and then move the symbol into the Movie Clips folder.**

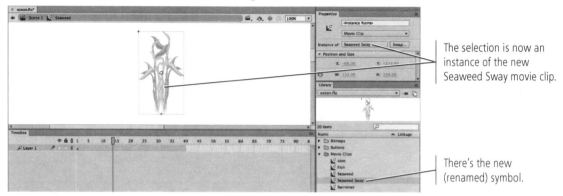

The selection is now an instance of the new Seaweed Sway movie clip.

There's the new (renamed) symbol.

7. **Choose the Free Transform tool in the Tools panel. Select the object on the Stage, and drag the transformation point to the bottom-center handle.**

8. **Select Frame 10 on the timeline. In the Transform panel, activate the Skew radio button, then change the Skew Horizontal value to 5°.**

   The concept here is the same as in the previous exercise: select the frame, and then change the object properties to what you want at that particular point in time.

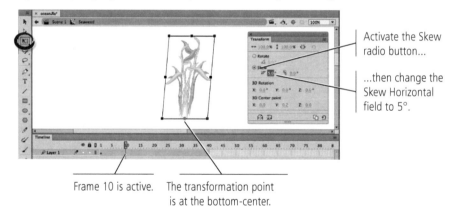

Activate the Skew radio button...

...then change the Skew Horizontal field to 5°.

Note:

The object must be selected to change its properties. Selecting the frame in the timeline also selects the object on that frame.

Frame 10 is active.   The transformation point is at the bottom-center.

9. **Move the playhead to Frame 30 in the timeline. In the Transform panel, change the Skew Horizontal value to -5°.**

   You don't need to manually move the skew back to 0°; the tween frames do that for you.

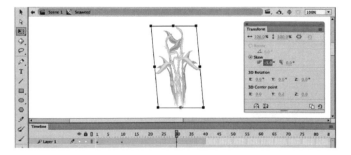

10. Move the playhead to Frame 40 in the timeline. Make sure the symbol instance is selected on the Stage, then change the Skew Horizontal value (in the Transform panel) to 0°.

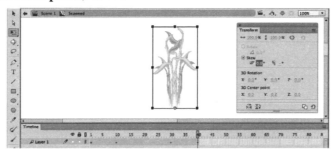

11. Click Scene 1 in the Edit bar to return to the main Stage.

12. Press Command-Return/Control-Enter to test the movie in a Player window.

Because you created the animation inside of the Seaweed movie clip symbol, all three instances of the symbol sway continuously as long as the animation is open.

13. Close the Player window and return to Animate. Save the file and continue to the next exercise.

Graphics vs. Movie Clips

Both graphics and movie clips can include animation. However, there are two fundamental differences in the capabilities of the two symbol types.

First, movie clip symbol instances can be named, which means they can be addressed by code. You can write scripts to control the timeline within a movie clip symbol independently of other objects in the file. Graphic symbol instances can't be named, which means you can't affect them with code.

Second, if you create animation inside of a graphic symbol, the timeline where you place the instance determines how much of the graphic symbol's animation plays. In other words, frames in the graphic symbol must correspond to frames on the parent timeline (they are "timeline dependent").

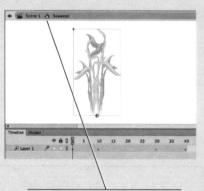

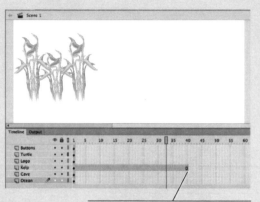

In this example, the seaweed animation was created in a graphic symbol instead of a movie clip.

On the main Stage, playing the animation requires the same number of frames that are contained in the graphic symbol timeline.

In the example here, the 40-frame seaweed animation was created in a graphic symbol (as you can see in the Edit bar above the symbol Stage, above left). For the instances on the main Stage to play properly, you need to extend the layer containing the graphic symbol to include all 40 required frames (above right).

If the parent timeline includes more frames than the graphic symbol (as in the example on the right, where the timeline has 95 frames) the graphic symbol's timeline will play slightly less than 2.5 times before looping back to the beginning — causing a visible jump in the animation.

If you have a number of animations of different length, you should use movie clip symbols, which function independently of the timeline where they are placed and can loop continuously regardless of the length of other animations on the same parent timeline.

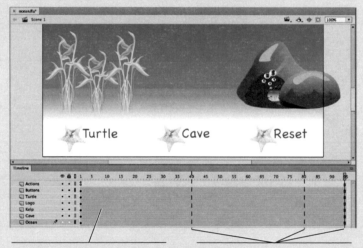

If you extend the timeline to create other animations, the graphic symbol animation repeats as long as the timeline allows.

The 40-frame seaweed animation would play 2 full times plus 15 frames before the main timeline looped back to Frame 1.

In addition to changing the common symbol properties — position, size, etc. — a motion tween can be used to animate a number of other options. Effects and filters, which can add visual interest to most objects on the Stage, can also be animated to change over time. In this exercise, you are going to cause the client's logo to fade into view over time, changing from blurry to clear and fully visible.

1. With **ocean.fla** open, use the Selection tool to select the logo instance on the Stage, then press the F8 key to convert it to a symbol.

2. Define the following settings in the Convert to Symbol dialog box:

Name:	**BOP**
Type:	**Movie Clip**
Registration:	**Center**
Location:	**Movie Clips folder**

3. Click OK to create the symbol.

4. Using the Selection tool, double-click the Logo instance on the Stage to edit the symbol in place. Select Frame 60 on the Layer 1 timeline and press F5 to add a new regular frame.

   Because movie clips are self-contained animations, every movie clip in the file can last a different amount of time. You also need to be able to control this animation separately from other animations, which is why you are creating the tween inside of the symbol.

5. Control/right-click between Frame 1 and Frame 60 and choose Create Motion Tween from the contextual menu.

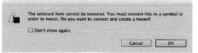

6. Click **OK** in the resulting warning. Rename the new Symbol 1 as **BOP Animated**, and then move the symbol into the Movie Clips folder.

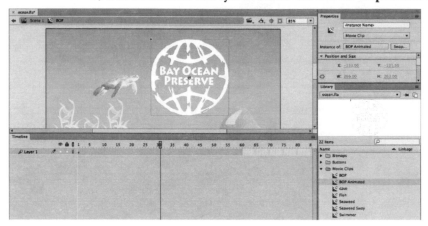

7. Move the playhead to Frame 1 in the timeline, and then click the symbol instance on the Stage to select it.

8. In the Properties panel, expand the **Filters** section (if necessary).

9. Click the **+** button and choose **Blur** from the pop-up menu.

Click the + button to add a new filter to the selected instance.

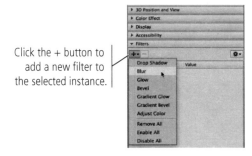

10. Make sure the Blur X and Blur Y values are linked, and then change the Blur X value to **30 px**.

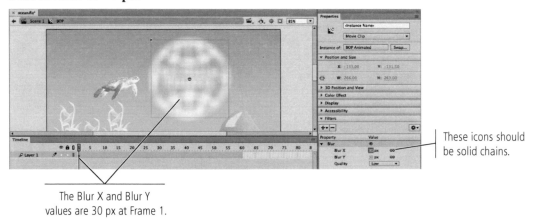

These icons should be solid chains.

The Blur X and Blur Y values are 30 px at Frame 1.

11. In the Properties panel, expand the **Color Effect** section (if necessary).

12. **Open the Style menu and choose Alpha. Drag the resulting slider all the way to the left to change the Alpha value to 0.**

The Alpha value controls an object's opacity; a value of 0 means the object is not visible.

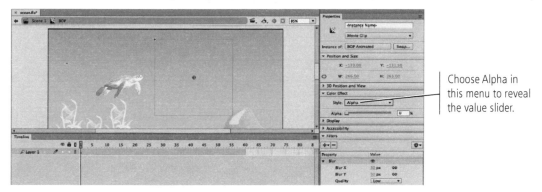

Choose Alpha in this menu to reveal the value slider.

13. **Move the playhead to Frame 30 on the Layer 1 timeline, and then click the symbol registration point on the Stage to select the symbol instance.**

Because the current Alpha value is 0, you can't see the actual object to select it; you have to rely on the registration point to select the instance on the Stage.

14. **In the Color Effects section of the Properties panel, change the Alpha value back to 100.**

15. **In the Filters section of the Properties panel, change the Blur X value to 0 px.**

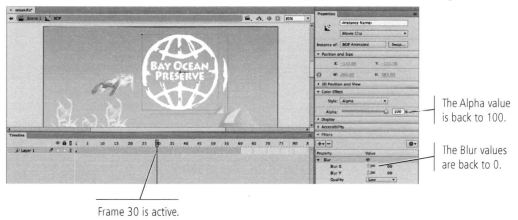

The Alpha value is back to 100.

The Blur values are back to 0.

Frame 30 is active.

16. **Return the playhead to Frame 1, and then press Return/Enter to preview the animation.**

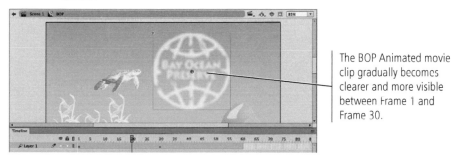

The BOP Animated movie clip gradually becomes clearer and more visible between Frame 1 and Frame 30.

17. **Click Scene 1 in the Edit bar to return to the main Stage.**

18. **Save the file and continue to the next stage of the project.**

Stage 3 Programming Basic Timeline Control

You now have all of the pieces in place for the ocean scene, including a number of animations that play automatically when the movie opens. According to the project specs, however, most of these animations should not play until a user clicks the appropriate button at the bottom of the screen. For everything to work properly, you need to complete several additional steps to accomplish the following goals:

- Play the logo animation only once when the movie first loads.

- Play the swimming turtle when the Turtle button is clicked.

- Show the cave with the bubbly fish when the Cave button is clicked.

- Hide the cave, stop the turtle and school of fish, and replay the logo animation when the Reset button is clicked.

 CONVERT A MOTION TWEEN TO A MOVIE CLIP

At this point, all but the swimming turtle animations are contained inside of various movie clip symbols. In order to add code that controls the turtle animation independently of the main timeline, you need to move the symbol instance and motion tween into a symbol, and then place an instance of that symbol on the Stage.

1. **With ocean.fla open, click the Turtle layer name in the Timeline panel to select everything on that layer.**

   Remember, the animation on this layer includes two motion tweens. Clicking the layer name selects both tweens on the layer.

2. **Control/right-click inside the selected frames and choose Copy Frames in the contextual menu.**

Clicking the layer name selects the entire layer timeline.

Both tweens are selected.

3. **Choose Insert>New Symbol. In the resulting dialog box, define the following settings:**

Name:	Swimming Turtle
Type:	Movie Clip
Location:	Movie Clips folder

   You are creating a new symbol, so there is no Registration option in the Create New Symbol dialog box. The new symbol Stage will include a registration point, around which you can place or create artwork.

4. **Click OK to create the new symbol.**

5. **Control/right-click Frame 1 of the new symbol's timeline and choose Paste Frames from the contextual menu.**

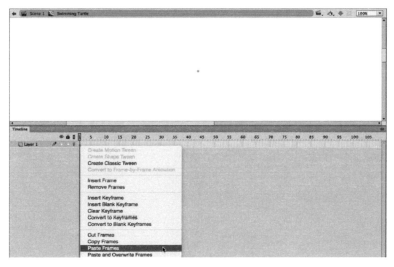

This pastes the full set of contents of the selected frames — including the turtle instance and the motion tweens — inside the symbol.

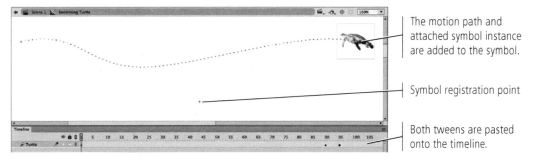

The motion path and attached symbol instance are added to the symbol.

Symbol registration point

Both tweens are pasted onto the timeline.

6. **Click anywhere within the Frame 1–94 tween, then choose Edit>Select All to select the motion path and the turtle symbol instance.**

This command selects both the motion path and the attached instance, so you can drag the entire piece as a single group.

7. **Use the Selection tool to drag the selection until the right end of the motion path aligns to the symbol registration point.**

The existing Swimmer symbol uses the center registration point. You're going to swap symbols, and the registration point in this symbol will align to the position of the previous one. For the tween to work as it does on the main timeline, you need to place the right end of the motion path at the registration point. (This will make more sense shortly).

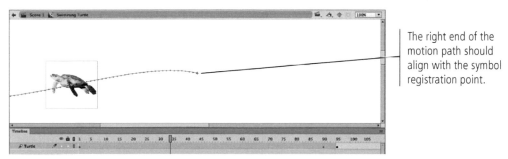

The right end of the motion path should align with the symbol registration point.

8. **Repeat Steps 6–7 for the Frame 95–184 tween.**

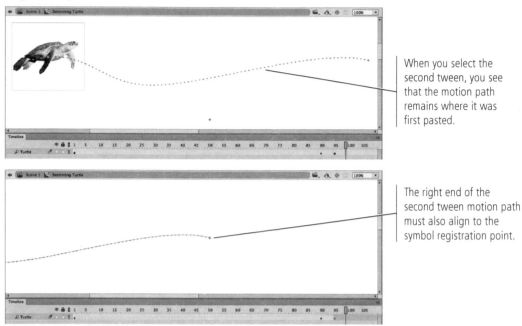

When you select the second tween, you see that the motion path remains where it was first pasted.

The right end of the second tween motion path must also align to the symbol registration point.

9. **Click Scene 1 in the Edit bar to return to the main Stage.**

10. **Control/right-click the Frame 1–94 tween on the Turtle layer and choose Remove Motion from the contextual menu.**

    The tweens now exist in the new Swimming Turtle movie clip symbol, so they are no longer needed on the main timeline.

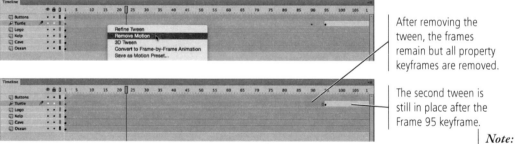

After removing the tween, the frames remain but all property keyframes are removed.

The second tween is still in place after the Frame 95 keyframe.

Note:

After removing both motion tweens, the Turtle layer is converted back to a regular layer.

11. **Repeat Step 10 for the Frame 95–184 tween on the same layer.**

12. **Click Frame 2 of the topmost layer to select it.**

13. **Scroll the Timeline panel as necessary until you see Frame 184. Press Shift, then click the last frame on the bottommost layer to select all frames from 2–184 on all layers.**

Click Frame 2 of the top layer...

...then Shift-click Frame 184 of the bottom layer to select all contiguous frames between the two you click.

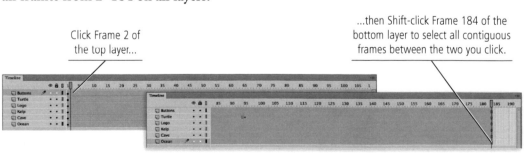

14. Control/right-click anywhere within the selected frames and choose Remove Frames from the contextual menu.

Because all animation in this movie occurs within the timelines of various movie clip symbols, you don't need 184 frames on each layer of the main timeline. However, you can't simply press the Delete key to remove frames. You must use the contextual menu (or the related commands in the Edit>Timeline submenu).

15. Click the existing turtle instance on the Stage to select it.

Because all of the animations are now contained within movie clip symbols, the main timeline now has only a single frame for each layer.

As you can see in the Properties panel, the selected object is currently an instance of the Swimmer movie clip. You need to replace it with the Swimming Turtle movie clip.

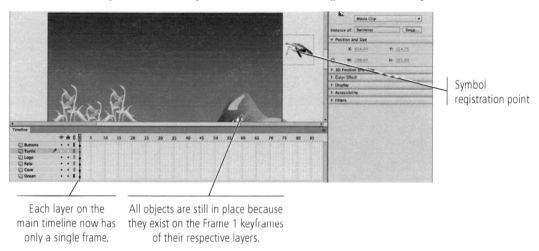

Symbol registration point

Each layer on the main timeline now has only a single frame.

All objects are still in place because they exist on the Frame 1 keyframes of their respective layers.

16. In the Properties panel, click the Swap button. Choose the Swimming Turtle movie clip in the resulting dialog box and click OK.

When you swap symbols, the registration point of the new symbol is put in exactly the same spot as the registration point of the replacement symbol — which is why you moved the right end of the motion path to align with the symbol's registration point.

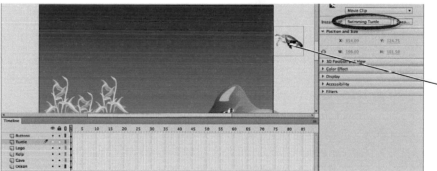

Although you can't see the motion path, you know the center of the turtle was aligned to the right end of the path at Frame 1.

17. Save the file and continue to the next exercise.

PREPARE SYMBOL INSTANCES FOR ACTIONSCRIPT

As you know, when you drag a symbol from the Library panel to the Stage, you create an instance of the symbol. **Named instances** are instances that have been assigned a unique identifier or name, which allows them to be targeted with ActionScript code.

1. **With `ocean.fla` open, make sure you are working on the main Stage.**

2. **Using the Selection tool, click the Swimming Turtle instance to the left of the Stage. In the top field of the Properties panel, type `turtle_mc`.**

Use the Properties panel to assign instance names.

3. **Define names for the rest of the placed instances as follows:**

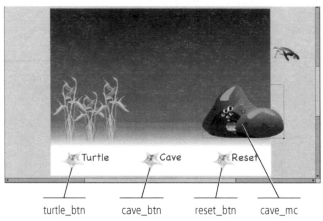

turtle_btn   cave_btn   reset_btn   cave_mc

Note:

You don't need to name the seaweed instances because those will not be targeted with scripts.

4. **In the Timeline panel, click the Logo layer name to select the layer.**

   Remember, selecting a layer reveals the bounding boxes for all objects on the layer.

5. **Click the symbol registration point to select the logo.**

   Because the logo object has an Alpha value of 0, this is the easiest way to select the instance so you can name it.

6. **In the Properties panel, type `bop_mc` as the instance name.**

Note:

The "_mc" and "_btn" naming convention is common in the world of Animate development. This convention allows programmers to easily recognize the type of a particular instance when they add scripts to the file.

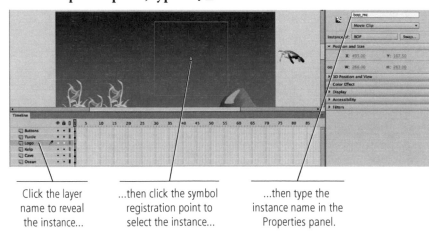

Click the layer name to reveal the instance...

...then click the symbol registration point to select the instance...

...then type the instance name in the Properties panel.

7. **Save the file and continue to the next exercise.**

ADD MOVIE CLIP CONTROLS

If you completed Project 3: Animated Internet Ads, you saw that the Code Snippets panel makes it relatively easy for non-programmers to add basic code to an Animate movie. Items in the panel, written in plain English, automatically add whatever code is necessary to perform the listed function. In this exercise, you will use code snippets to determine what is visible when you first open the movie.

1. **With ocean.fla open, open the Code Snippets panel from the Window menu.**

   Different types of common commands are available, grouped into logical sets or folders.

2. **Expand the ActionScript>Actions folder in the Code Snippets panel. Move your mouse cursor over the Stop a Movie Clip item to get more information about that snippet.**

3. **Select the Swimming Turtle instance on the stage and then double-click the Stop a Movie Clip item.**

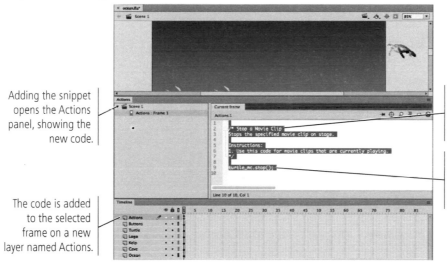

Adding the snippet opens the Actions panel, showing the new code.

The code is added to the selected frame on a new layer named Actions.

Code snippets include instructions in the form of comments, which are enclosed by /* and */.

The actual command uses dot syntax to define what instance is affected and what will happen to that instance.

It might seem that by first selecting the object, you are attaching script to that object. Instead, you are telling Animate which object you want the command to address. In ActionScript 3.0, all scripts are placed on the timeline frames rather than attached to specific objects on the Stage. In the Timeline panel, a new layer named Actions is added to the top of the layer stack. (Although not required, this separate layer for the code is a common convention among developers.)

In the Actions panel, which opens automatically when you add the snippet, you can see that the stop command has been added to Frame 1 of the Actions layer. The command references turtle_mc, which is the instance name you defined. In other words, this command stops the turtle_mc instance from playing. The instance is stopped as soon as the main timeline reaches the command; because the command is on Frame 1 of the main timeline, the instance is stopped as soon as the movie opens.

Note:

*The format or syntax of the added code is called **dot syntax**: it first defines the object you are addressing, then adds a dot, then defines what you want to do to that object.*

4. **Select the Cave instance and then double-click the Stop a Movie Clip item in the Snippets panel.**

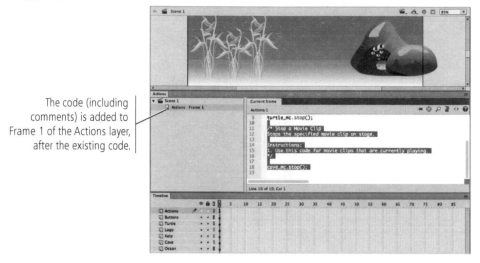

The code (including comments) is added to Frame 1 of the Actions layer, after the existing code.

5. **Select the Cave instance again and double-click the Show an Object item.**

Unfortunately, there is no snippet to simply hide an item without requiring the user to click something. (The Click to Hide an Object item is not appropriate because you want to hide the instance as soon as the movie opens, and not as a reaction to the user's click.)

However, the added Show an Object statement shows that the value "true" is attached to the visible property of the instance. To make the instance *not* visible, you simply have to change the property's value in the code.

6. **In the Actions panel, change the word true to false on Line 27.**

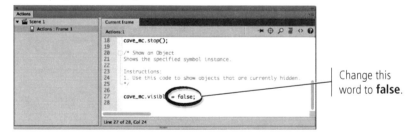

Change this word to **false**.

7. Press Command-Return/Control-Enter to test the movie.

The two movie clips are stopped, and the cave is hidden. However, the logo animation still plays continuously, and you want it to play only once when the movie opens.

8. Close the Player window and return to Animate.

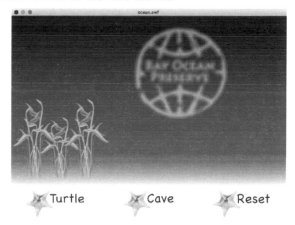

⭑ Turtle   ⭑ Cave   ⭑ Reset

9. In the Library panel, double-click the BOP movie clip symbol icon to enter into the symbol's Stage.

You can't stop the BOP instance on the main Stage because you want the animation to play one time when the movie first opens. To accomplish this goal, you need to add a stop command to the end of the movie clip timeline.

10. Move the playhead to the last frame in the timeline, then click the logo instance on the Stage to select it.

11. Expand the ActionScript>Timeline Navigation folder in the Code Snippets panel, then double-click the Stop at this Frame item to add the necessary code.

Timeline Navigation snippets can be used to control the timeline (and thus, the playback) of specific symbols. The Stop at this Frame command affects the active timeline at the selected frame, so a specific instance is not referenced in the resulting code.

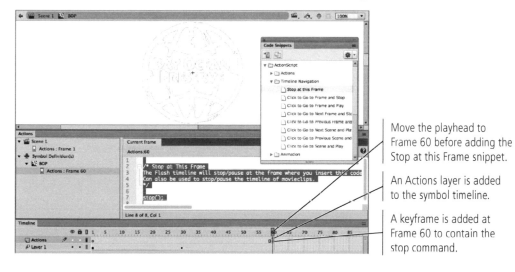

Move the playhead to Frame 60 before adding the Stop at this Frame snippet.

An Actions layer is added to the symbol timeline.

A keyframe is added at Frame 60 to contain the stop command.

12. Click Scene 1 in the Edit bar to return to the main Stage, then press Command-Return/Control-Enter to test the movie.

The logo animation now plays only once and then stops.

13. Close the Player window and return to Animate, then save the file and continue to the next exercise.

As you saw in the previous exercise, ActionScript 3.0 requires code to be attached to a frame on the timeline. To affect a specific object on the Stage, you have to use the defined instance names as reference in the code. Programming a button requires more complex code called an **event handler**, with (at least) two referenced objects — the event that triggers the action, and the name of the function that is affected by the event.

The Code Snippets panel includes options for creating event handlers with the proper syntax, although defining what occurs as a result of the event might require a few workaround steps. Even using code snippets, it is helpful if you are familiar with the basics of ActionScript code.

1. **With ocean.fla open, expand the ActionScript>Timeline Navigation folder in the Code Snippets panel.**

2. **Select the Turtle button instance on the Stage, then double-click the Click to Go to Frame and Play item in the Code Snippets panel.**

   The added code is not attached to the selected instance; it is added to Frame 1 of the existing Actions layer, after all code that you already added.

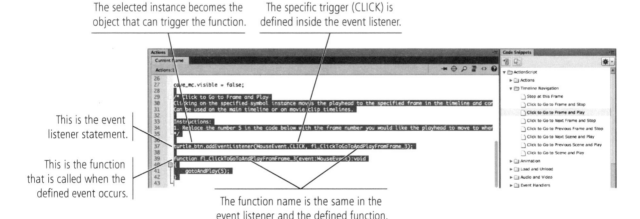

The selected instance becomes the object that can trigger the function.

The specific trigger (CLICK) is defined inside the event listener.

This is the event listener statement.

This is the function that is called when the defined event occurs.

The function name is the same in the event listener and the defined function.

Although you do not need to know every detail of ActionScript code to use Code Snippets, there are a few important points that you should understand:

- The first line of added code defines what will happen to trigger the function (the **event listener**). Inside the parentheses, the MouseEvent.CLICK statement says that the following function will be called when the turtle_btn instance is *clicked*.

- The first line of code includes a **function name** immediately before the closing parenthesis. That same name is defined at the beginning of the following function, so the file knows which function to play when the defined button is clicked.

- The **function body** — between the two braces — defines what occurs when the event is triggered.

3. **Place the insertion point before the gotoAndPlay command inside the function body and click the Insert Instance Path and Name button at the top of the Actions panel.**

The statement inside this function currently says "go to Frame 5 and play the timeline". Because the statement does not address a specific instance, the code will be interpreted to mean the timeline on which the code is placed (in this case, the main Stage timeline). You want the function to play the School movie clip instance, so you have to add the appropriate reference.

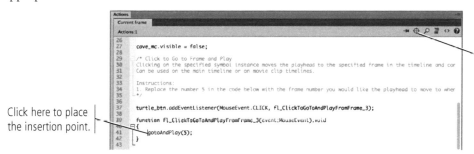

Click here to place the insertion point.

Insert Instance Path and Name button

4. **Choose turtle_mc in the Insert Target Path dialog box and click OK.**

This dialog box lists every nameable instance on the Stage, so you can choose from the list instead of trying to remember the exact name you defined for a specific object.

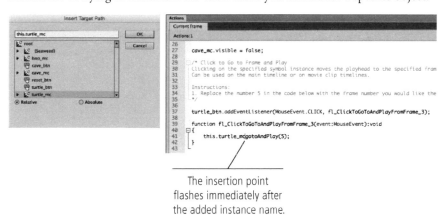

The insertion point flashes immediately after the added instance name.

Note:

If an item in the Insert Target Path dialog box appears in parentheses, the instance is not yet named; selecting it will prompt you to define an instance name.

Note:

The word "this" is automatically included when you use the Insert Target Path dialog box. It is not strictly necessary in this case because the instances are all on the main timeline of the file you are building, but you do not need to remove it from the code.

The word "this" in the instance name refers to the timeline where the code is written. The overall statement is essentially saying, "On *this* timeline, you will find something called school_mc. Tell school_mc to execute its gotoAndPlay() method."

5. **Type a period (dot) immediately after the instance name to separate it from the gotoAndPlay command.**

Remember, dot syntax requires a period separating the different parts of code — in this case, the instance that will be affected by the gotoAndPlay command.

6. **Change the number inside the parentheses to 1.**

This number defines the frame number of the instance that will be called when a user clicks the button. You want the instance to start at the beginning, so you are changing the frame reference to 1.

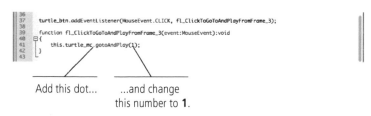

Add this dot...   ...and change this number to **1**.

7. **Repeat Steps 2–6 to create an event handler for the Cave button that plays the cave_mc movie clip instance from Frame 1.**

8. **Select the cave_mc instance on the Stage (not the Cave button) and double-click the Show an Object item in the ActionScript>Actions folder of the Code Snippets panel.**

   The Cave button needs to show the instance before it plays, so this button function needs two lines of code. However, the Code Snippets panel was not designed to add code inside of an existing function. The Show an Object snippet is added at the end of the existing code, *after* the function that is called when a user clicks the cave_btn instance. As a work-around, you have to add the necessary command and then paste it into the function body.

The "show" command is added outside of the existing function.

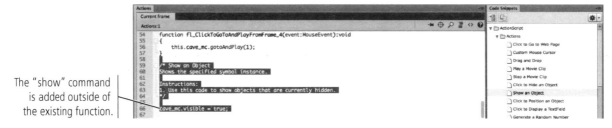

9. **Select the line of code that makes the cave_mc instance visible (Line 66 in the above example) and press Command/Control-X to cut the selected code.**

   You have to use the keyboard shortcuts to copy (Command/Control-C), cut (Command/Control-X), or paste (Command/Control-V) code in the Actions panel. The menu commands do not work while you are active in the Actions panel.

10. **Place the insertion point immediately after the opening brace in the previous function for the cave_btn instance (Line 55 in our example). Press Return/Enter to add a new line in the function body, then press Command/Control-V to paste the code that you cut in Step 9 into the function body.**

11. **Delete the extra lines of comments at the end of the code.**

Note:

The comments are the gray lines that are surrounded by /* and */. After you moved the actual code into the function body (Steps 9–10), the comments from the original code are unnecessary. Deleting them helps keep the code pane as clean as possible.

12. **Press Command-Return/Control-Enter to test the movie.**

Test the buttons that you just programmed. Each should play the relevant movie clip.

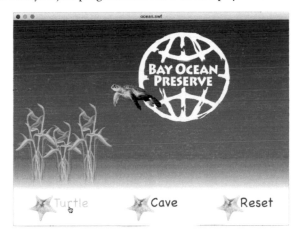

13. **Close the Player window and return to Animate, then save the file and continue to the next exercise.**

COMBINE MULTIPLE EVENT HANDLERS IN A BUTTON

The final element of this project is the Reset button, which needs to accomplish a number of things. As the name suggests, clicking this button should restore the movie to exactly what happens when it first opens. Because the symbols in this movie are controlled with code, you need to add more code that defines what happens when this button is clicked.

1. **With ocean.fla open, select the Reset button instance on the Stage.**

2. **Double-click the Click to Go To Frame and Stop item in the ActionScript>Timeline Navigation folder of the Code Snippets panel.**

3. **Inside the function body, add a reference to the turtle_mc instance before the gotoAndStop command, and change the referenced frame inside the parentheses to 1.**

4. **Select the line inside the function body (Line 72 in our example) and copy it.**

5. **Place the insertion point at the beginning of the existing function body (Line 72) and paste the copied code two times.**

Depending on how you copied the code in Step 4, you might have to press Return/Enter to move each pasted line onto a separate line in the code.

6. **Change the second line to reference the cave_mc instance.**

7. **Change the third line to reference the bop_mc instance, and change the command to gotoAndPlay.**

   When a user clicks the Reset button, the logo animation should replay from the first frame. It will replay only once because you already added the stop command inside the movie clip's timeline.

These lines will stop the first two animations, and effectively hide the turtle from the Stage.

This command will cause the logo animation to play once.

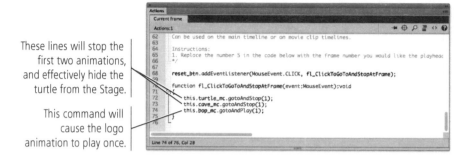

8. **Select the Reset button on the Stage again, and double-click the Click to Hide an Object item in the Actions folder of the Code Snippets panel.**

9. **In the resulting function, change the referenced instance to cave_mc.**

   By default, this snippet hides the object that triggers the function. Because you want to hide the cave and not the Reset button, you need to change the instance name inside of the function body.

Note:

You don't need to hide the turtle instance because Frame 1 of that movie clip exists entirely out of the Stage area; it won't be visible when its timeline is reset.

10. **Cut the function body (Line 89 in our example) from the code and then paste it inside the body of the previous function.**

   In this case, it is not necessary to have two separate event handlers for the same button.

Change the reference to cave_mc...

...then cut this line from this function...

...and paste it into this function.

11. **Delete all code related to the second reset_btn event handler (Lines 78–89 in our example above).**

Because you combined this function body with the other event handler for the same button, this code is no longer necessary.

12. **Press Command-Return/Control-Enter to test the movie.**

Test the buttons that you just programmed. The Reset button should stop and hide all animations except for the swaying seaweed.

13. **Close the Player window, then save the Animate file and close it.**

1. Objects from a Photoshop file should be created on _____ if they need to be managed separately when imported into Animate.

2. The _____ tool allows you to scale objects dynamically on the Stage.

3. The _____ defines the point around which object transformations are made.

4. The X and Y position of a symbol instance is based on the _____.

5. You can use the _____ panel to define numeric scale and skew values for the selected object.

6. Animation in a _____ requires the same number of frames on the timeline where the instance is placed.

7. Animation in a _____ plays regardless of the number of frames in the timeline where instances are placed.

8. _____ is the format required by ActionScript 3 code.

9. Using ActionScript 3, code is attached to a specific _____, and uses instance names to address specific objects.

10. In ActionScript, a(n) _____ includes a statement defining the instance that triggers an event and the function that is called when the defined event occurs.

1. Briefly explain the concept of "tweening."

2. Briefly explain the difference between a graphic symbol and a movie clip symbol.

3. Briefly define an event handler.

Portfolio Builder Project

Use what you learned in this project to complete the following freeform exercise.
Carefully read the art director and client comments, then create your own design to meet the needs of the project.
Use the space below to sketch ideas; when finished, write a brief explanation of your reasoning behind your final design.

art director comments

The media director for the Chicago Wild Animal Park is re-branding the facility from the "City Zoo" image it has had for the past twenty years. He has hired you to create a series of animated icons for the park's new interactive Web site.

To complete this project, you should:

❏ Create each icon in the same shape and size, and use the same general style for each.

❏ Add some kind of animation to each icon. Use any combination of frame animations, shape tweens, and/or motion tweens.

client comments

We've gotten rid of the cages and created realistic natural habitats for the animals. Our main goals now are rehabilitation, preservation, and education. We're going to have educational programs and exhibits throughout the facility, but we don't want people to be scared off by the idea of learning!

We have many international visitors, so most of our collateral — including our new Web site — is based on images that can be understood in any language. Although there will be text as well, the icons should very clearly indicate what users will find when they click on any specific one (even if they can't read the words).

We need a series of six animated icons that will label the different areas of the facility. The six main sections are: the tropics, the desert, the Arctic, the forest, the ocean, and the sky. There will also be a special children's section that needs its own icon.

project justification

This project incorporated artwork that was created in Adobe Photoshop, which is a common development workflow. You also worked with symbols that were created in another Animate file, which is also a common collaborative process.

The second stage of this project focused on different methods of creating animation — frame-by-frame to move something in jumps, motion tweening to move objects smoothly, tweening to change only certain properties over time, and even tweening to rotate an object in three-dimensional space. To create these animations, you have also learned a number of techniques for transforming objects on the Stage; the Transform panel, the Free Transform tool, the Properties panel, and the Motion Editor panel all play valuable roles in Animate development.

Finally, you were introduced to the object-oriented model of ActionScript 3 when you added button controls using the Code Snippets panel. With very little (if any) knowledge of coding or programming, you were able to use the built-in functionality to meet the project's interactive requirements.

Import artwork from an Adobe Photoshop file

Import symbols from an external Flash library

Animate Alpha properties and graphic filters

Define movie clip symbols to create tween animations

Create frame animations to move objects over time

Add code to control the playback of various movie clip instances.

Index

Index